Goodbye, World!
Looking at Art in the Digital Age

Omar Kholeif

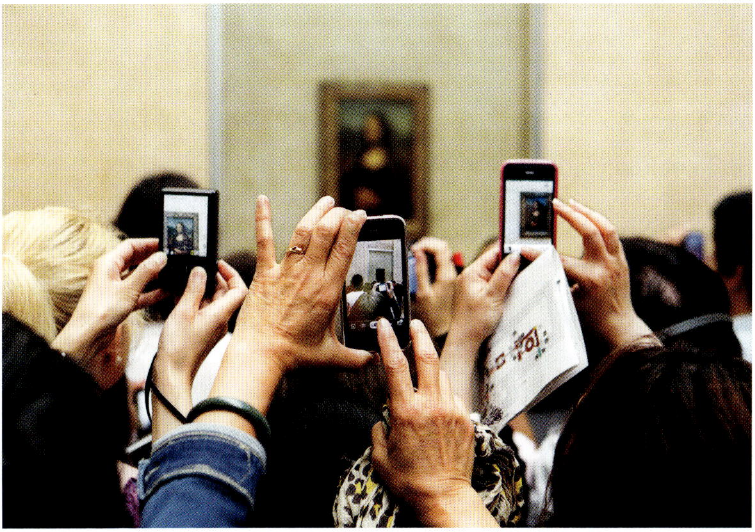

Sternberg Press

Goodbye, World!
Looking at Art in the Digital Age
Omar Kholeif

Published by Sternberg Press

Copyeditor: Michael Barron
Proofreading: Mark Soo
Image research: Isabella Ritchie
Graphic design: Zak Group
Printing: KOPA, Vilnius

ISBN 978-3-95679-309-7

Sternberg Press
Caroline Schneider
Karl-Marx-Allee 78
D-10243 Berlin
www.sternberg-press.com

With the support of:

Graham Foundation

Contents

Acknowledgments

Such a project has occupied my mind and being for as long as I have worked in the field of art and culture. I am indebted to the beginnings, to my early days as a researcher and then curator at FACT (Foundation for Art and Creative Technology) in Liverpool. My mentors and interlocutors during this time were Heather Corcoran, Michael Connor, and Mike Stubbs, as well as Karen Alexander, who continually encouraged me to interrogate the agency that emerging technologies could play in the visual field. I was also emboldened by working with Sarah Perks and Henriette Huldisch at Cornerhouse, and later HOME in Manchester, where I was offered the opportunity to commission numerous artworks that fundamentally questioned art's relationship to its audience. Is art made for the people, or "with" the people? This is a question that Perks encouraged me to ask, and it is a question that I shall forever examine.

Much of this thinking developed as I attempted to create a historical through-line from early artists who worked with the internet to how artists are doing so today. This began during my time at SPACE, London, where Anna Harding offered me the chance to run an experimental lab for artists who engaged with immersive technologies. This study led to my edited volume *You Are Here: Art after the Internet*, which came out in 2014. I took this experience with me to the Whitechapel Gallery, London, where Iwona Blazwick and Sofia Victorino, my two key advocates, helped me develop "Electronic Superhighway (2016–1966)," a major historical exhibition that examined the early collaborative spirit of Experiments in Art and Technology (E.A.T.) and investigated how that fed into the legacy of art's relationship to technology.

After leaving the Whitechapel Gallery, I moved to my current role at the Museum of Contemporary Art Chicago, where I was invited by Madeleine Grynsztejn and Michael Darling to consider in an exhibition how art that engaged the internet had changed the way we see the world around us. This led to *I Was Raised on the Internet*, which allowed me to focus my research on the post-millennium period. Here, I had incredible critics and confidants who helped me, including Susan Chun, Jared Quinton, and Nina Wexelblatt, to name but a few.

This project would not be possible without the belief of Caroline Schneider at Sternberg Press, who gave me the courage to put my thoughts on paper. Her stellar editorial team, including Tatjana Günthner, Isabella Ritchie, and Mark Soo, helped me shape this book to what it is today. Numerous other friends that have informally contributed to its realization include Judith Barry, Rosa Barba, Stephanie Bailey, Andrea Lissoni, Eva Respini, Joana Hadjithomas and Khalil Joreige, Hannah Feldman, Hans Ulrich Obrist, Ben Cook, Abina Manning, Richard Dyer, W. J. T. Mitchell, Sultan Sooud Al Qassemi, Todd Reisz, Sophia Al-Maria, Erika Balsom, Zach Blas, Simon Sakhai, Frank Gallacher, Sarah Herda, and Douglas Coupland. My greatest mentor in life has been the late Jean Fisher, to whom this book, as well as everything else that I ever do, will be forever dedicated. This book has also benefited from early financial support by the Barjeel Art Foundation, who enabled me to conduct preliminary research. Most importantly, I would like to thank the Graham Foundation, whose production grant helped bring this book to life.

I have been very much inspired by my family, including my brother, Yousef Kholeif, whose time working in Silicon Valley has informed my thinking. I would also like to thank my parents, Manar Farahat and Yasser Kholeif, as well as my late grandfather, Abdel Kader Kholeif, who always encouraged me to dream.

User's Guide

In his book *Bit Rot* (2015), Douglas Coupland articulates a current state of being in the twenty-first century. Discussing its contents with me, Coupland expressed that he believes our present condition is one where we feel that we are going down a continual rabbit hole. Indeed, the world has become a site of perpetual discovery, loss, confusion, and renewal: Will we ever come out the other end? This book functions as an introductory guide into this condition, and as a tool kit for understanding the different ways of looking at the world. It focuses particularly on the changing nature by which we experience art and the space around it. It takes cues from books such as John Berger's *Ways of Seeing* (1972) and Alvin Toffler's *Future Shock* (1970) to ask fundamental questions about whether the world we are starting to "see" is one of liberation or entrapment. This book's title looks back to the sense of possibility of "Hello, World," the output of Dennis Ritchie and Brian Kernighan's first computer program from 1978. Written in the first person, *Goodbye, World!* is based on my experiences as a curator who has spent the last decade wrestling with what it means to make and exhibit art in the changing world of the current century. This book, I should also note, is neither definitive nor conclusive, offering only a snapshot of the incredibly diverse works being produced by artists today. I seek to address evolving issues that I hope will help readers interrogate the ways they engage with contemporary visual culture.

Looking at Art after the Internet

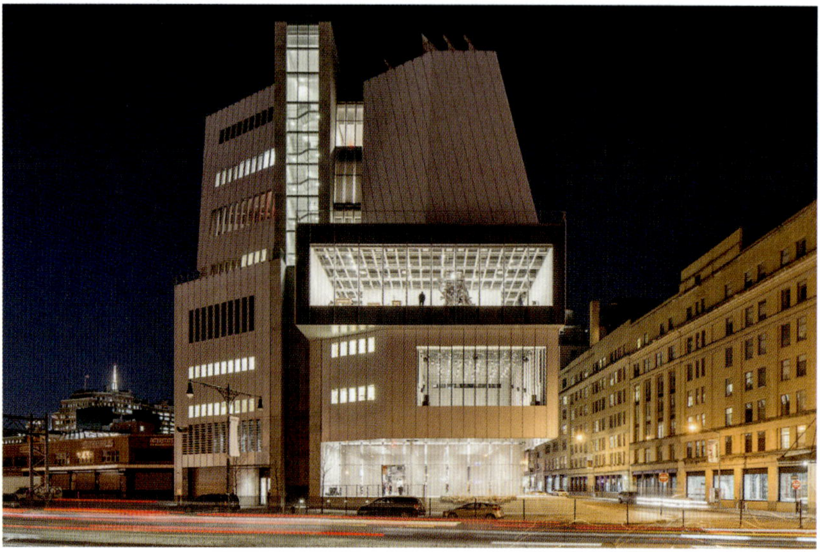

Renzo Piano Building Workshop's new Whitney Museum of American Art, New York, 2015

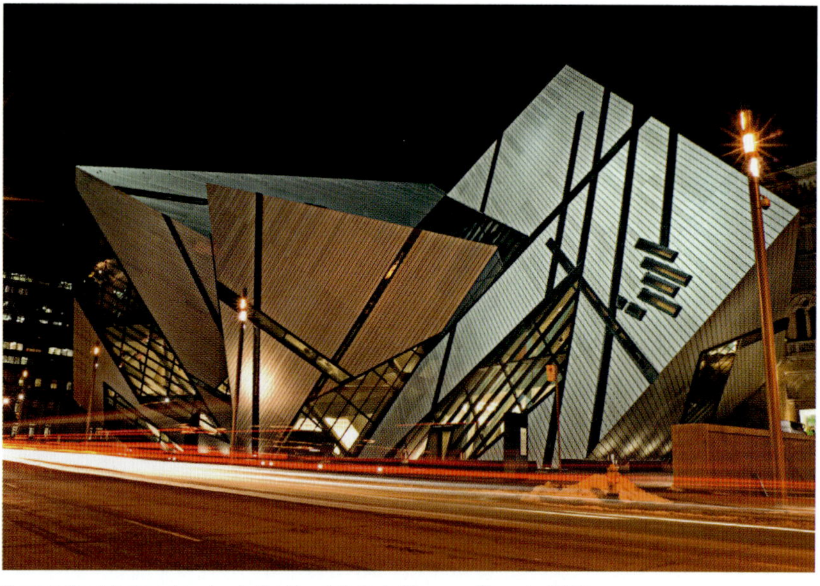

Daniel Libeskind's extension to the Royal Ontario Museum, Toronto, 2008

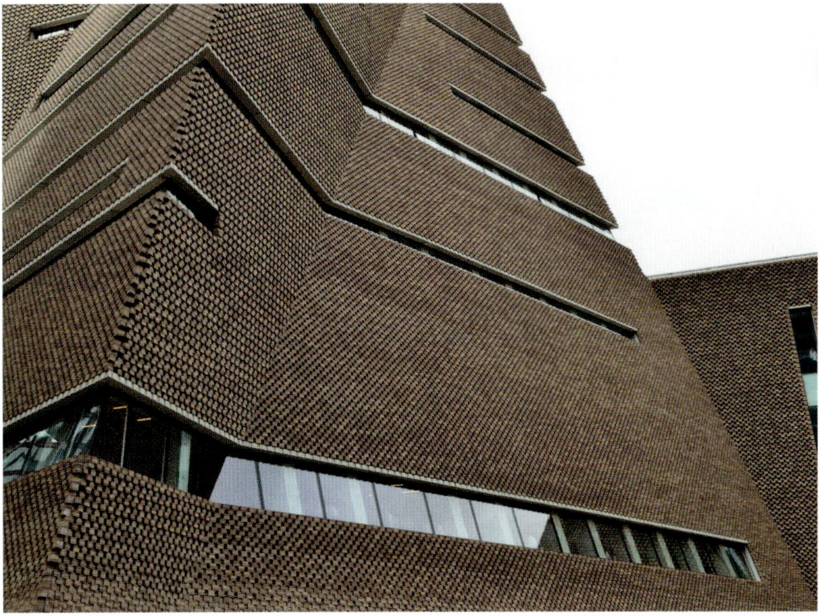

The Blavatnik Building, Herzog and de Meuron's extension to Tate Modern, London, 2016

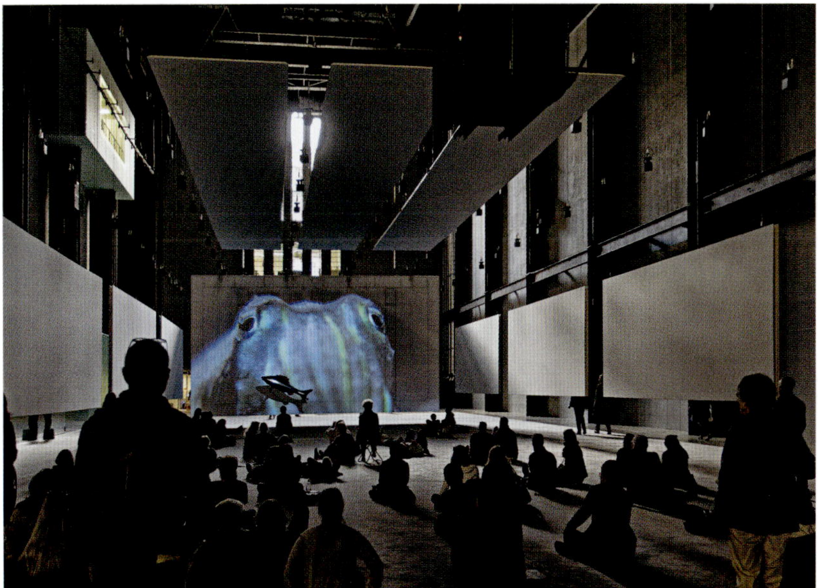

Philippe Parreno, *Anywhen*, 2016

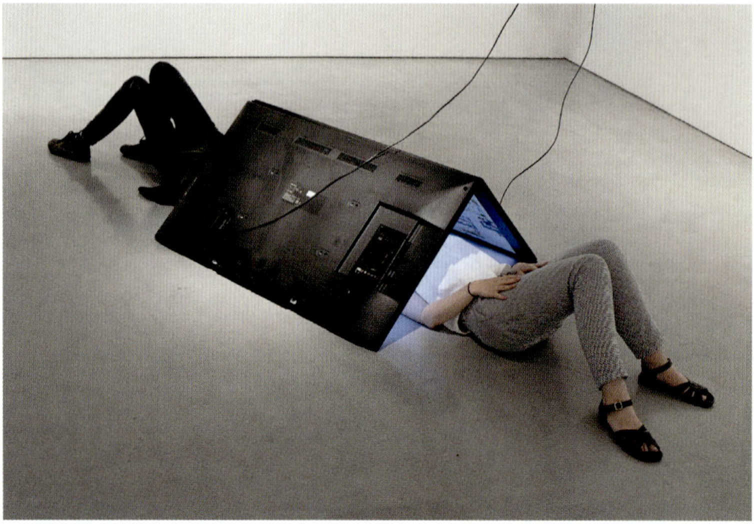

Eva and Franco Mattes, *BEFNOED*, 2016

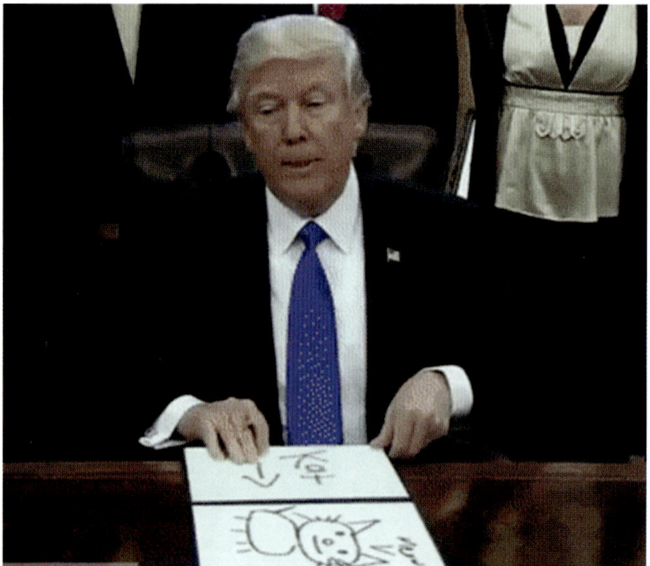

Trump GIF, 2017

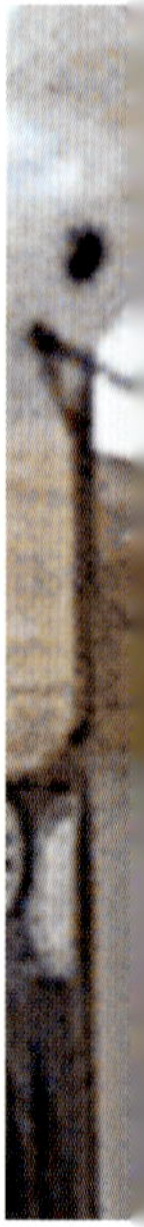

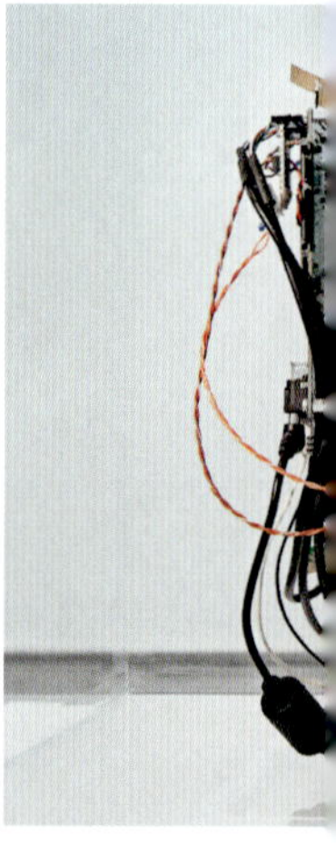

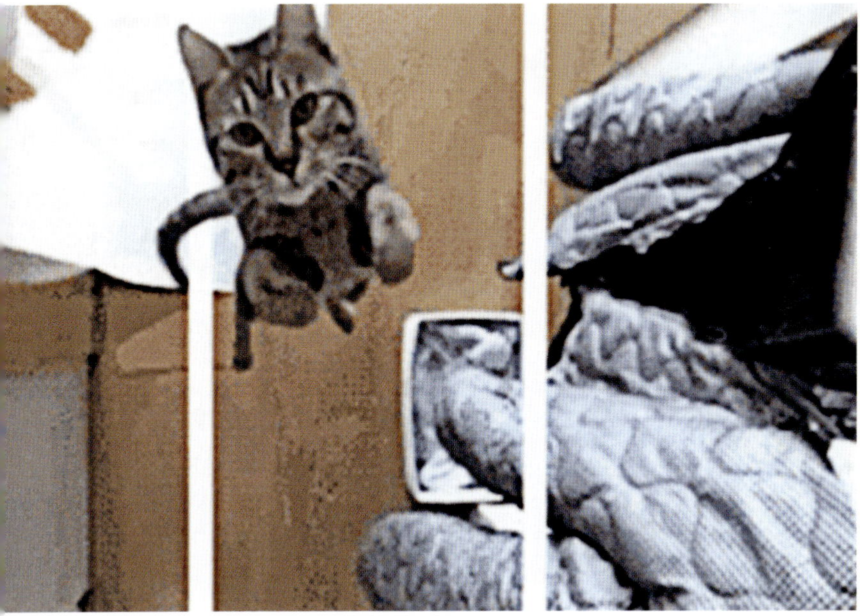

3-D cat jump GIF, 2015

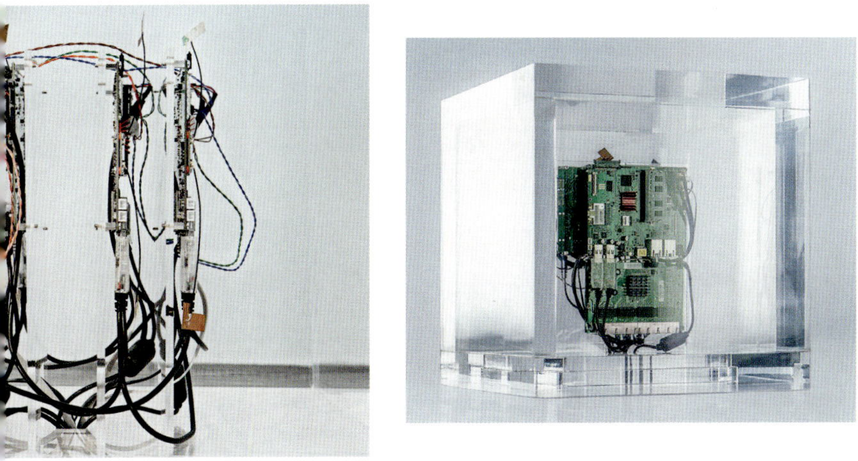

Trevor Paglen, *Autonomy Cube*, 2015

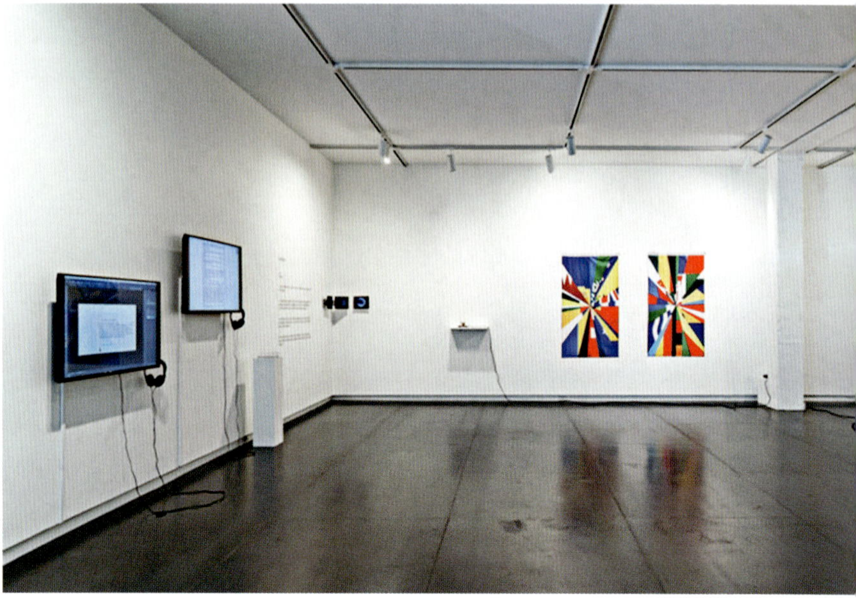

James Bridle, *Citizen Ex*, 2015

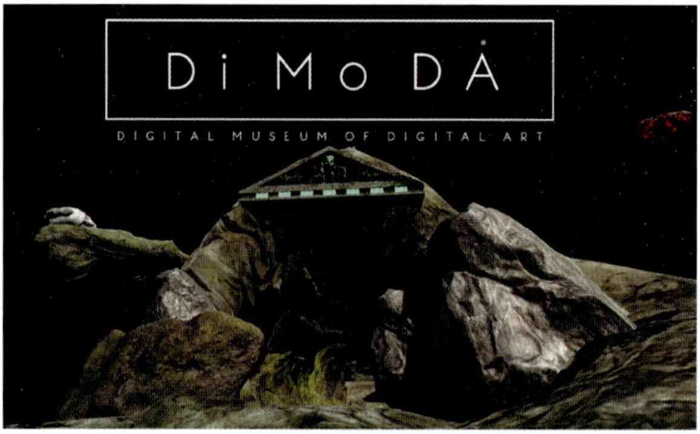

Exterior environment of DiMoDA, 2015

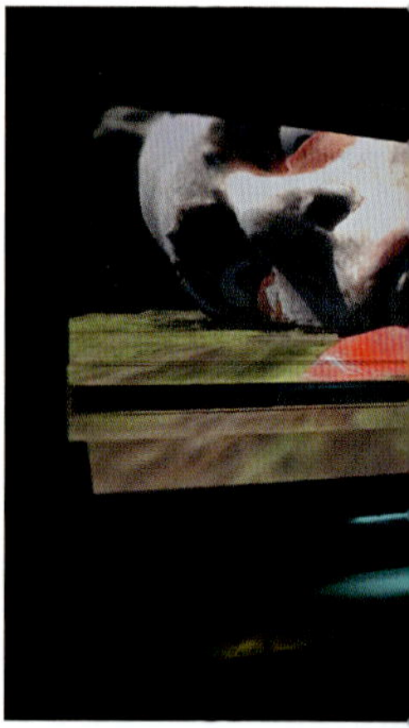

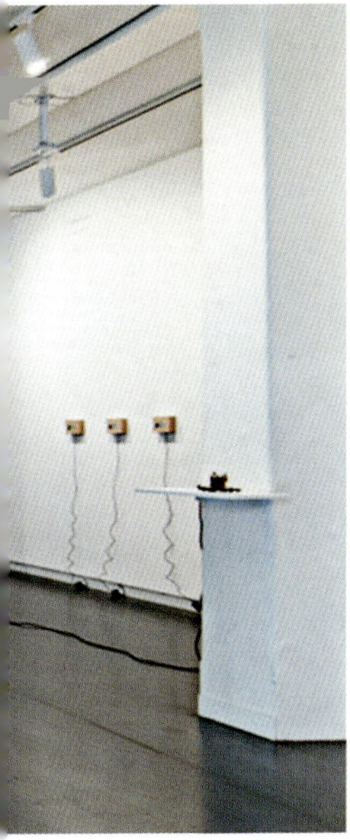

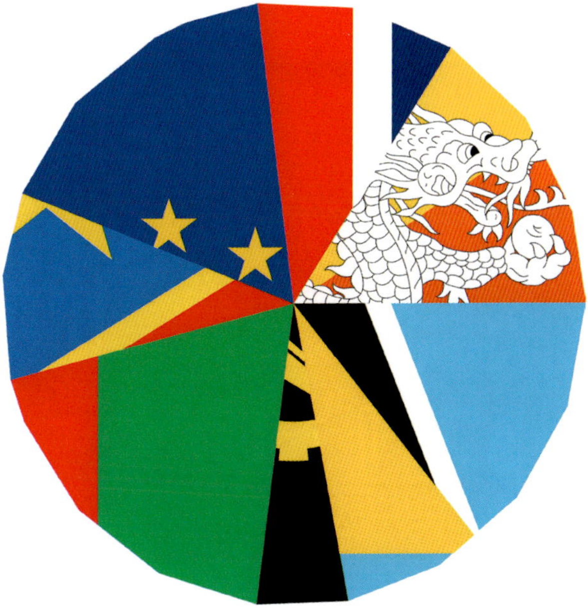

James Bridle, *Citizen Ex*, 2015

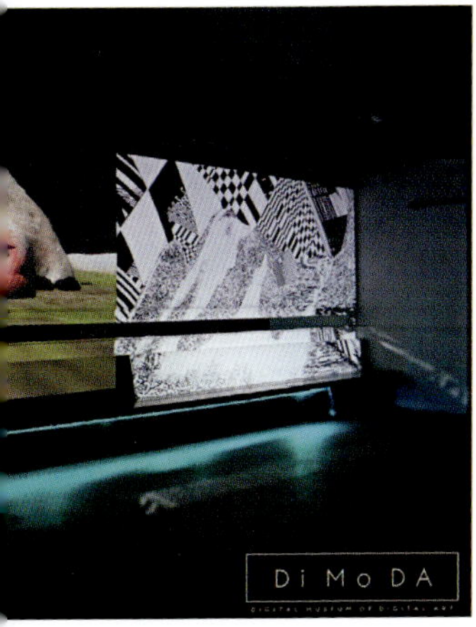

"DiMoDA 2.0: Morphé Presence,"
Superchief Gallery, Brooklyn, 2016

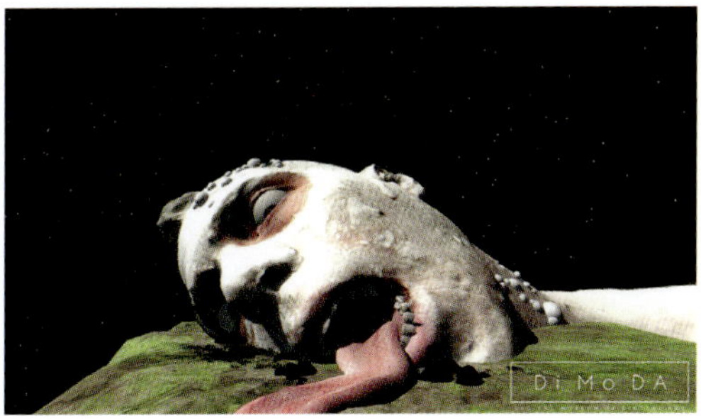

Still from Theo Triantafyllidis, *Self Portrait (Interior)*, 2016

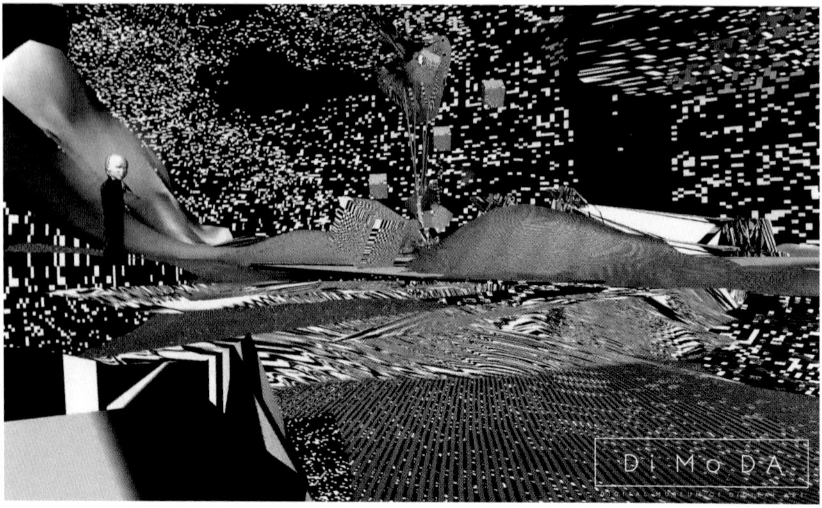

Still from Rosa Menkman, *DCT: Syphoning. The 64th Interval*, 2016

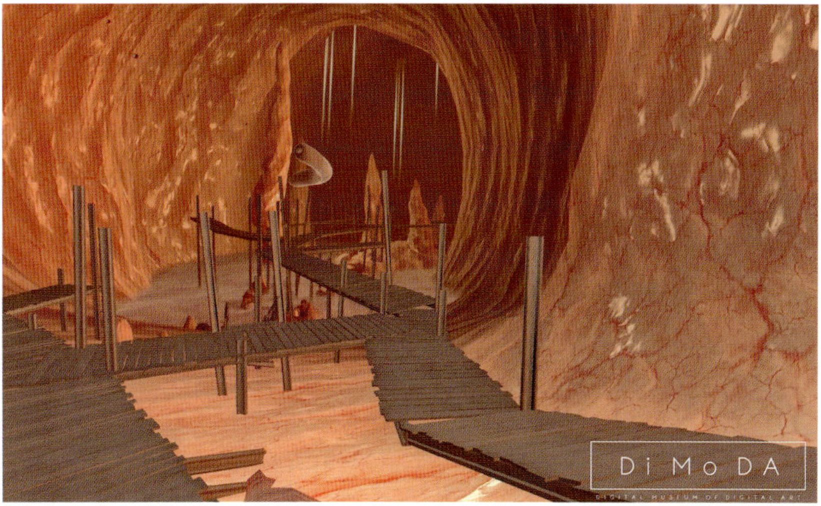

Still from Theo Triantafyllidis, *Self Portrait (Interior)*, 2016

The New Self

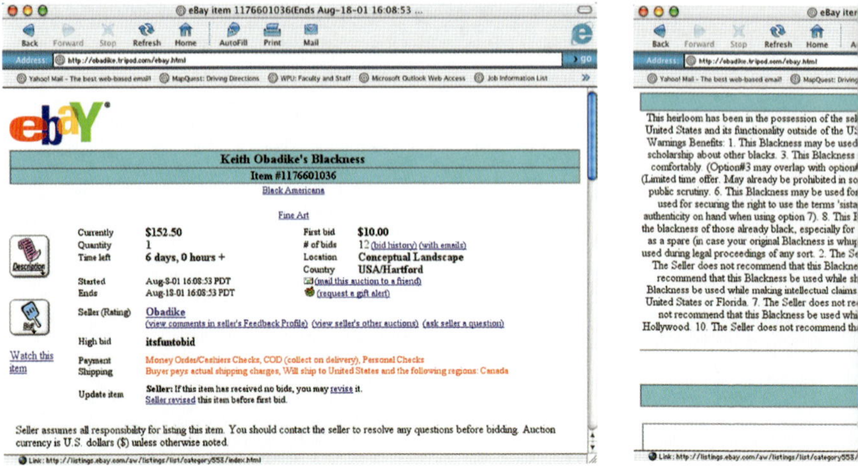

Mendi + Keith Obadike, *Blackness for Sale*, 2001

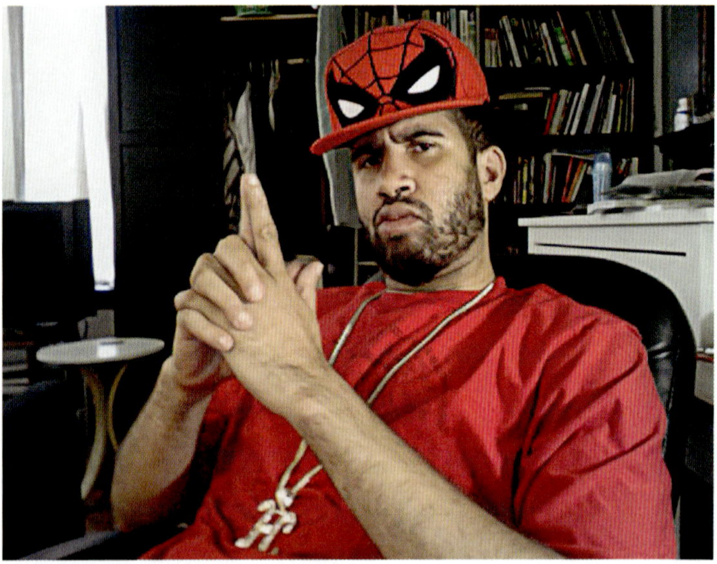

Jayson Musson as Hennessy Youngman, 2010

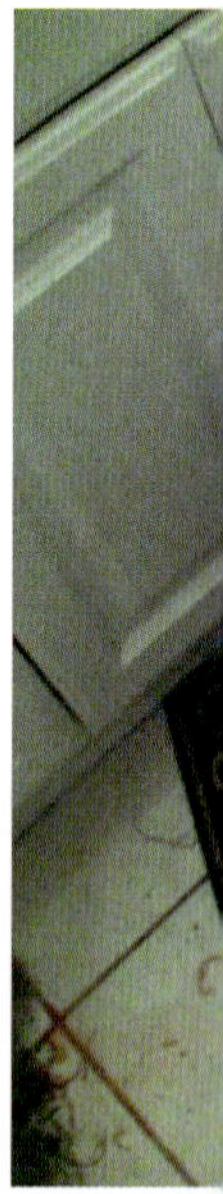

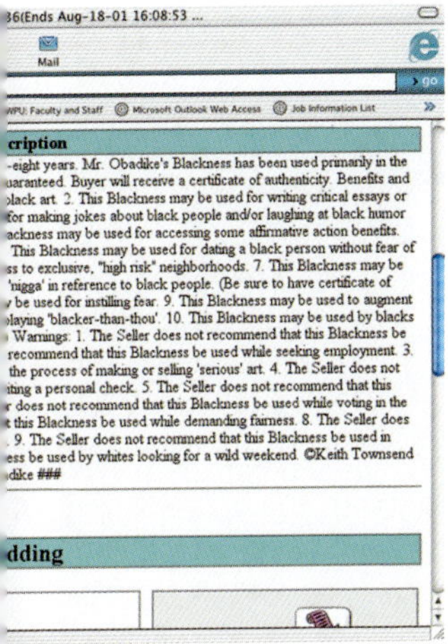

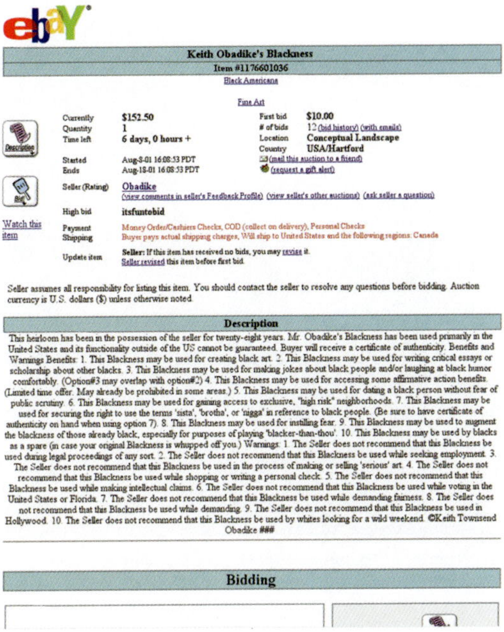

Keith Obadike's Blackness

Item #1176601036

Black Americana

Fine Art

Currently	$152.50	First bid	$10.00
Quantity	1	# of bids	12 (bid history) (with emails)
Time left	6 days, 0 hours +	Location	Conceptual Landscape
		Country	USA/Hartford
Started	Aug-8-01 16:08:53 PDT		(mail this auction to a friend)
Ends	Aug-18-01 16:08:53 PDT		(request a gift alert)
Seller (Rating)	Obadike (view comments in seller's Feedback Profile) (view seller's other auctions) (ask seller a question)		
High bid	itsfuntobid		
Payment	Money Order/Cashiers Checks, COD (collect on delivery), Personal Checks		
Shipping	Buyer pays actual shipping charges, Will ship to United States and the following regions: Canada		
Update item	Seller: If this item has received no bids, you may revise it. Seller revised this item before first bid.		

Watch this item

Seller assumes all responsibility for listing this item. You should contact the seller to resolve any questions before bidding. Auction currency is U.S. dollars ($) unless otherwise noted.

Description

This heirloom has been in the possession of the seller for twenty-eight years. Mr. Obadike's Blackness has been used primarily in the United States and its functionality outside of the US cannot be guaranteed. Buyer will receive a certificate of authenticity. Benefits and Warnings Benefits: 1. This Blackness may be used for creating black art. 2. This Blackness may be used for writing critical essays or scholarship about other blacks. 3. This Blackness may be used for making jokes about black people and/or laughing at black humor comfortably. (Option#3 may overlap with option#2) 4. This Blackness may be used for accessing some affirmative action benefits. (Limited time offer. May already be prohibited in some areas.) 5. This Blackness may be used for dating a black person without fear of public scrutiny. 6. This Blackness may be used for gaining access to exclusive, "high risk" neighborhoods. 7. This Blackness may be used for securing the right to use the terms 'sista', 'brotha', or 'nigga' in reference to black people. (Be sure to have certificate of authenticity on hand when using option 7). 8. This Blackness may be used for instilling fear. 9. This Blackness may be used to augment the blackness of those already black, especially for purposes of playing 'blacker-than-thou'. 10. This Blackness may be used by blacks as a spare (in case your original Blackness is whupped off you.) Warnings: 1. The Seller does not recommend that this Blackness be used during legal proceedings of any sort. 2. The Seller does not recommend that this Blackness be used while seeking employment. 3. The Seller does not recommend that this Blackness be used in the process of making or selling 'serious' art. 4. The Seller does not recommend that this Blackness be used while shopping or writing a personal check. 5. The Seller does not recommend that this Blackness be used while making intellectual claims. 6. The Seller does not recommend that this Blackness be used while voting in the United States or Florida. 7. The Seller does not recommend that this Blackness be used while demanding fairness. 8. The Seller does not recommend that this Blackness be used while demanding. 9. The Seller does not recommend that this Blackness be used in Hollywood. 10. The Seller does not recommend that this Blackness be used by whites looking for a wild weekend. ©Keith Townsend Obadike ###

Bidding

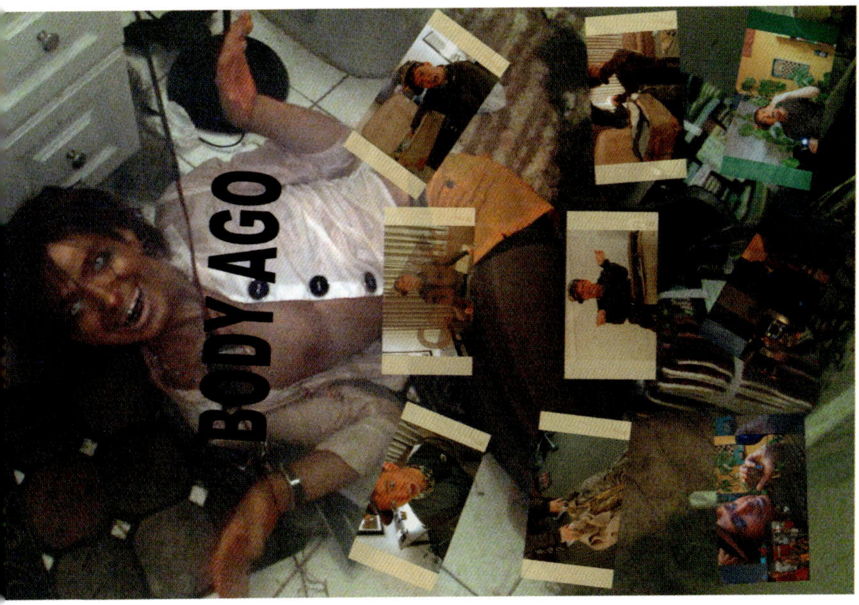

Still from Ryan Trecartin, *P.opular S.ky (section ish)*, 2009

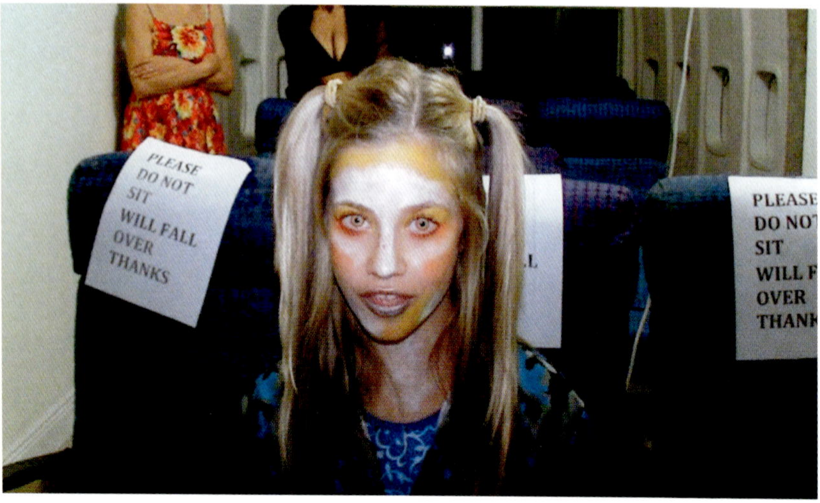

Still from Ryan Trecartin, *P.opular S.ky (section ish)*, 2009

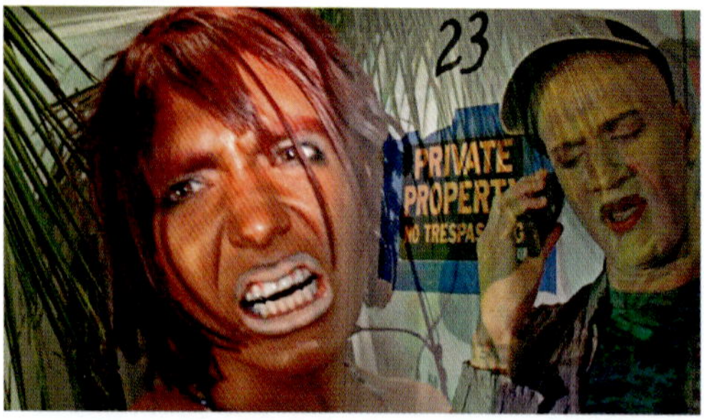

Still from Ryan Trecartin, *Sibling Topics (section a)*, 2009

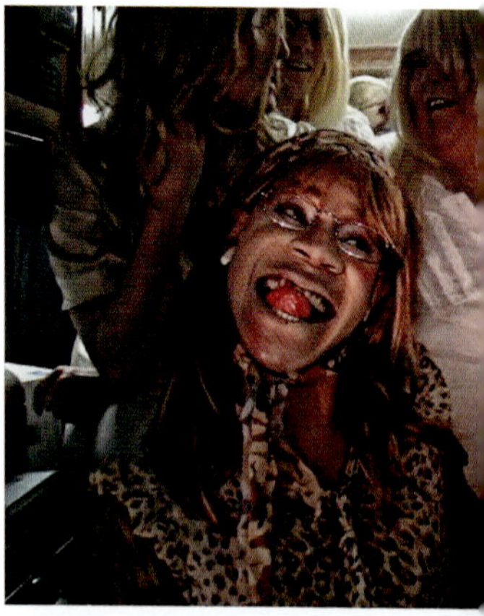

Still from Ryan Trecartin, *KCorealNC.K (section a)*, 2009

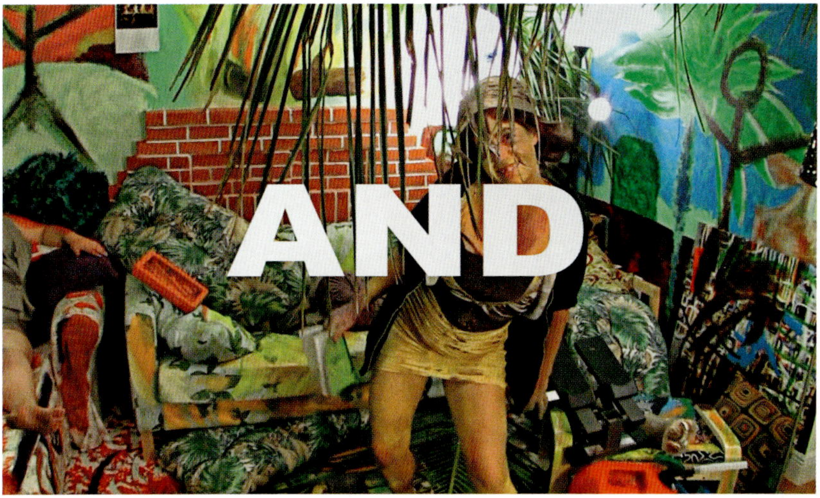

Still from Ryan Trecartin, *Sibling Topics (section a)*, 2009

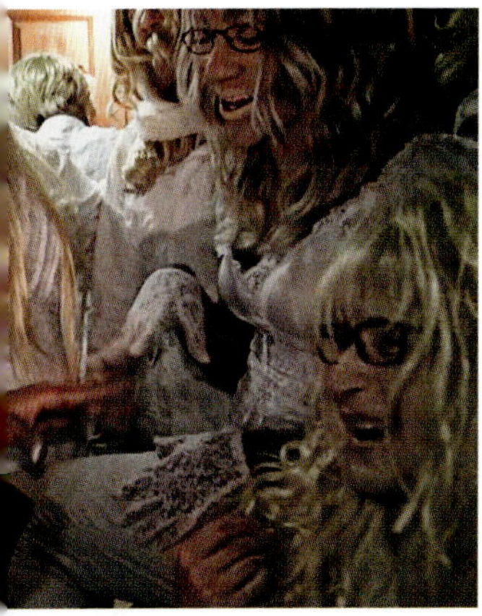

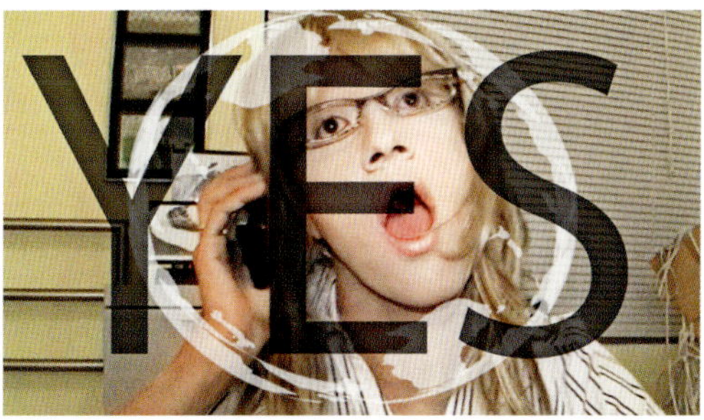

Still from Ryan Trecartin, *KCorealNC.K (section a)*, 2009

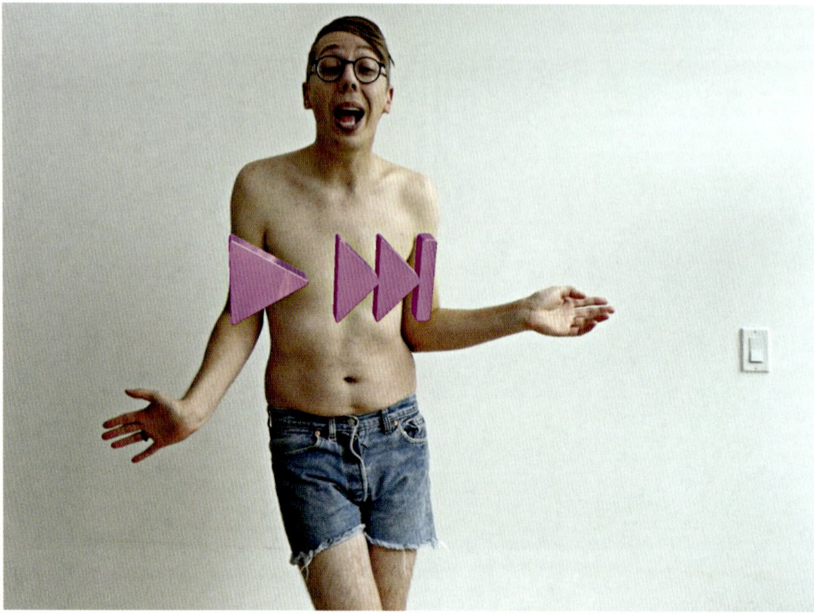

Still from Jeremy Bailey, *The Web I Want*, 2015

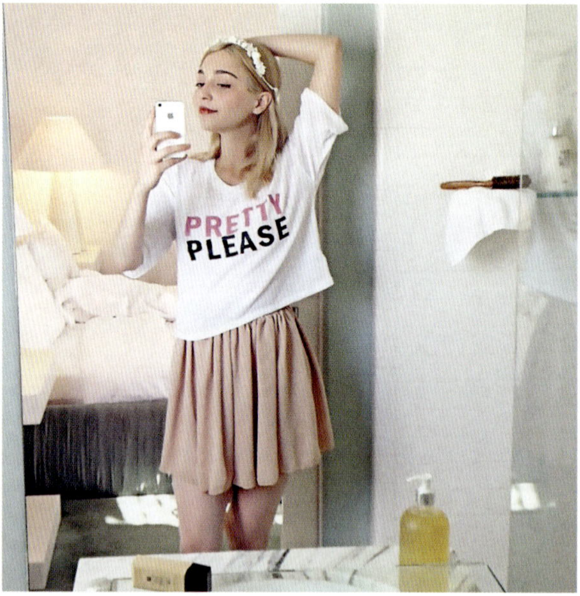

Amalia Ulman, *Excellences & Perfections (Instagram Update, 1st June 2014)*, 2015

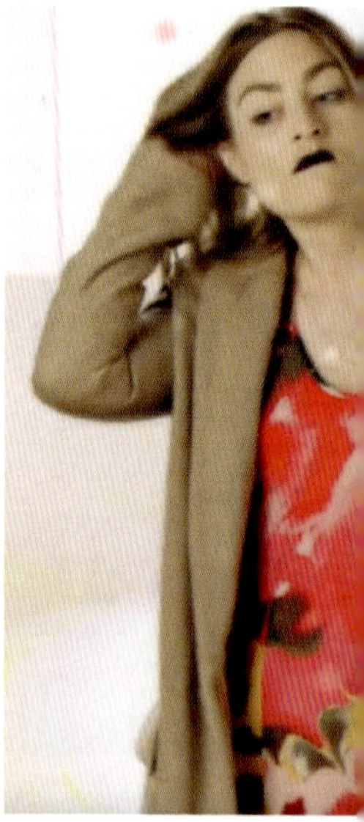

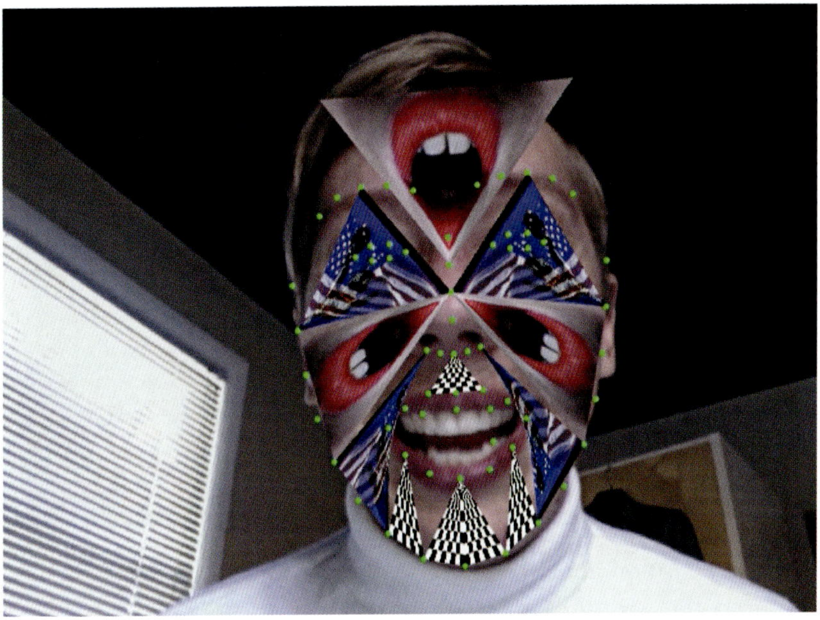

Still from Jeremy Bailey, *The Future of Television*, 2012

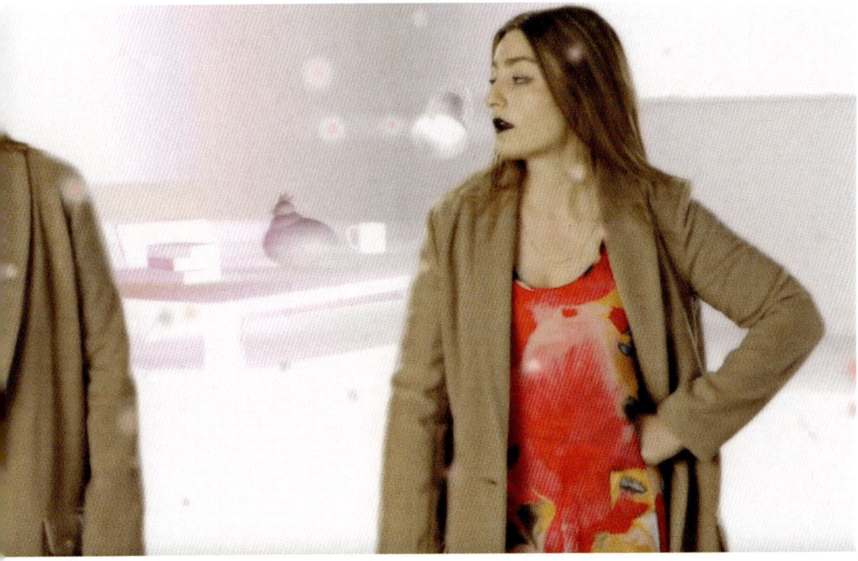

Still from Casey Jane Ellison, *The Right & Left Brains of Casey Jane's—Episode 1*, 2015

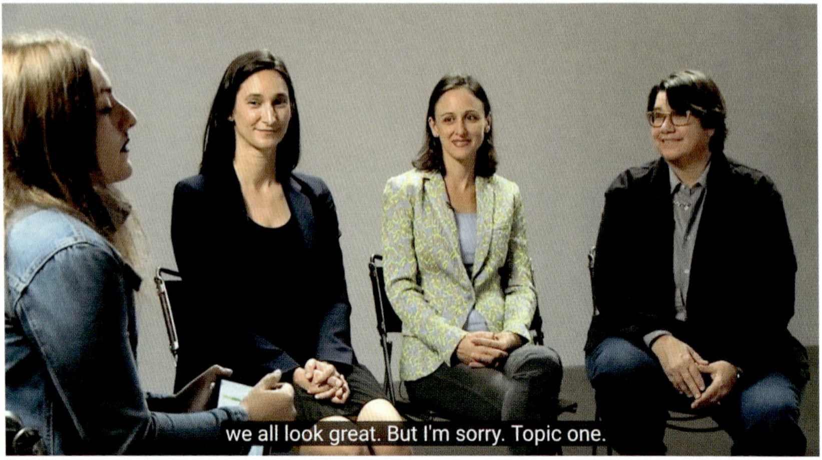

Still from Casey Jane Ellison, *Touching the Art—Episode 1: Catherine Opie, Bettina Korek, Jori Finkel*, 2014

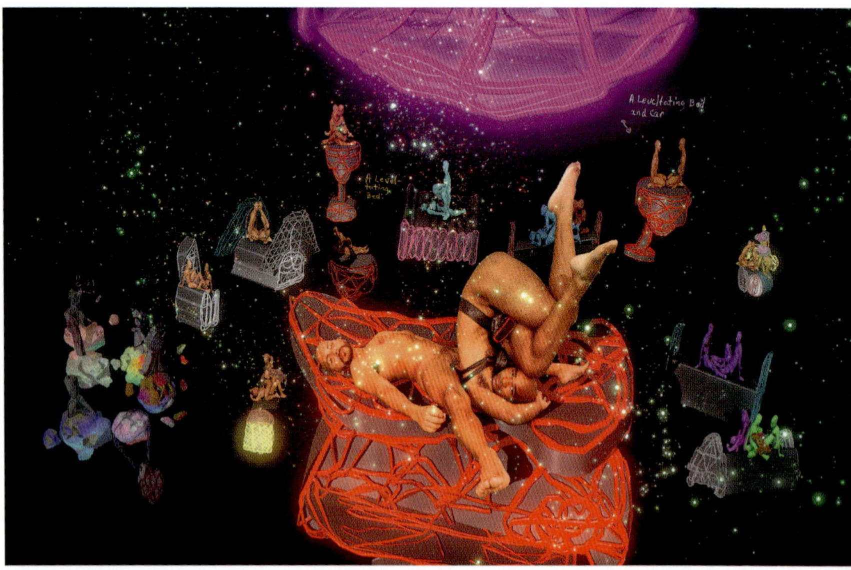

Still from Jacolby Satterwhite, *Reifying Desire 6*, 2014

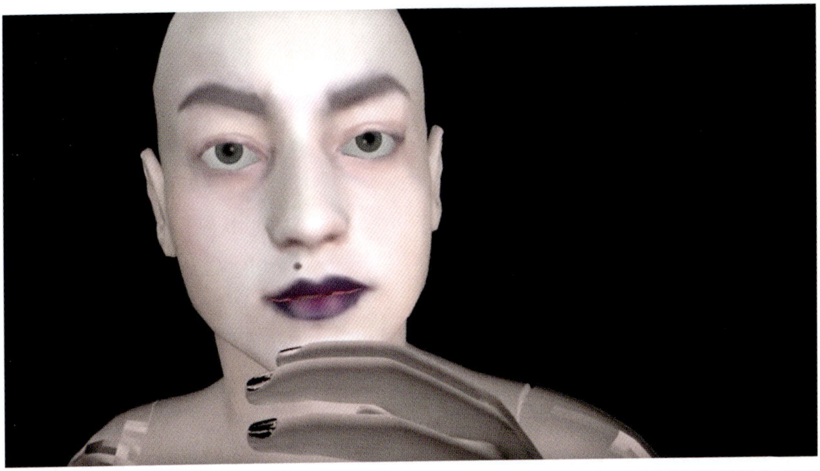

Still from Casey Jane Ellison, *IT'S SO IMPORTANT TO SEEM WONDERFUL*, 2012

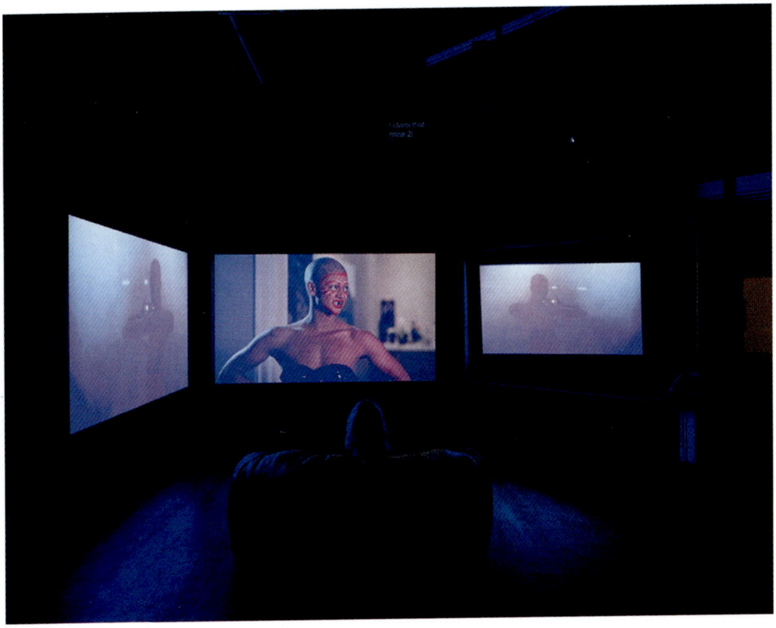

Wu Tsang, *A day in the life of bliss*, 2014

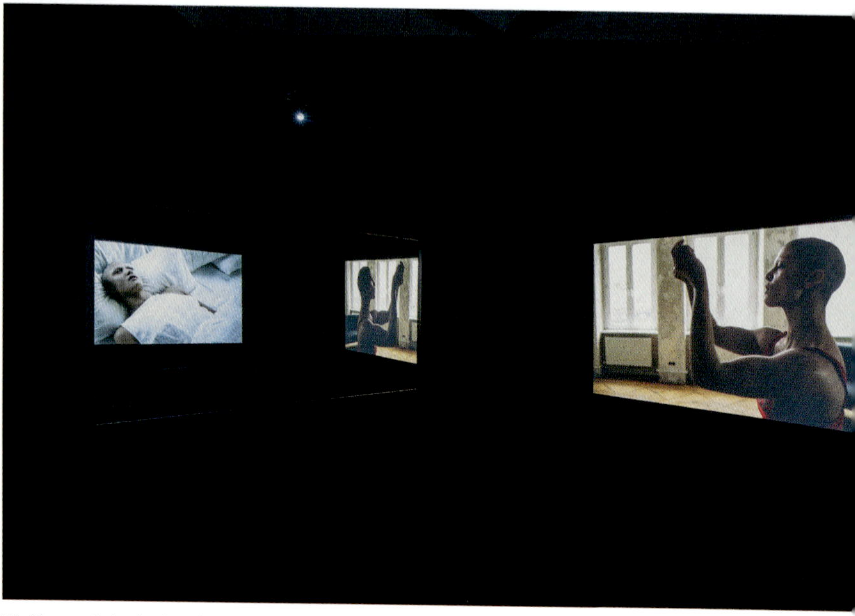

Wu Tsang, *A day in the life of bliss*, 2014

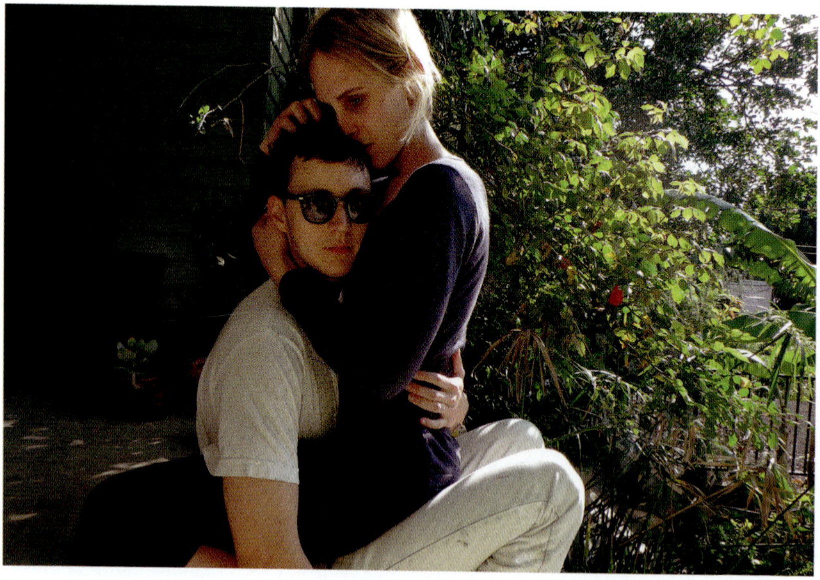

Zackary Drucker and Rhys Ernst, *Relationship, #23 (The Longest Day of the Year)*, 2008–14

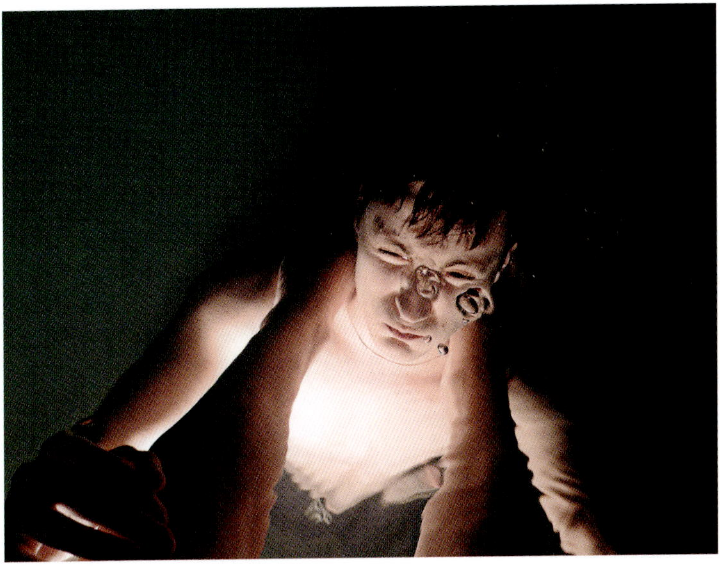

Zackary Drucker and Rhys Ernst, *Relationship, #58*, 2008–14

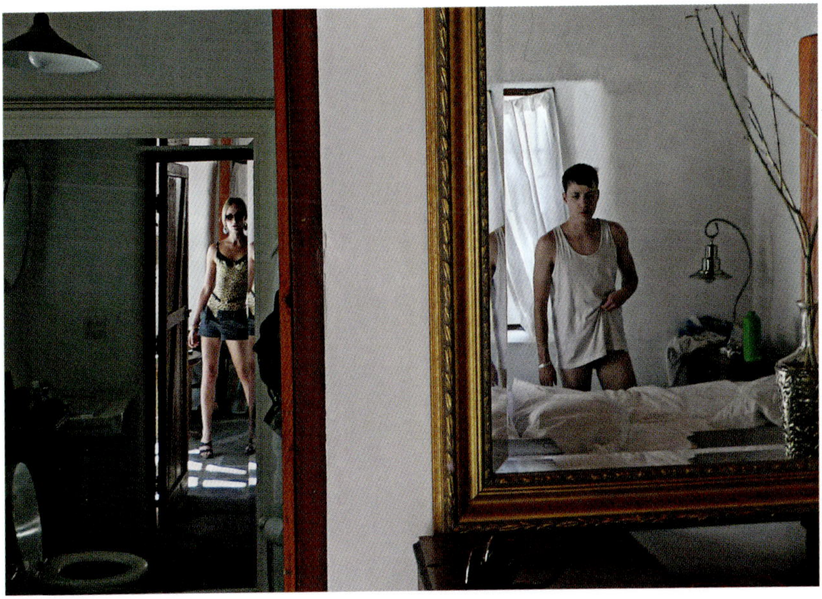

Zackary Drucker and Rhys Ernst, *Relationship, #33*, 2008–14

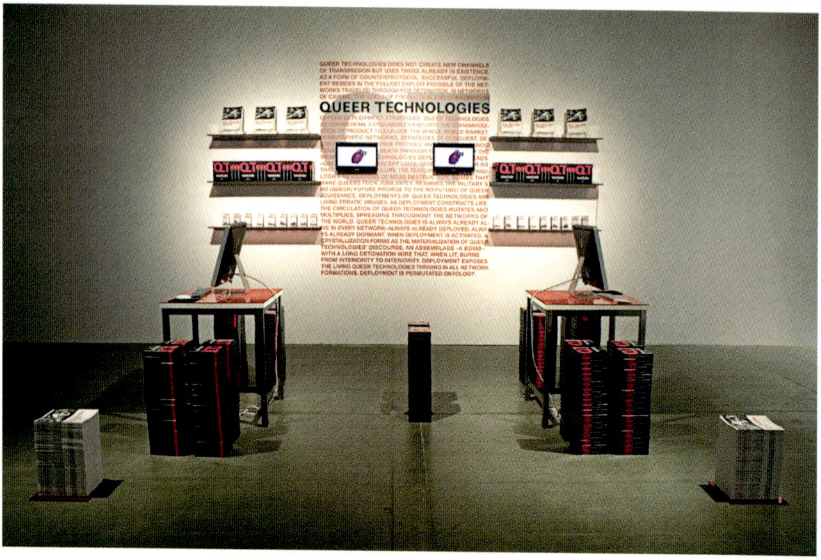

Zach Blas, *Queer Technologies: Disingenuous Bar*, 2008

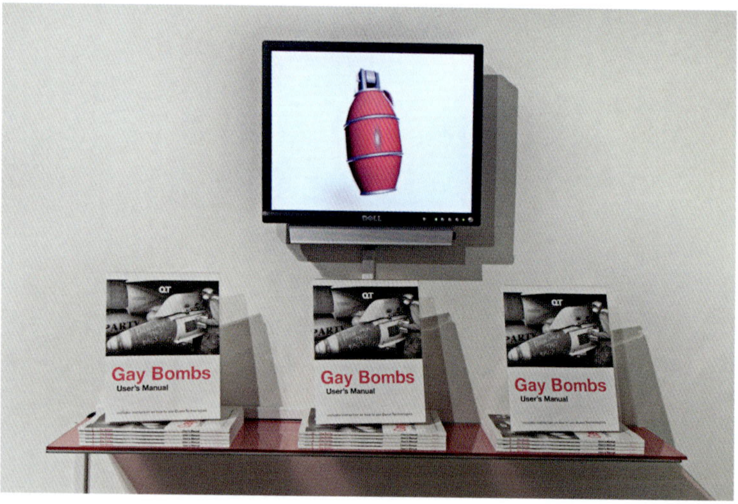

Zach Blas, *Queer Technologies: Gay Bombs: User's Manual*, 2011

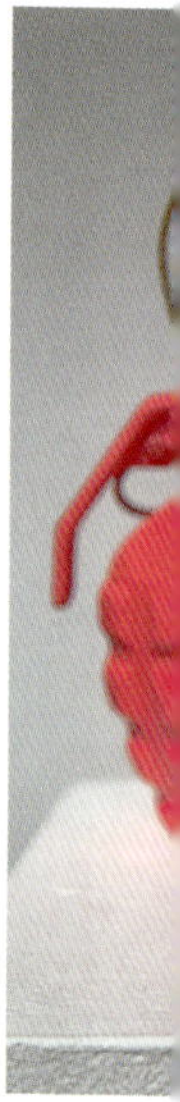

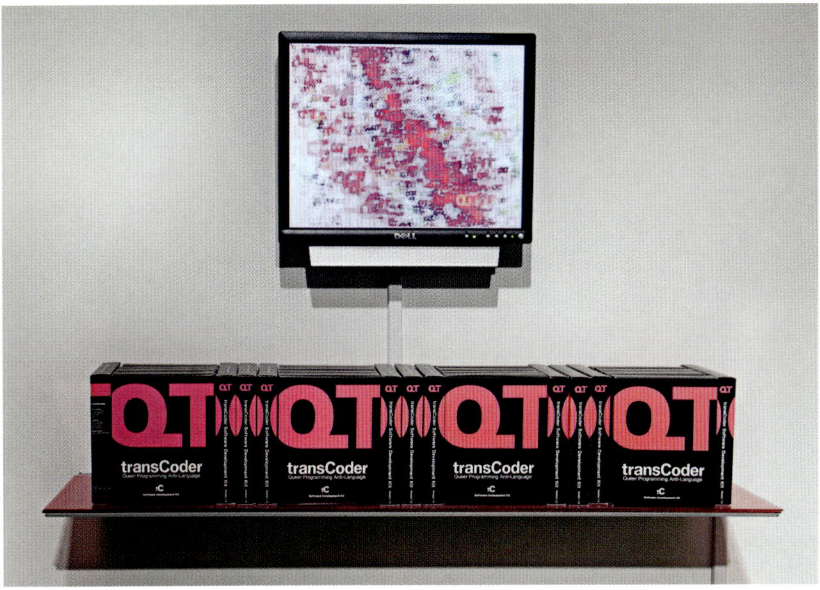

Zach Blas, *Queer Technologies: transCoder*, 2011

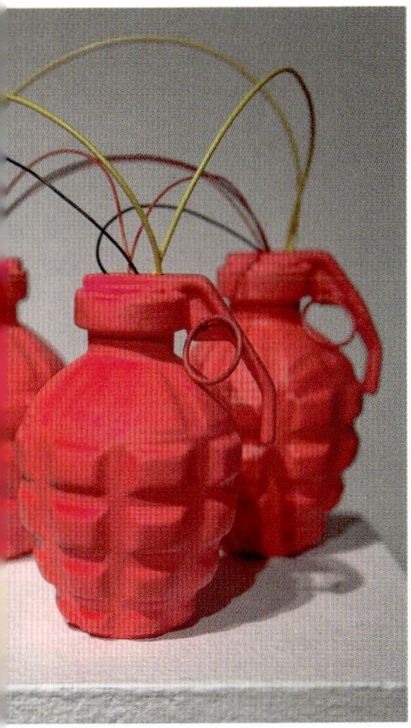

Zach Blas, *Queer Technologies: Gay Bombs*, 2011

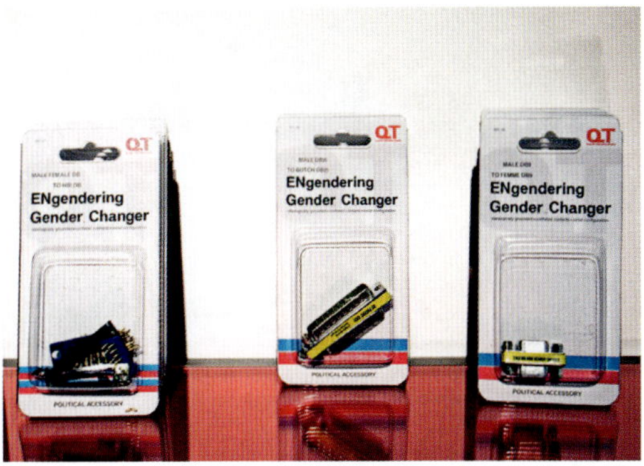

Zach Blas, *Queer Technologies: ENgenderingGenderChangers*, 2008

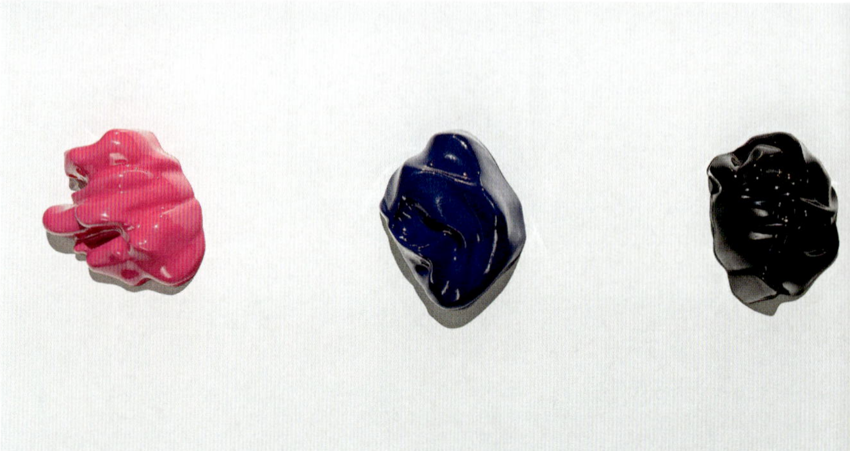

Zach Blas, *Facial Weaponization Suite*, 2015

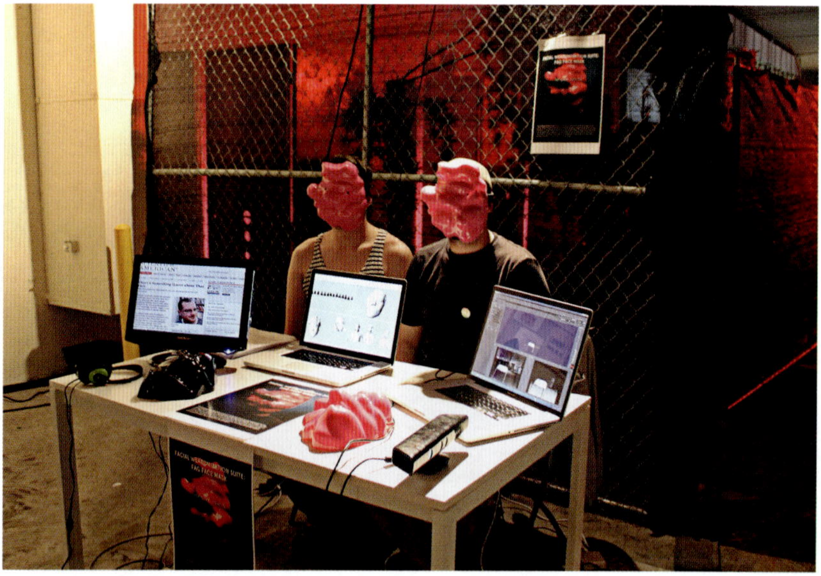

Zach Blas, *Facial Weaponization Suite: Fag Face Scanning Station*, 2013

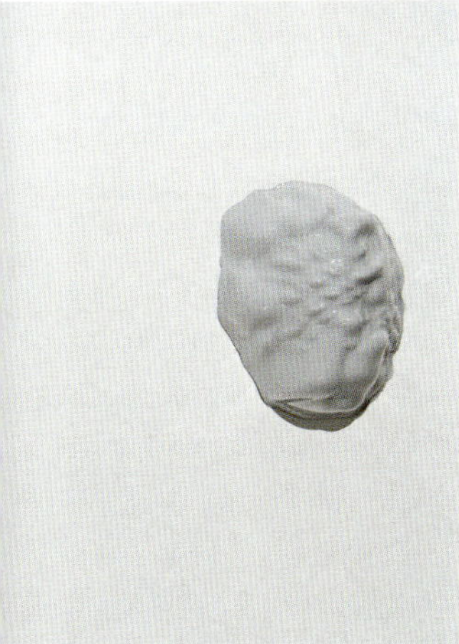

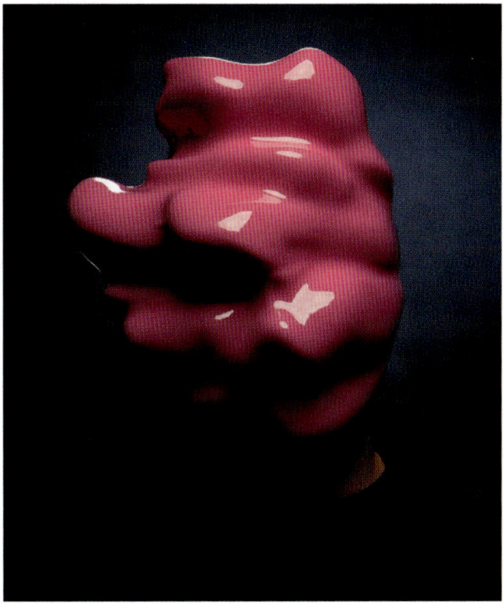

Zach Blas, *Facial Weaponization Suite: Fag Face Mask*, 2012

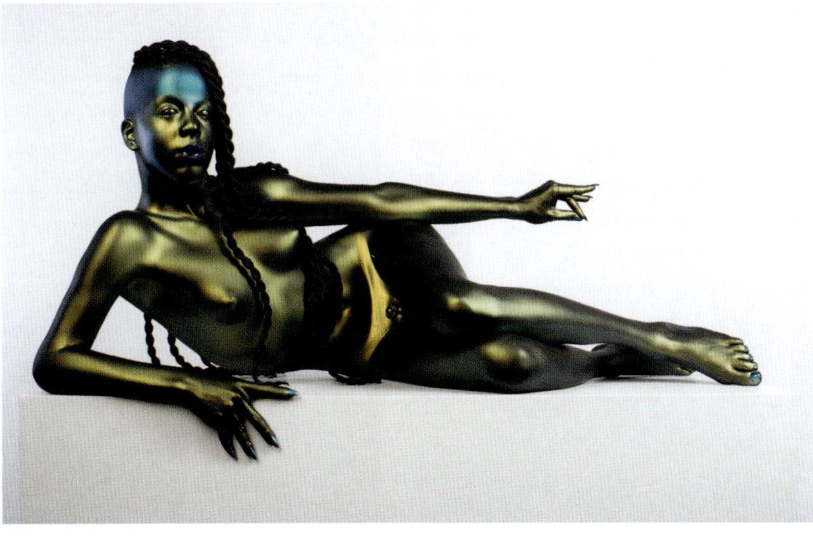

Frank Benson, *Juliana*, 2014–15

Touch Me

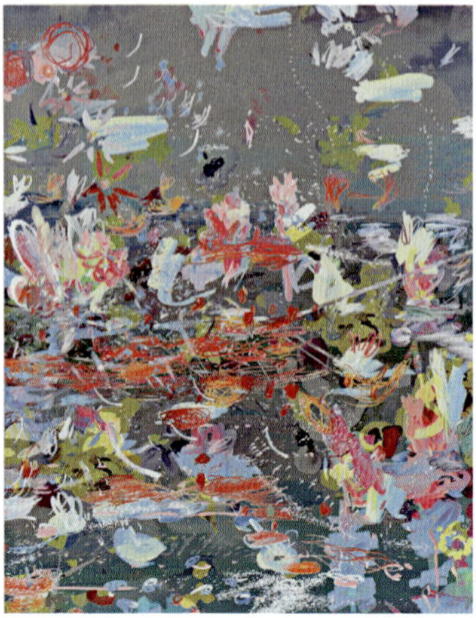

Petra Cortright, *Call Trees VC++*, 2014

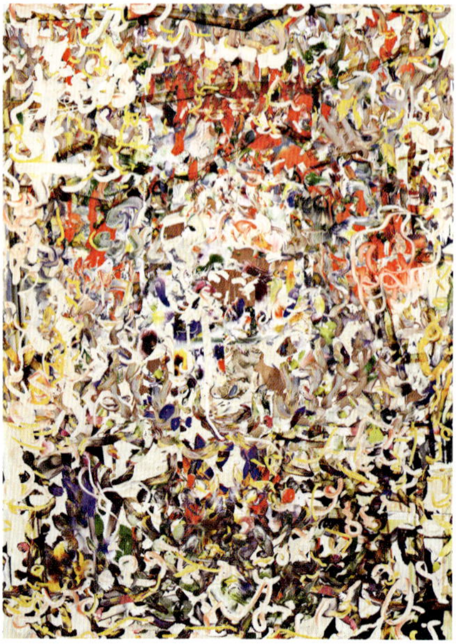

Petra Cortright, *photo_graphicStudent-CreditCard:foun@clicnetSRVR*, 2016

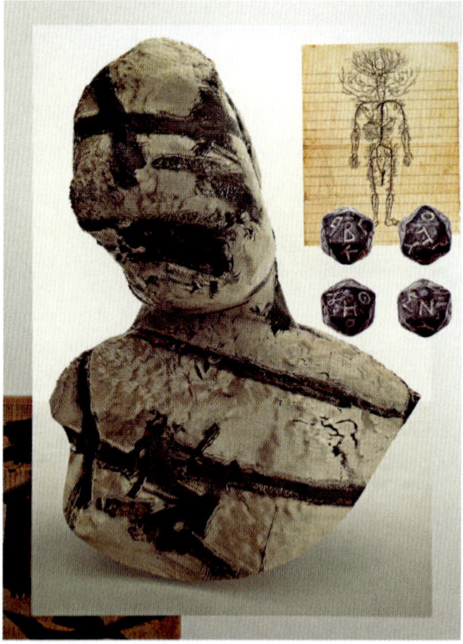

Jon Rafman, *New Age Demanded (Kline)*, 2011

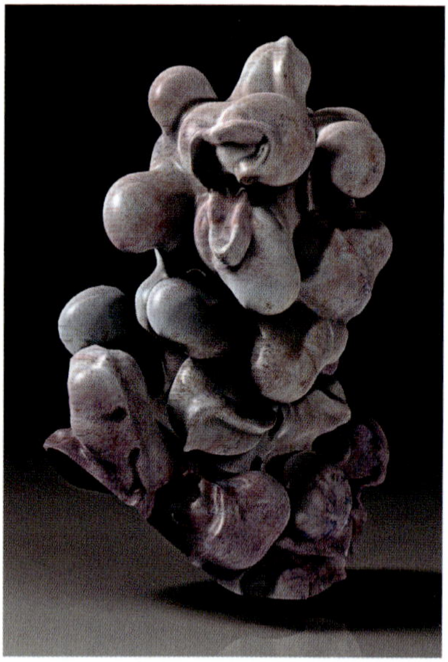

Jon Rafman, *New Age Demanded (Globular Marble)*, 2014

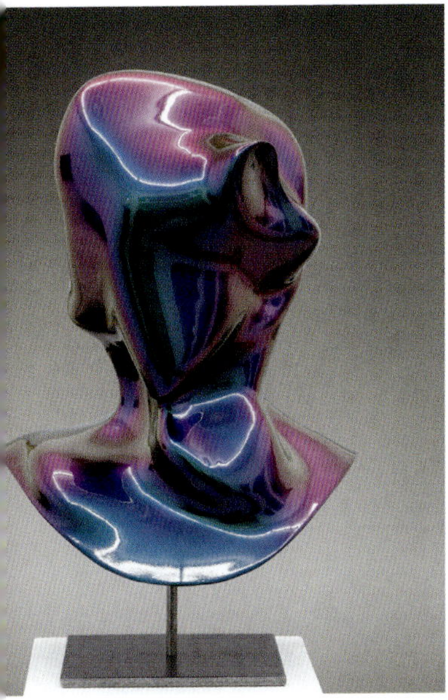

Jon Rafman, *New Age Demanded (Futurisimo Red to Green)*, 2013

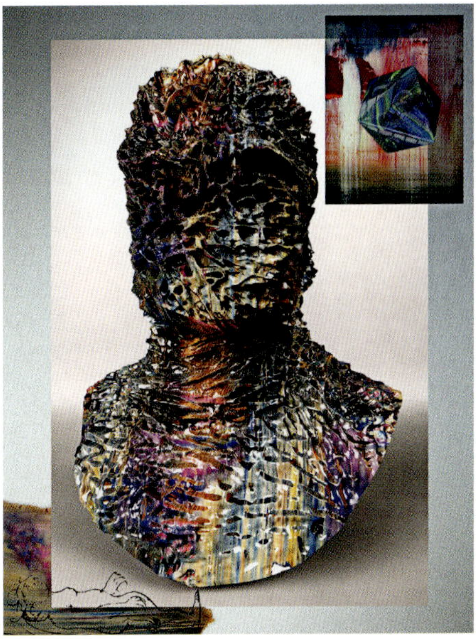

Jon Rafman, *New Age Demanded (Richter)*, 2011

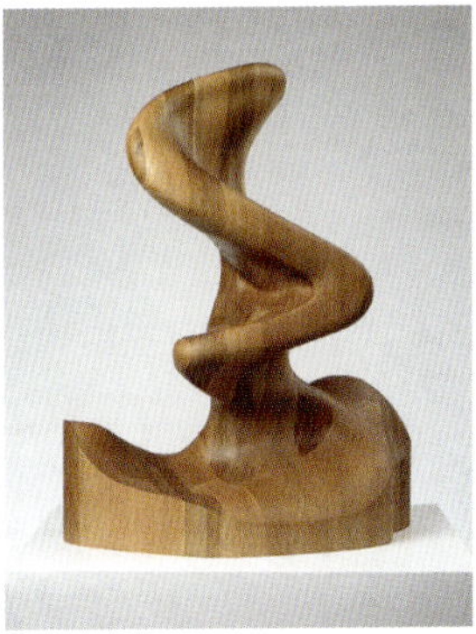

Jon Rafman, *New Age Demanded (Sface Oak)*, 2017

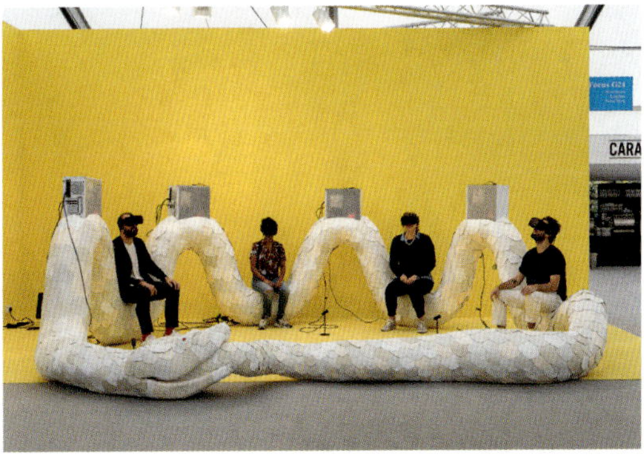

Jon Rafman, *Trans-dimensional Serpent*, 2016

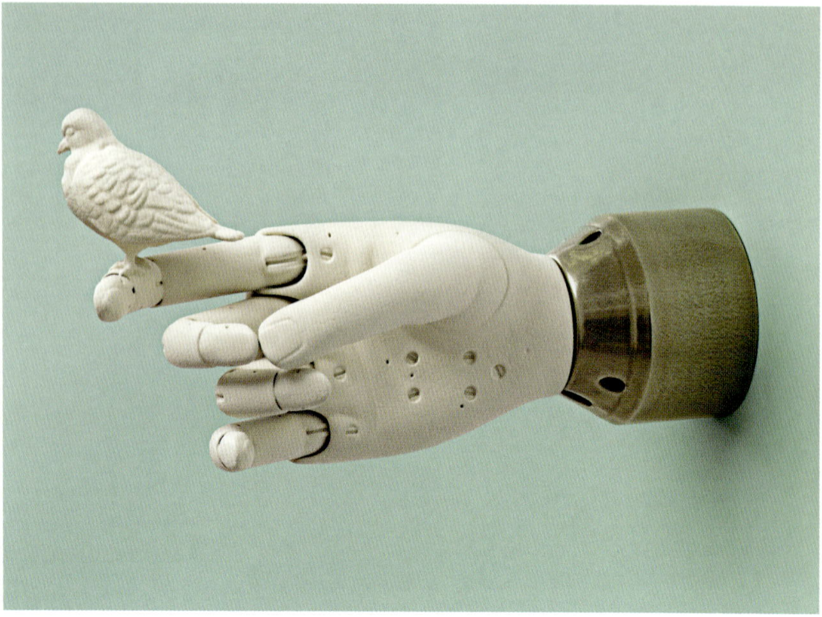

Aleksandra Domanović, *Little Sister II*, 2013

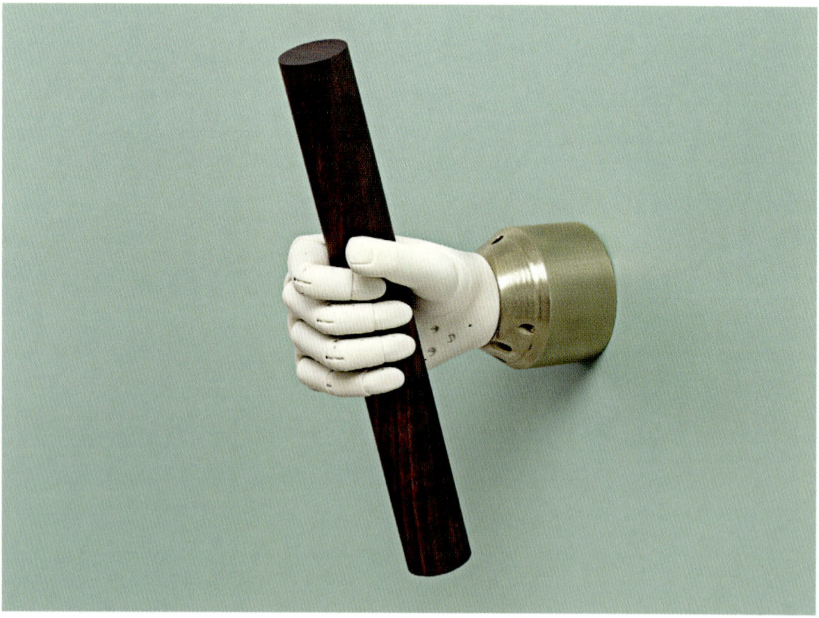

Aleksandra Domanović, *Relay Runner (Sanija Hyseni 1979)*, 2013

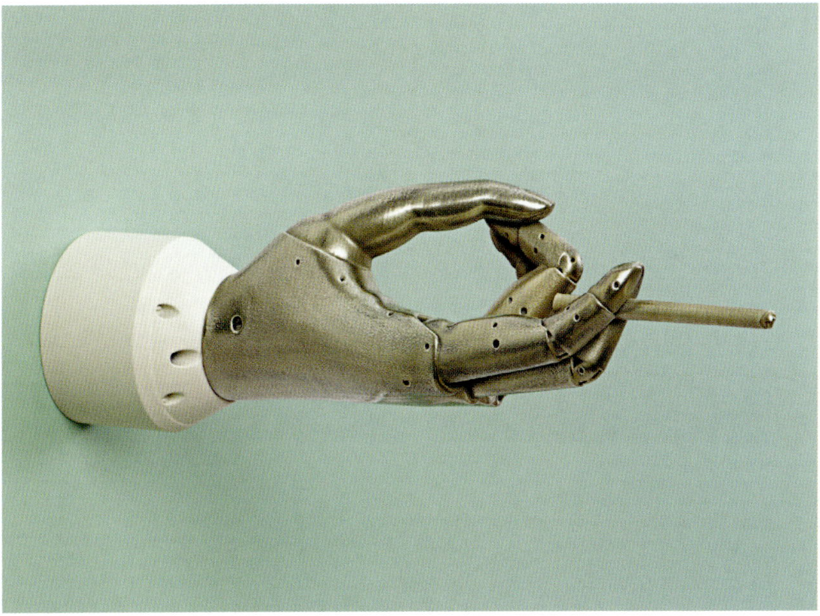

Aleksandra Domanović, *Torches of Freedom*, 2013

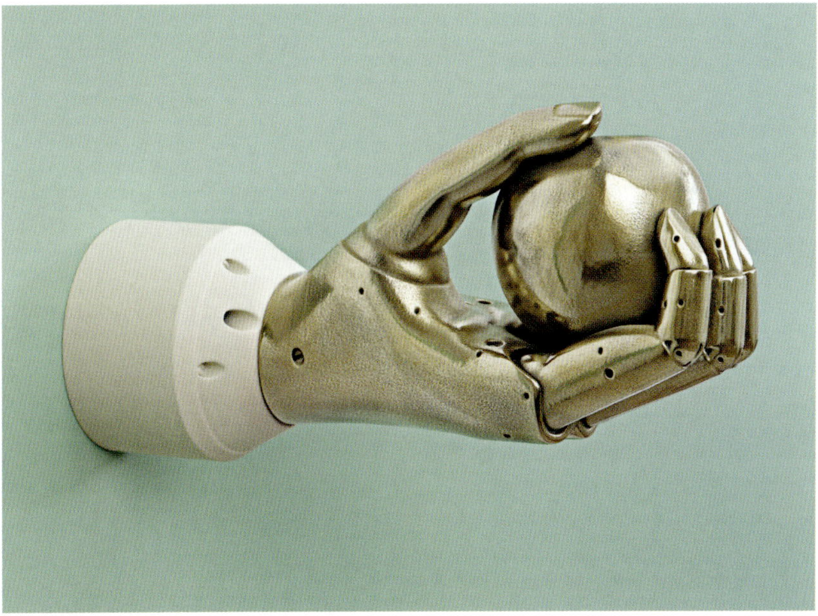

Aleksandra Domanović, *Alan's Apple*, 2013

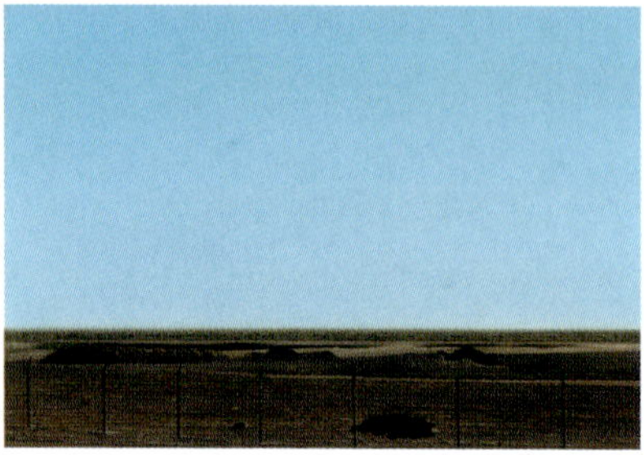

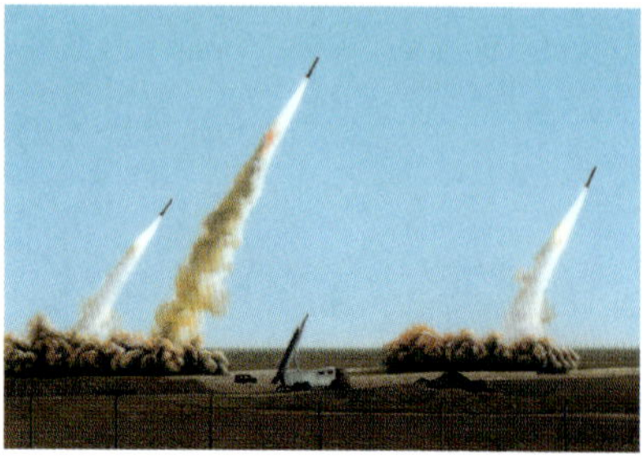

Oliver Laric, *Versions (Missile Variations)*, 2010

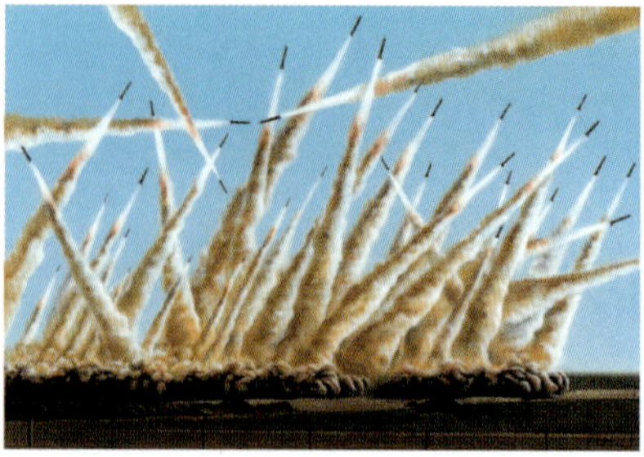

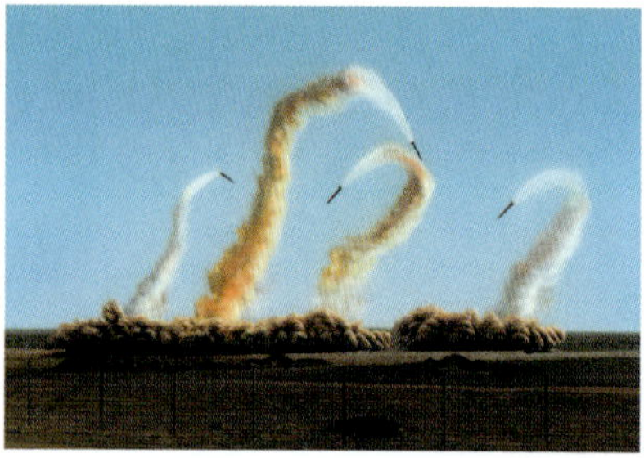

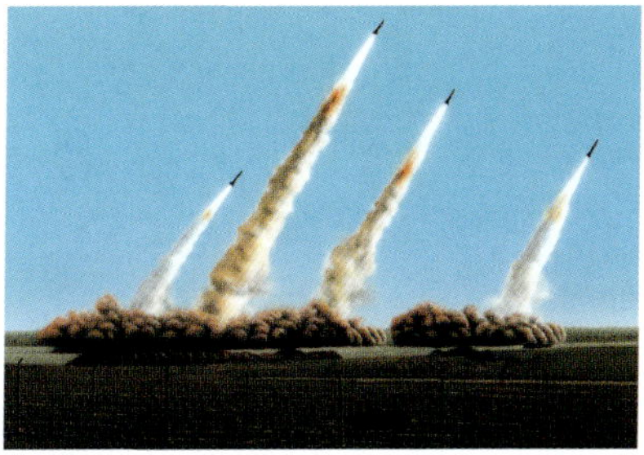
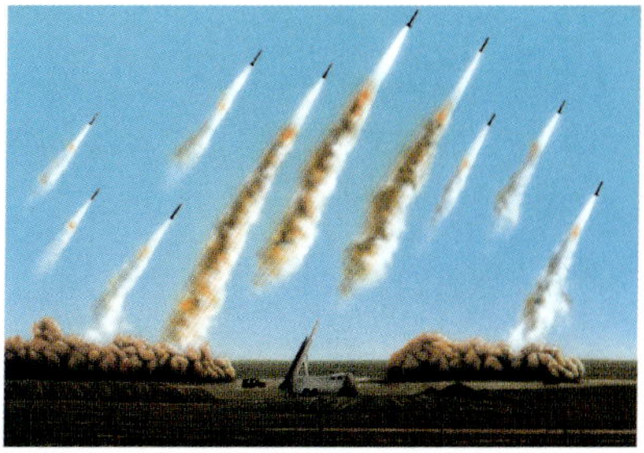
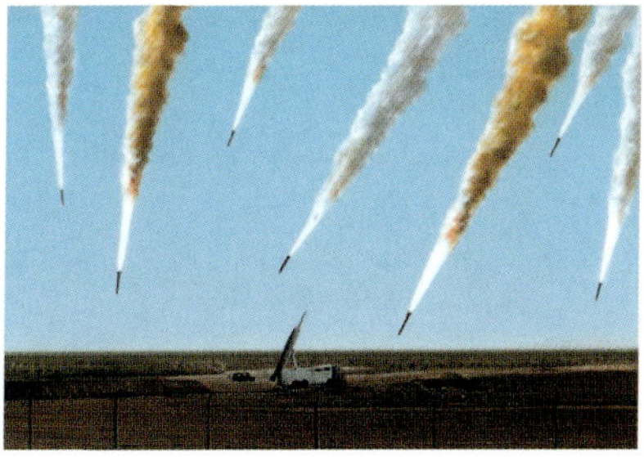
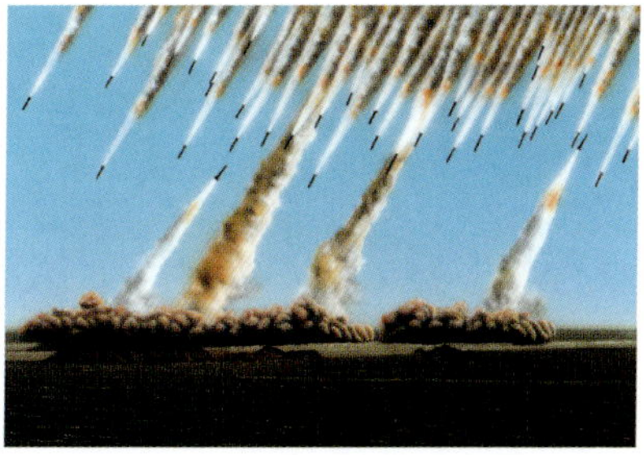

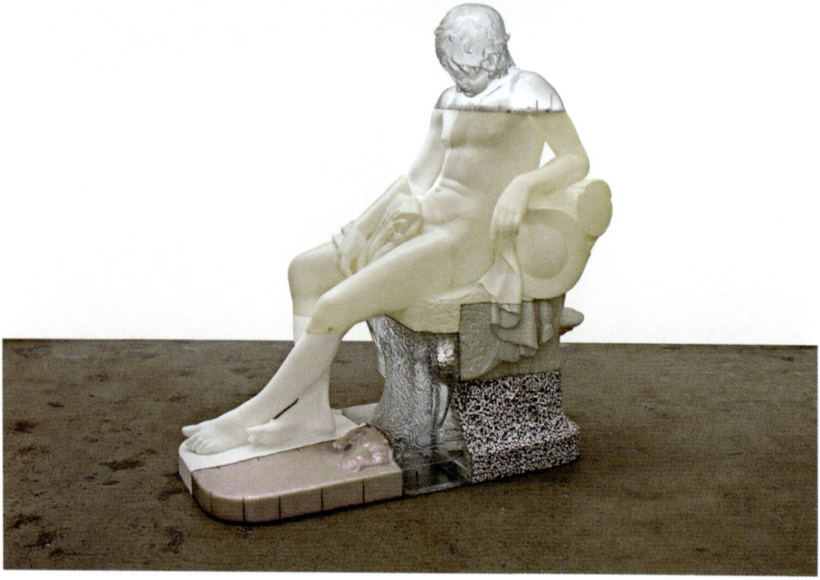

Oliver Laric, *Sleeping Boy*, 2016

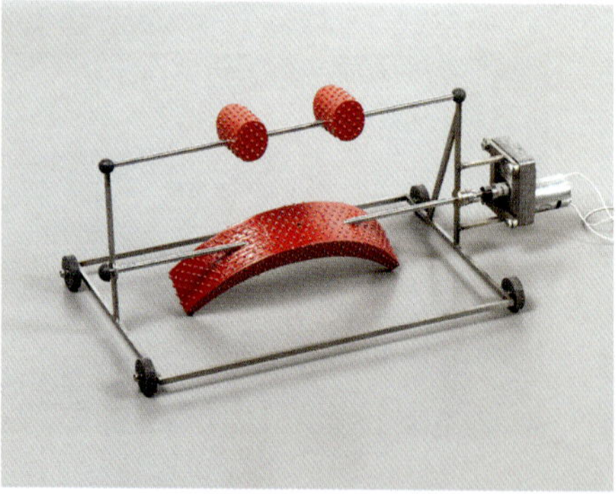

Antoine Catala, *:)*, 2014

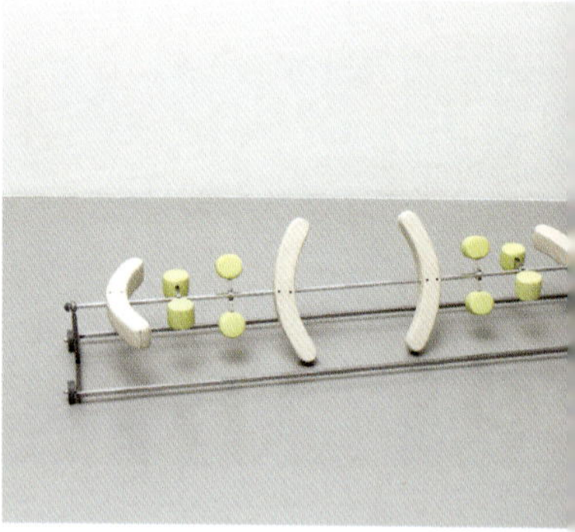

Antoine Catala, *(::( )::) (band-aid)*, 2014

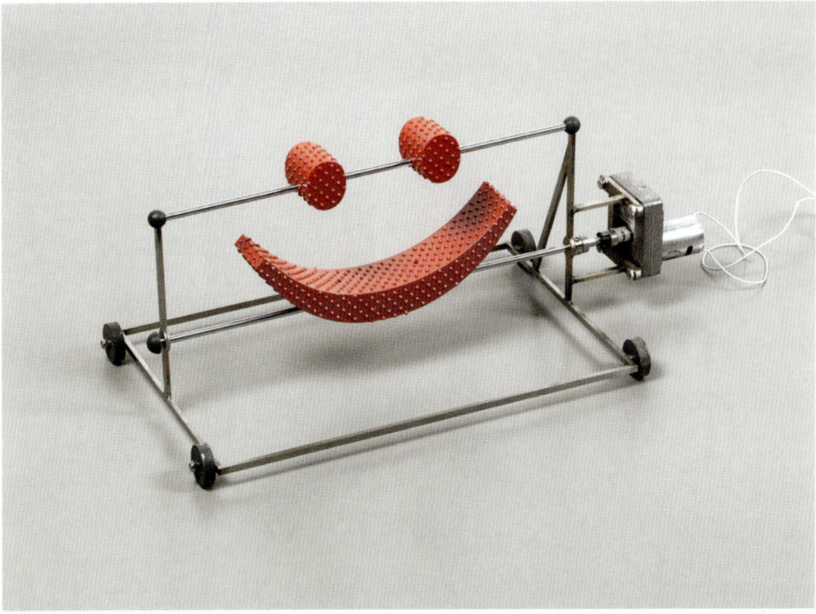

Antoine Catala, *:)*, 2014

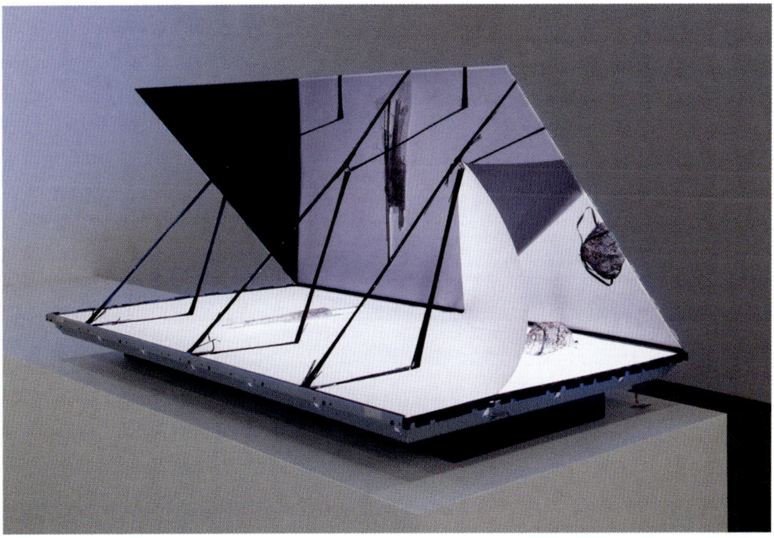

Josh Tonsfeldt, *Untitled*, 2015

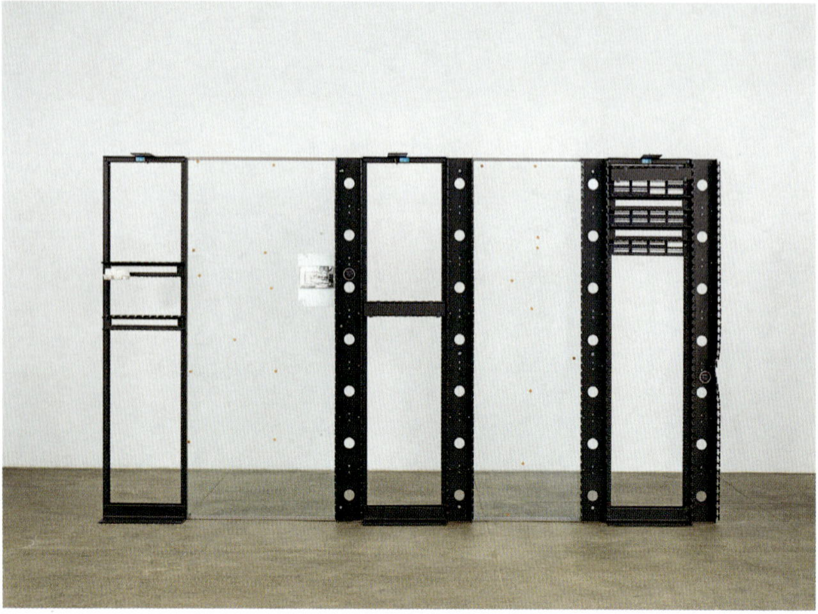

Ben Schumacher, *Rebirth of the Bathhouse, server room detail 1:1*, 2014

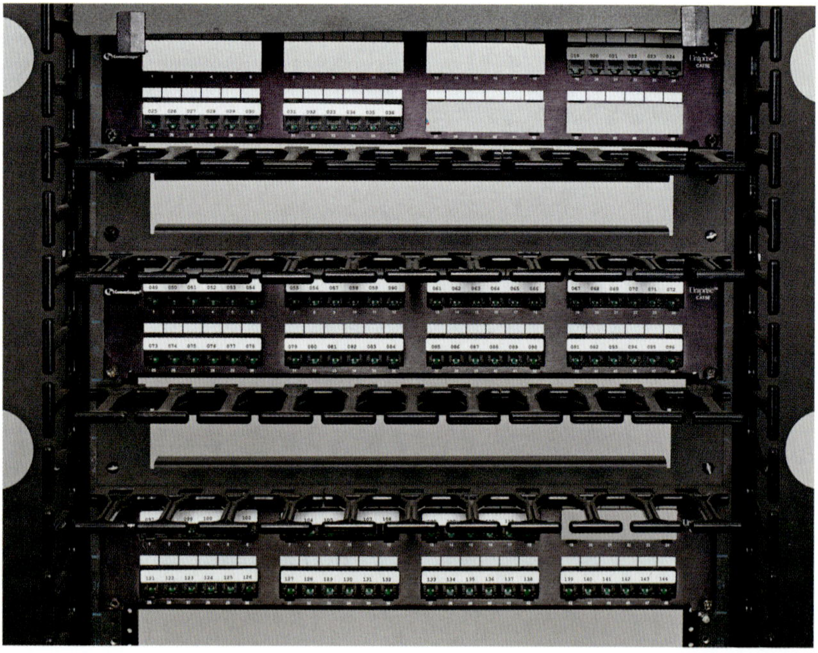

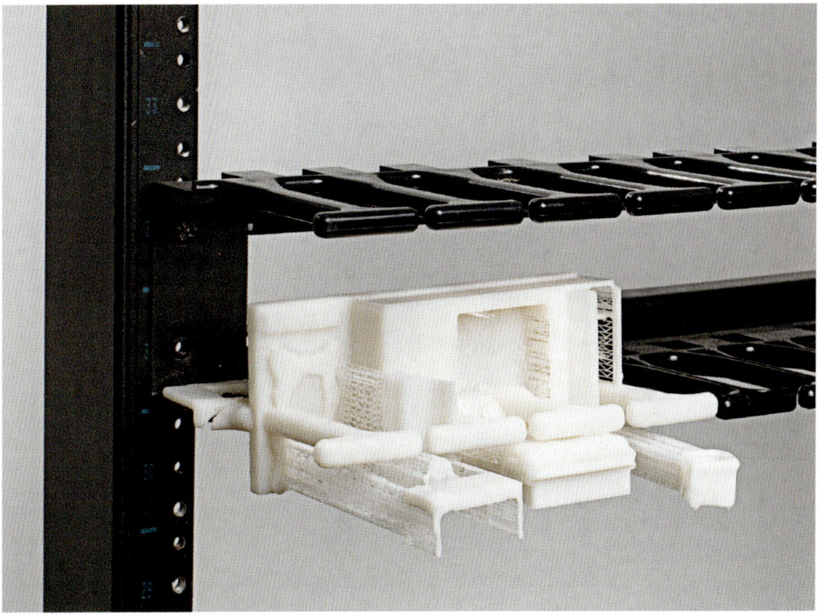

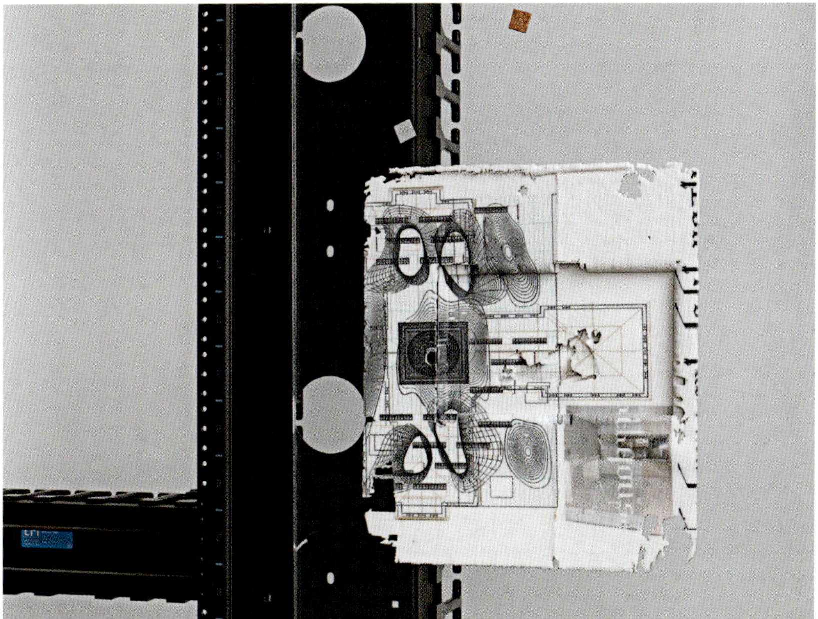

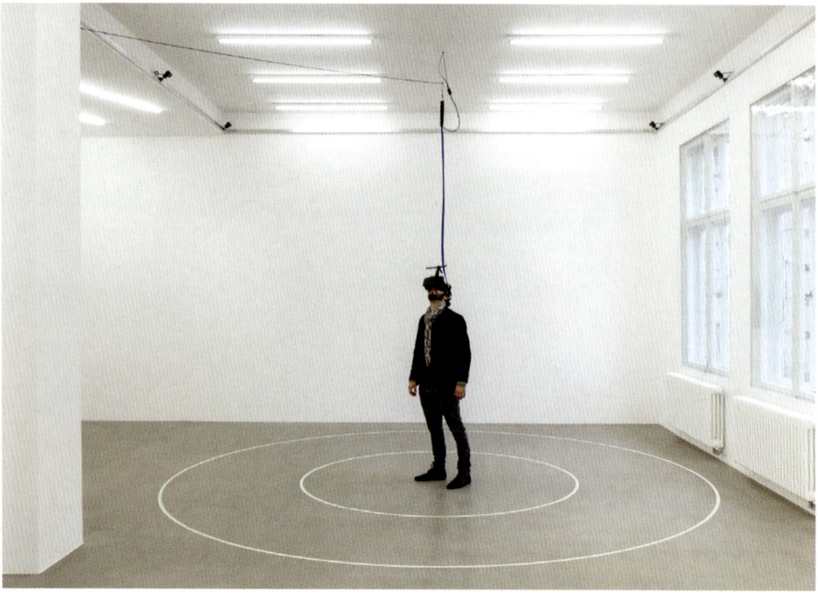

Daniel Steegmann Mangrané, *Phantom (Kingdom of all the animals and all the beasts is my name)*, 2014–15

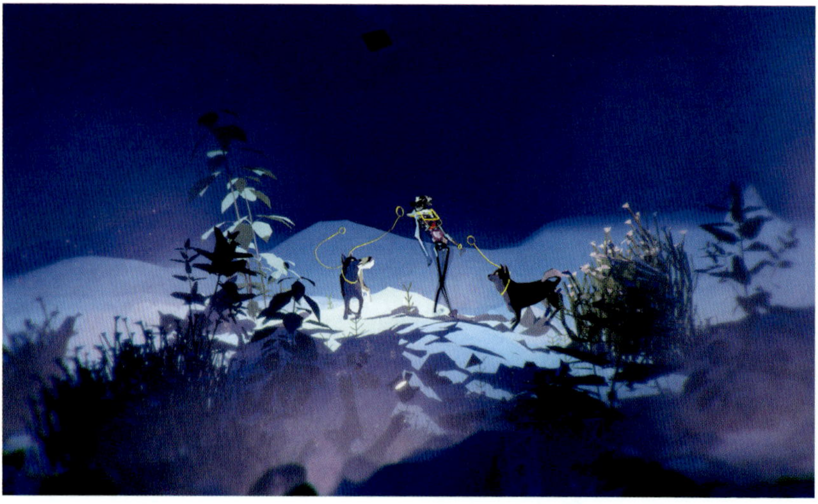

Ian Cheng, *Emissary Forks at Perfection*, 2015–16

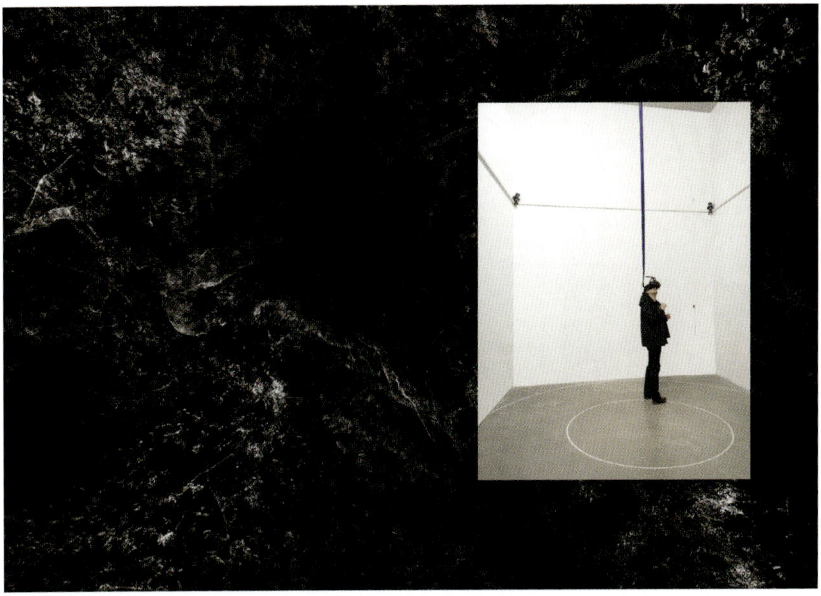

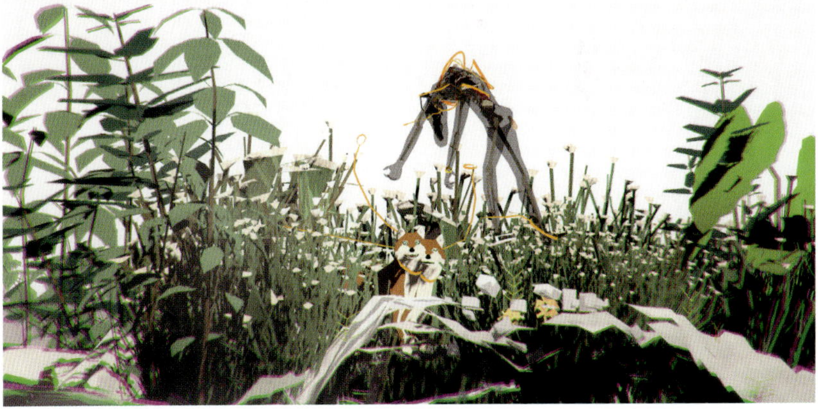

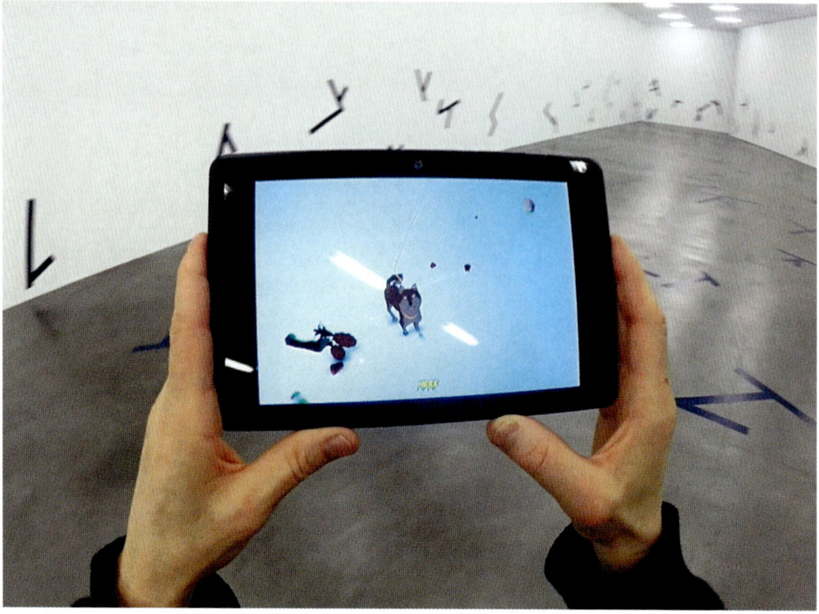

Ian Cheng, *Emissary Forks for You*, 2016

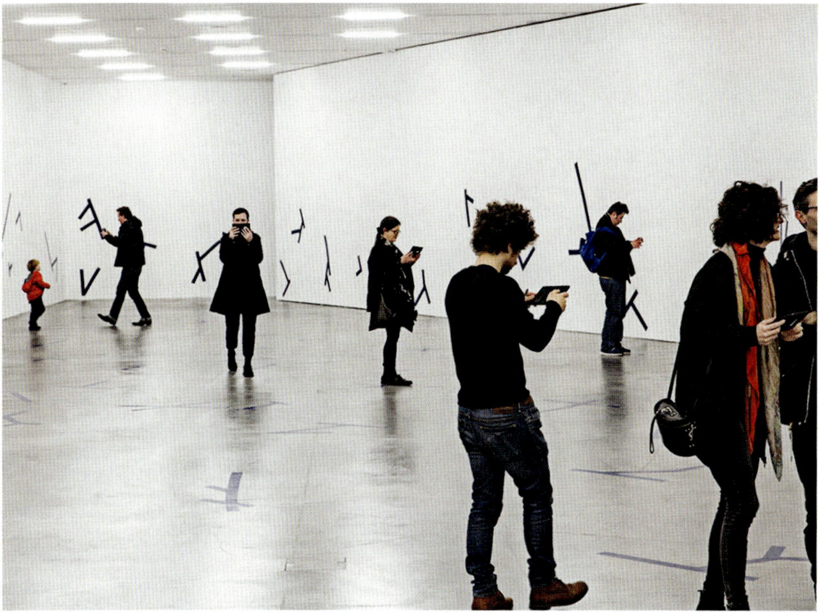

Don't Control Me

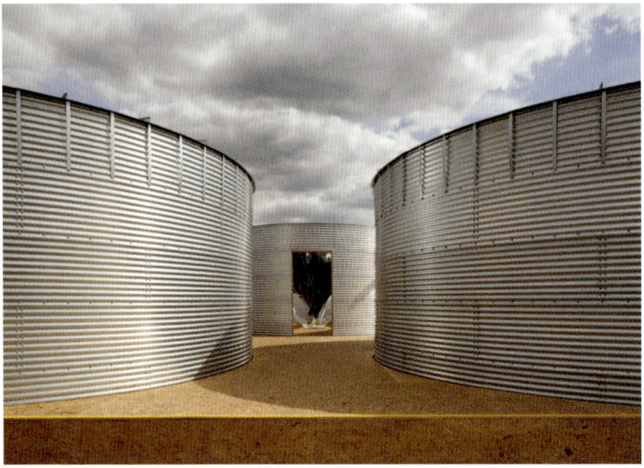

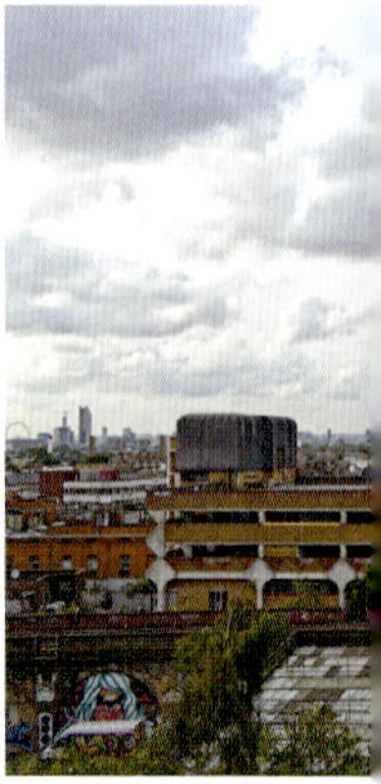

James Bridle, *The Right To Flight*, 2014

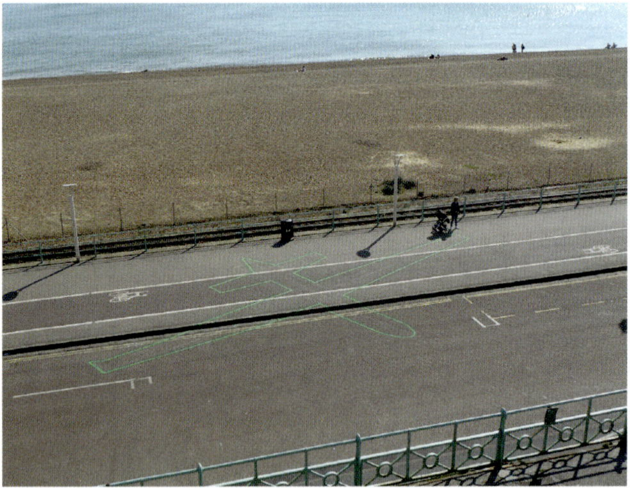

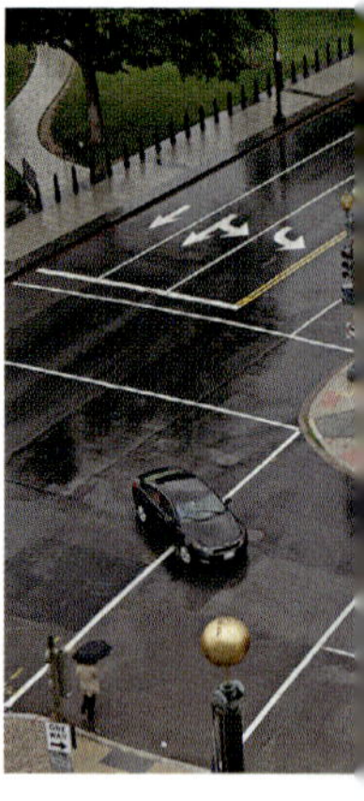

James Bridle, *Drone Shadow 003*, 2013

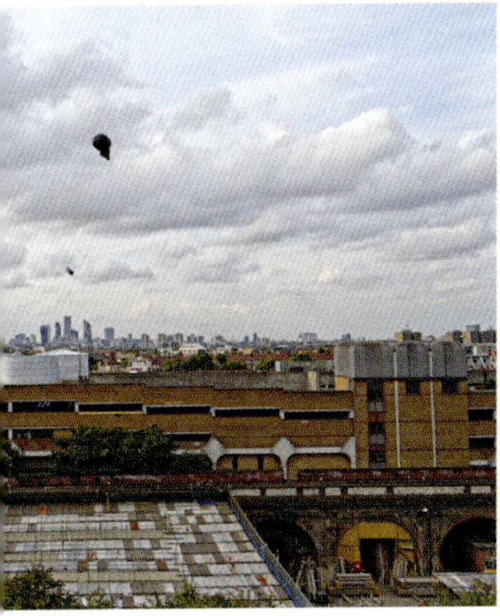

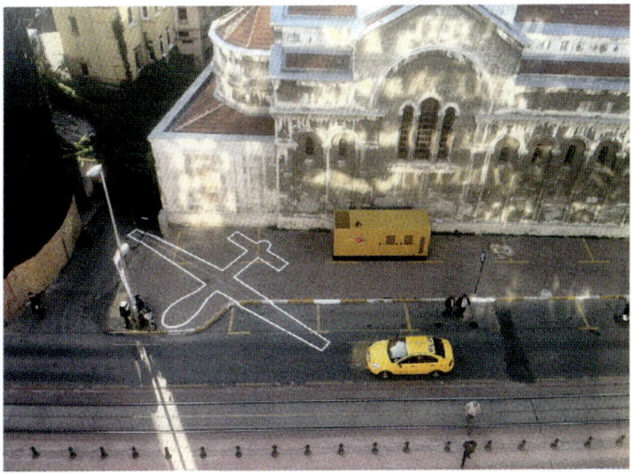

James Bridle, *Drone Shadow 002*, 2012

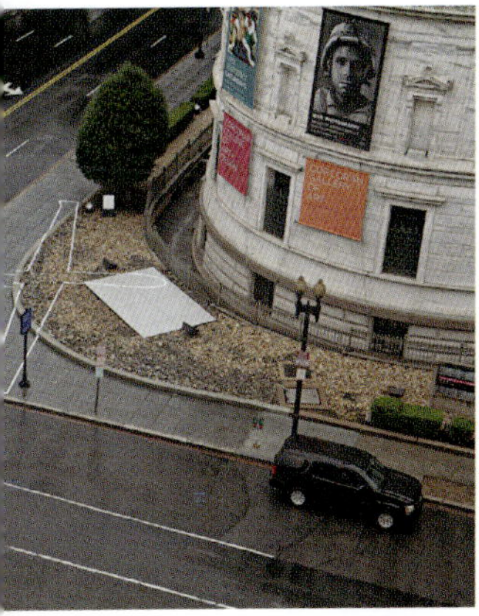

James Bridle,
Drone Shadow 004, 2013

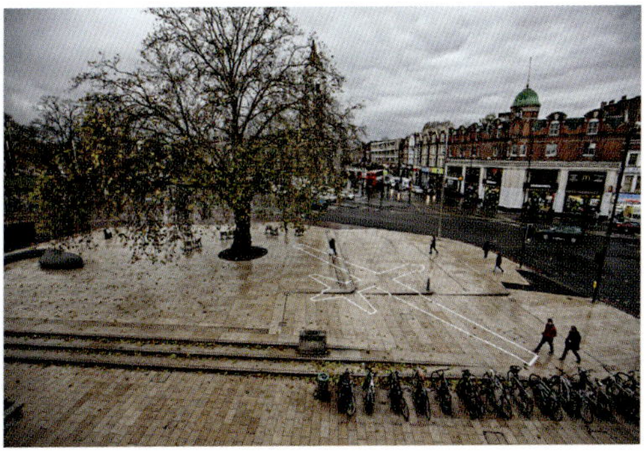

James Bridle, *Drone Shadow 006*, 2013

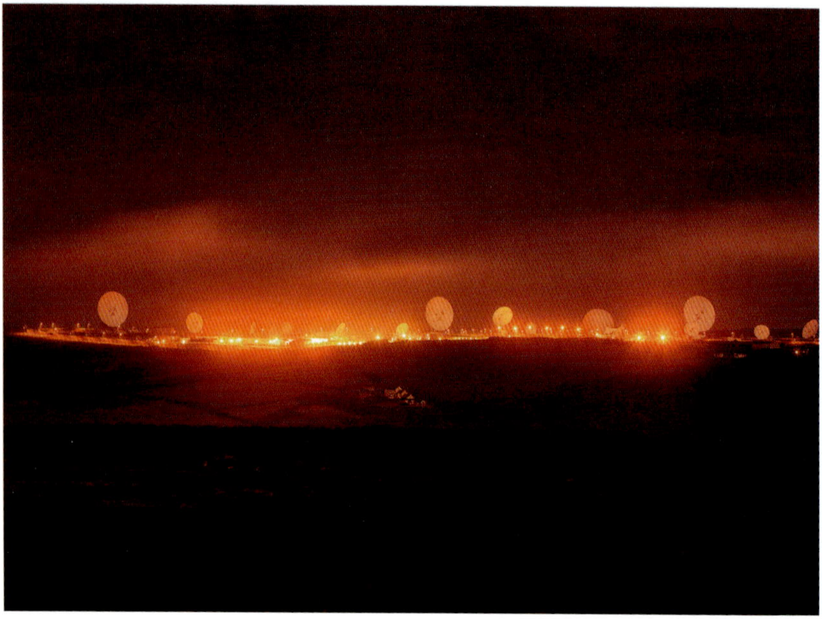

Trevor Paglen, *NSA/GCHQ Surveillance Base, Bude, Cornwall, UK*, 2015

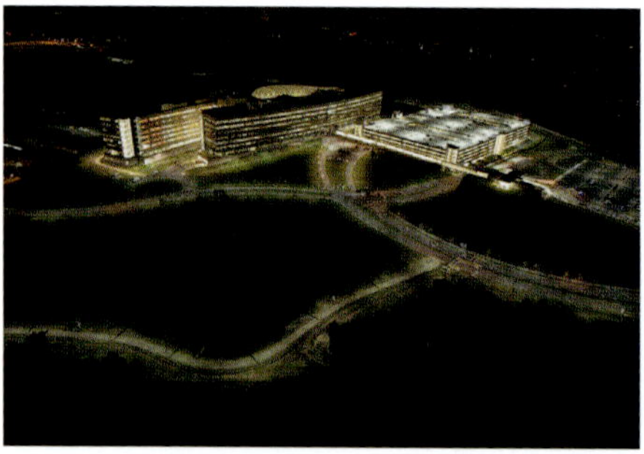

Trevor Paglen, *National Geospatial-Intelligence Agency, Springfield, Virginia*, 2014

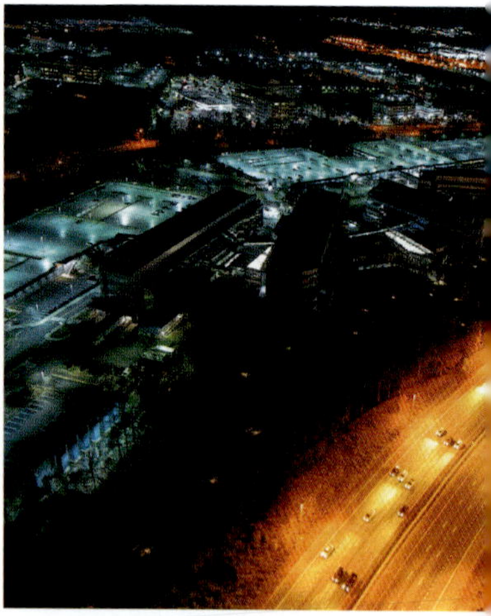

Trevor Paglen, *National Reconnaissance Office, Chantilly, Virginia*, 2014

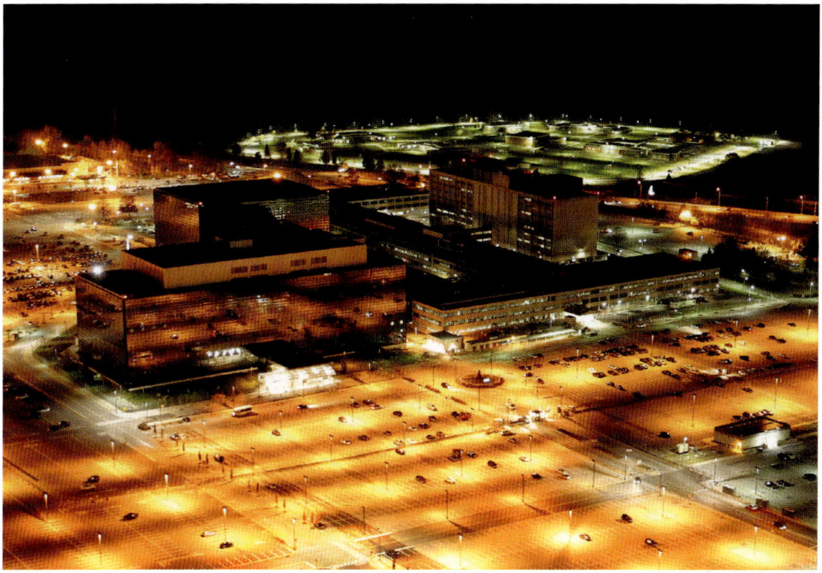

Trevor Paglen, *National Security Agency, Ft. Meade, Maryland*, 2014

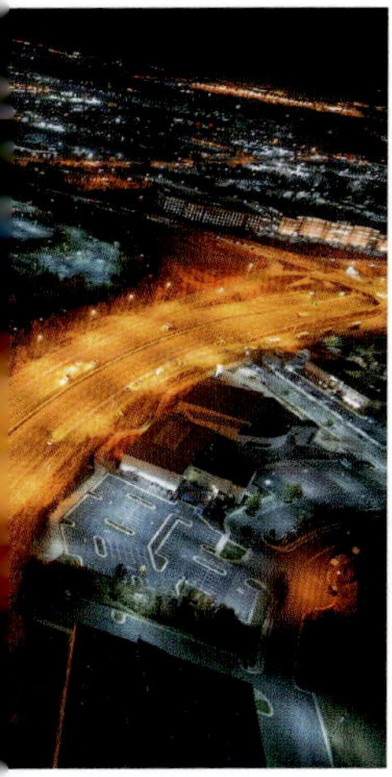

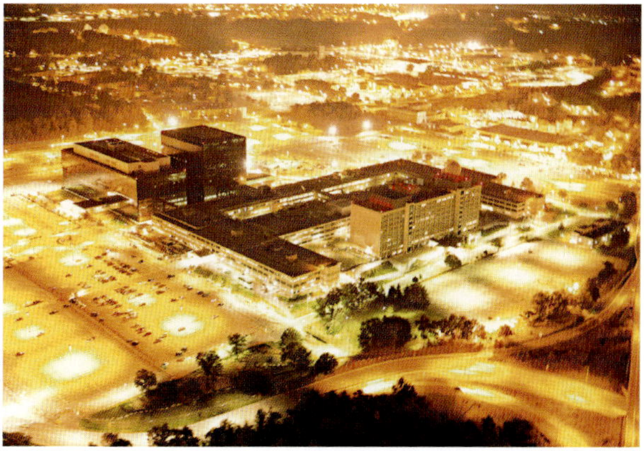

Trevor Paglen, *National Security Agency, Ft. Meade, Maryland*, 2013

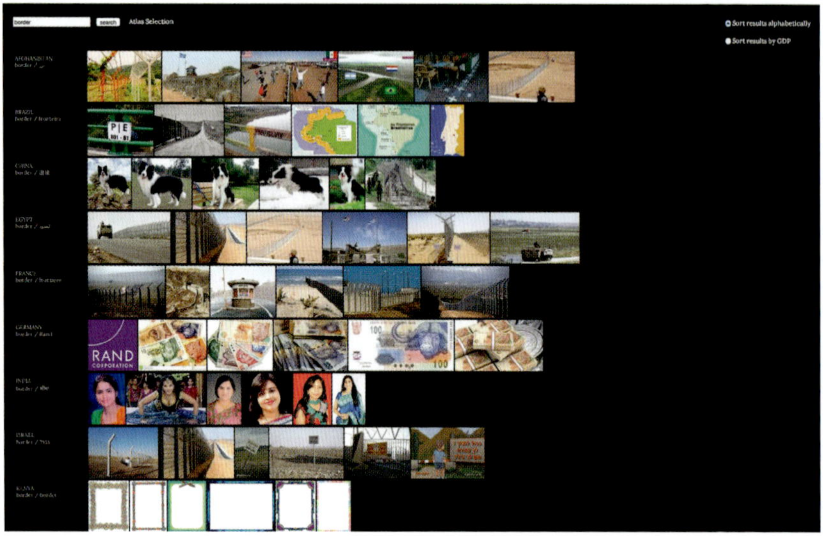

Tayrn Simon and Aaron Swartz, *Image Atlas: Border, 9/30/16, 12:19 PM (Eastern Standard Time)*, 2012

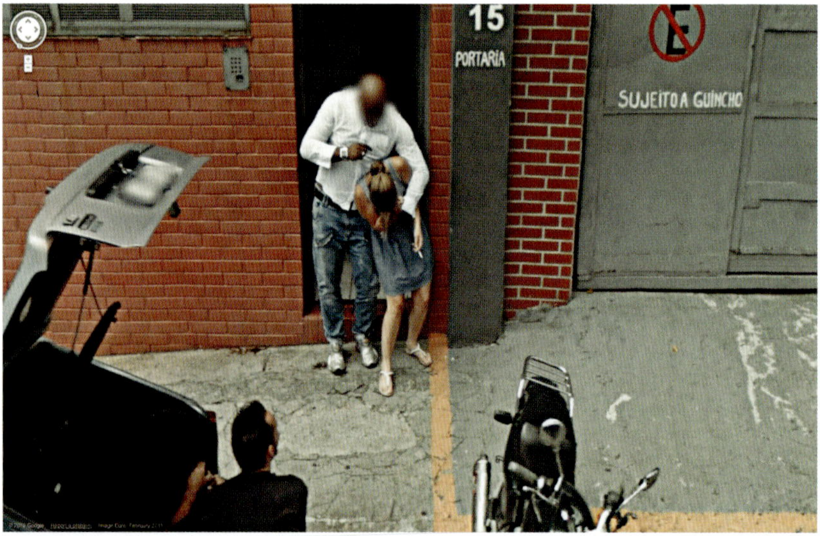

Jon Rafman, *24 Rua Maria Ortiz, Santo André, São Paulo, Brazil*, 2012

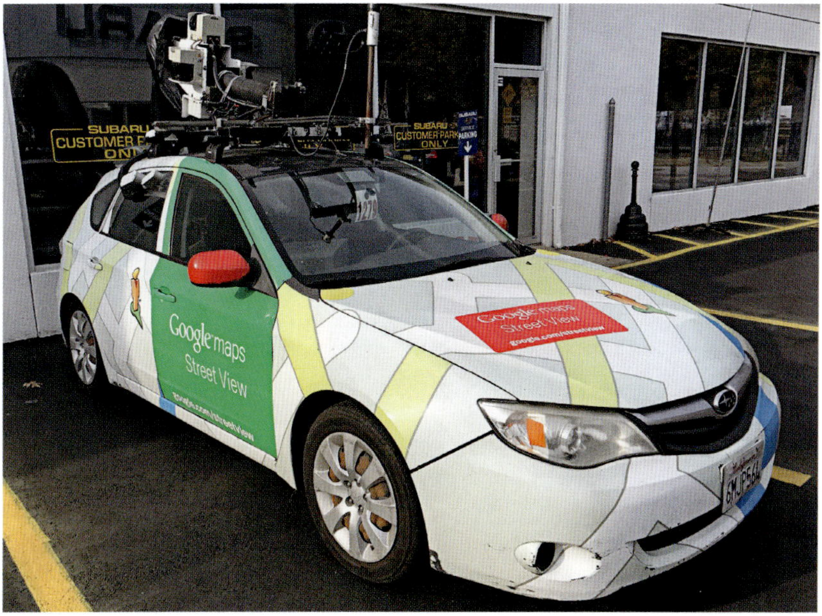

Google Street View car, November 2, 2016

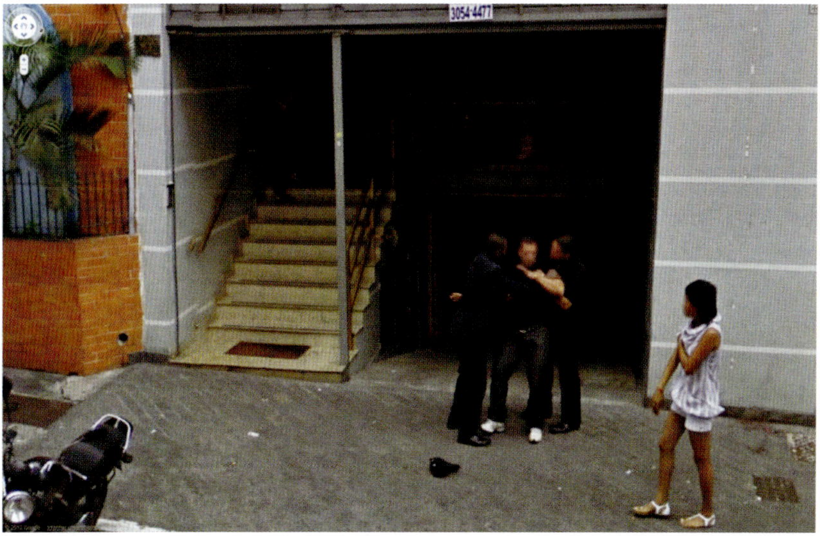

Jon Rafman, *353 Rua Bento Freitas, São Paulo, Brazil*, 2010

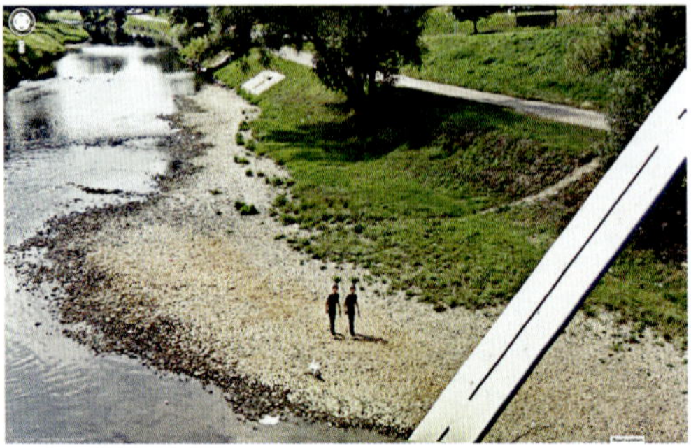

Jon Rafman, *Havlíčkovo nábřeží, Ostrava, Czech Republic*, 2013

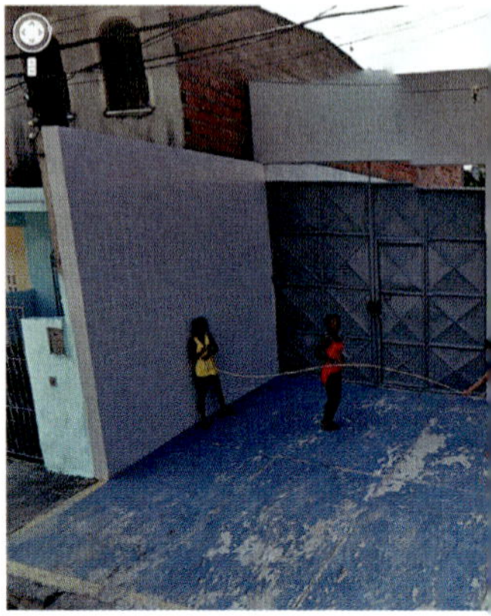

Jon Rafman, *176 Rua Ligia Maria, Salvador, Bahia, Brazil*, 2013

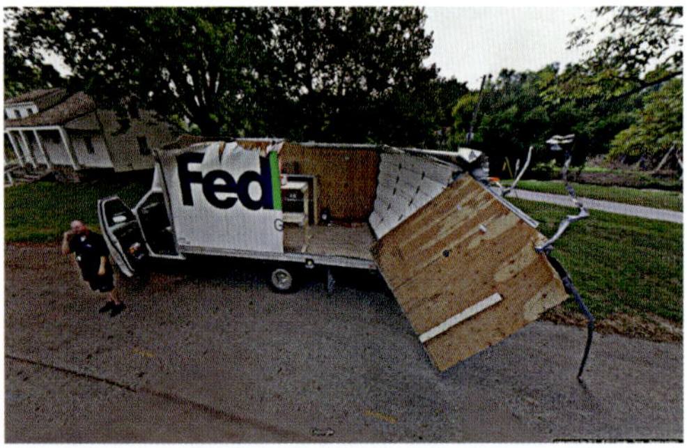

Jon Rafman, *77 S Gabouri St, Ste. Genevieve, Missouri, United States*, 2017

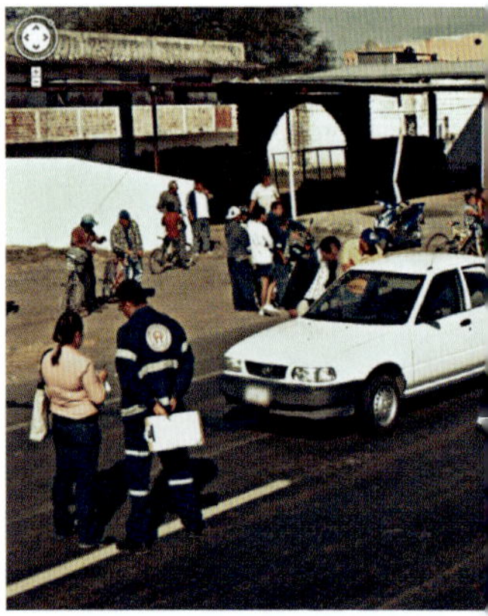

Jon Rafman, *Mexico 45, Silao Guanajuato, Mexico*, 2011

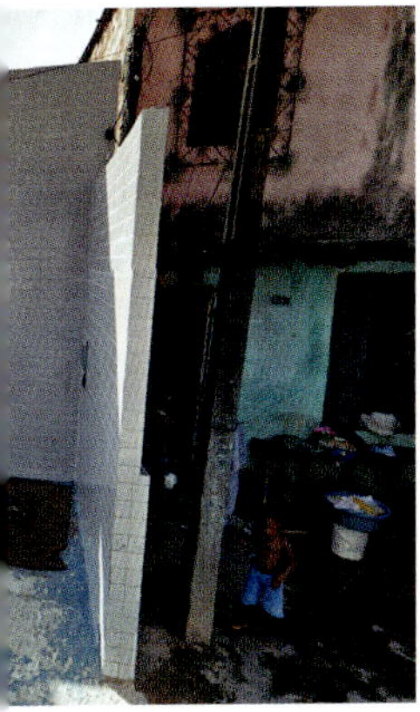

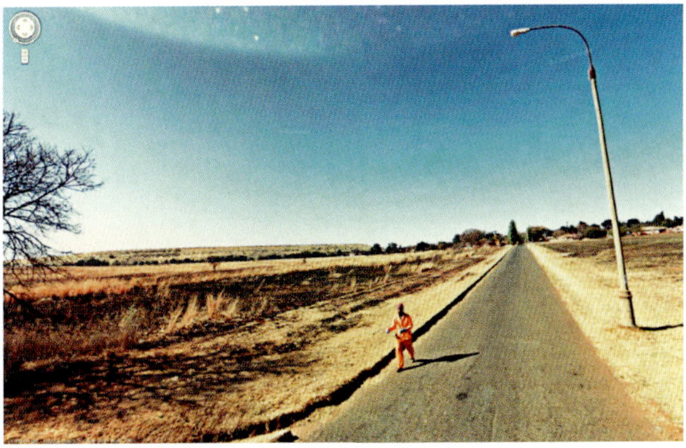

Jon Rafman, *Unknown Road, Carltonville, Johannesburg, South Africa*, 2012

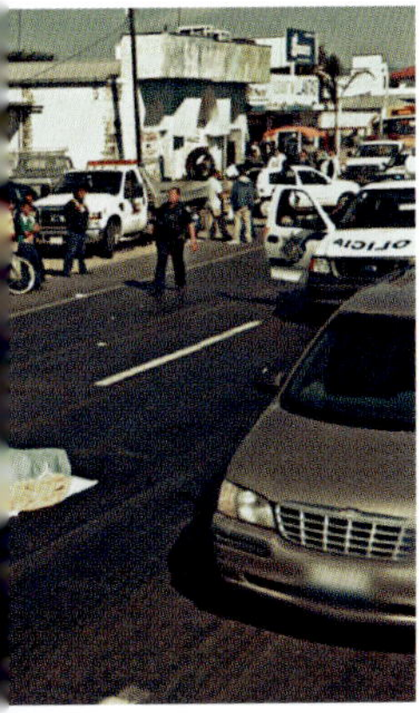

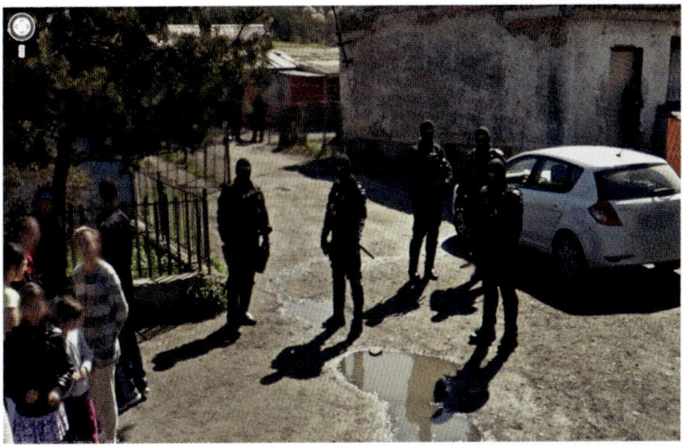

Jon Rafman, *75 Na Podskaiku, Humenne, Presov Region, Slovakia #1*, 2012

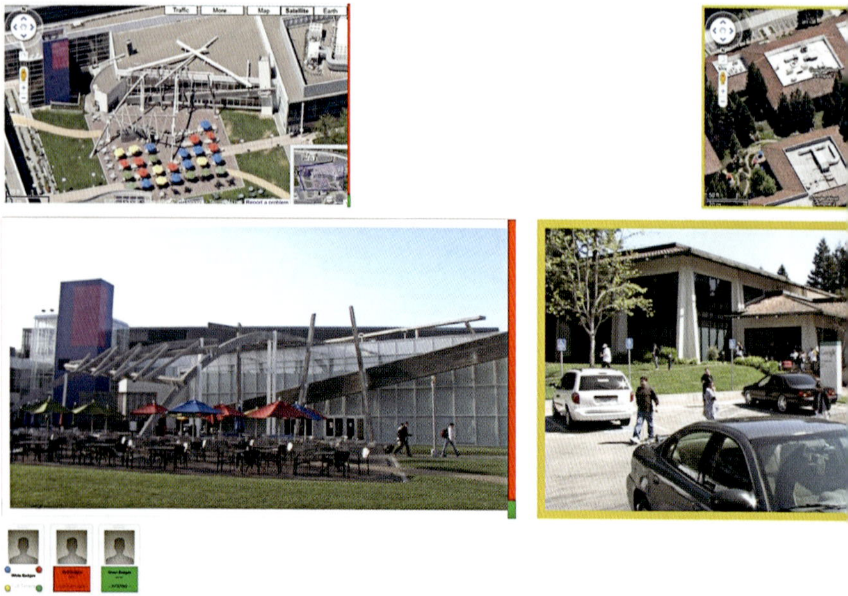

Andrew Norman Wilson, *Workers Leaving the Googleplex*, 2009–11

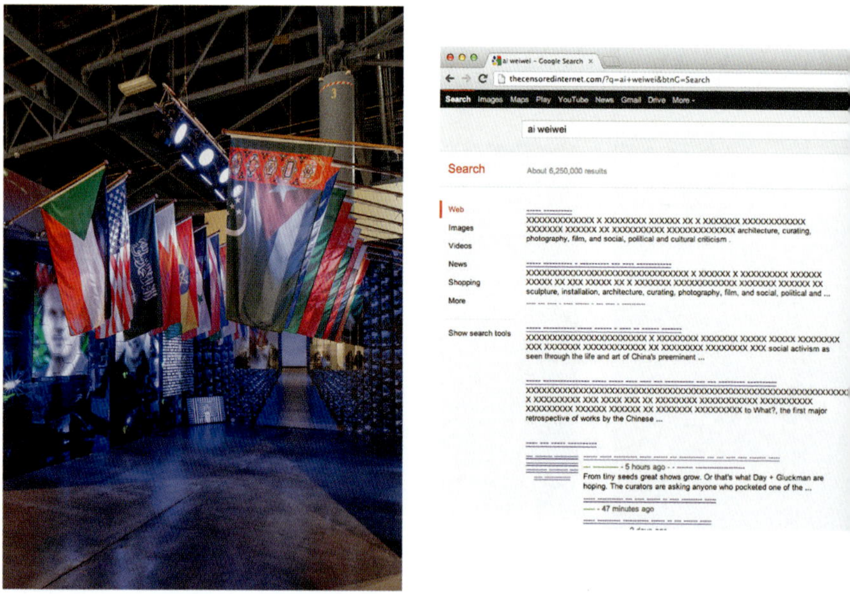

Constant Dullaart, *The Censored Internet*, 2013–14

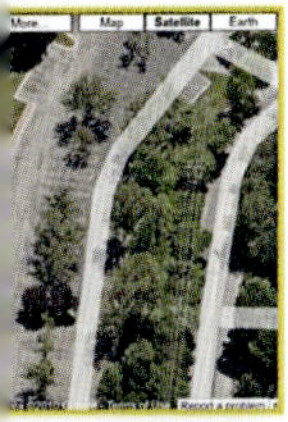

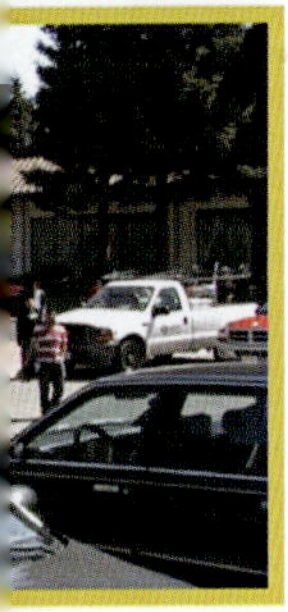

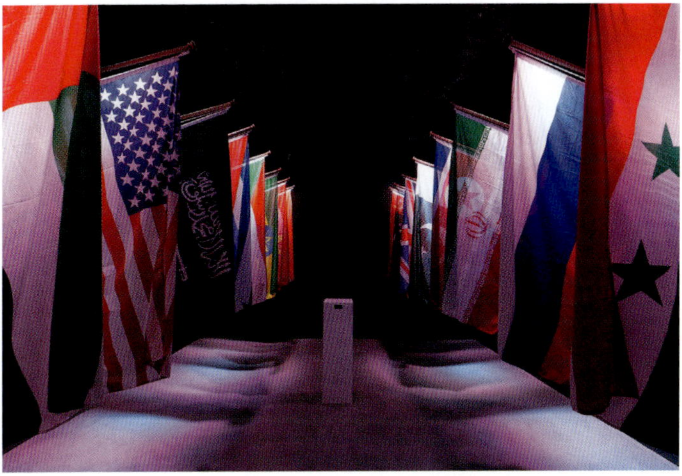

Constant Dullaart, *The Censored Internet*, 2013–14

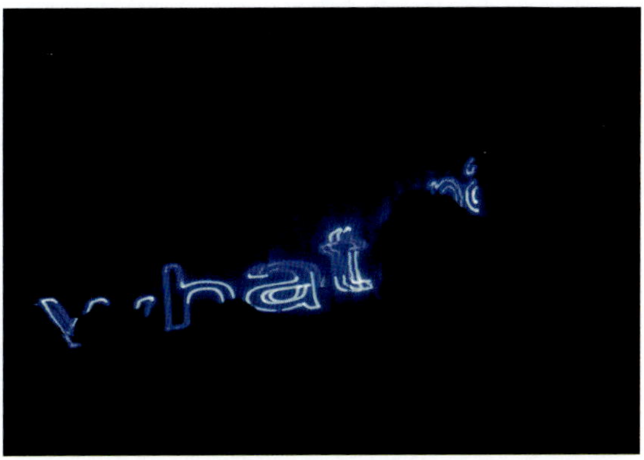

Constant Dullart, *Rave Lecture*, 2013–15

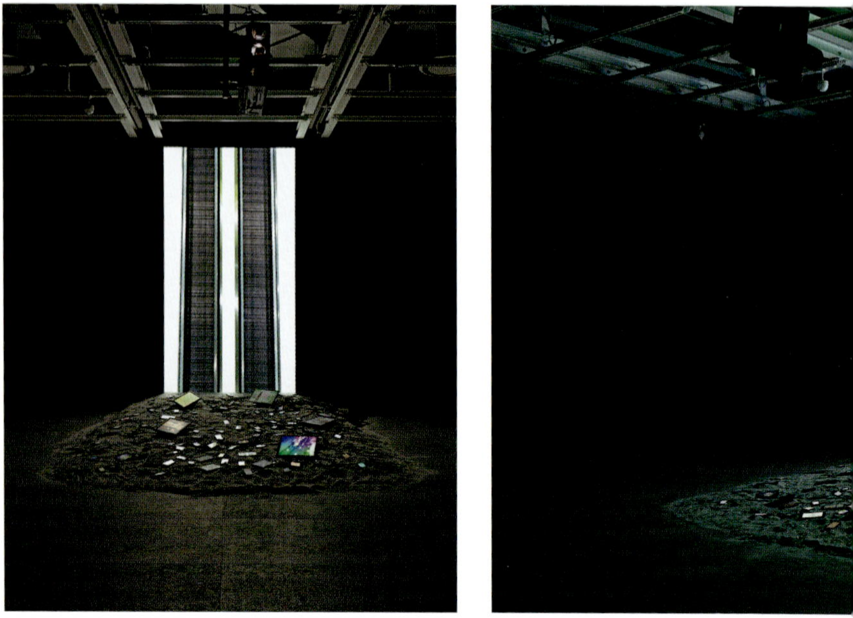

Sophia Al-Maria, *Black Friday* and *The Litany*, 2016

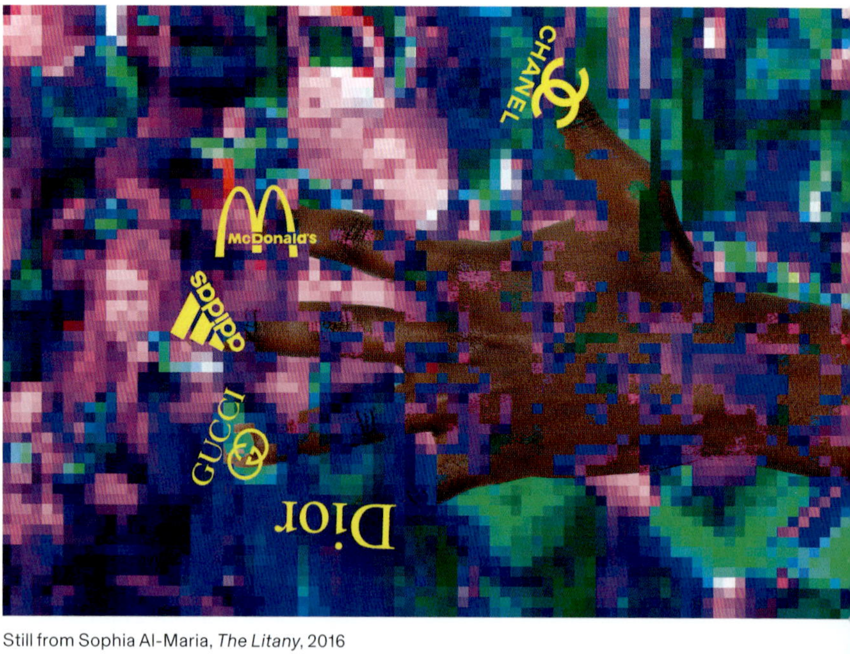

Still from Sophia Al-Maria, *The Litany*, 2016

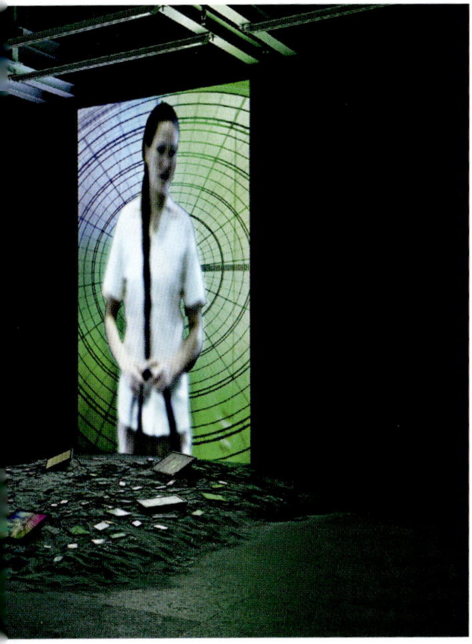

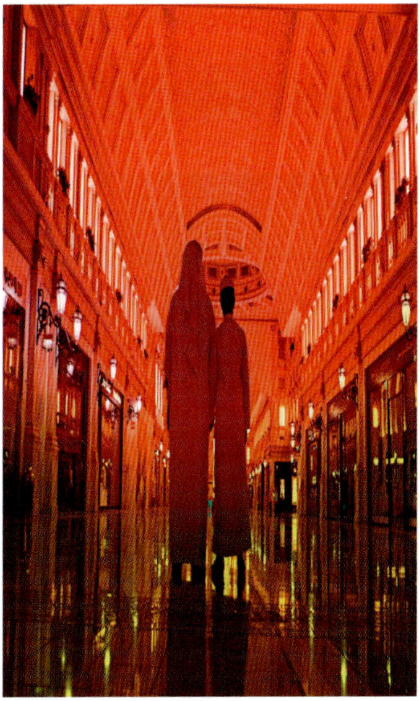

Still from Sophia Al-Maria, *Black Friday*, 2016

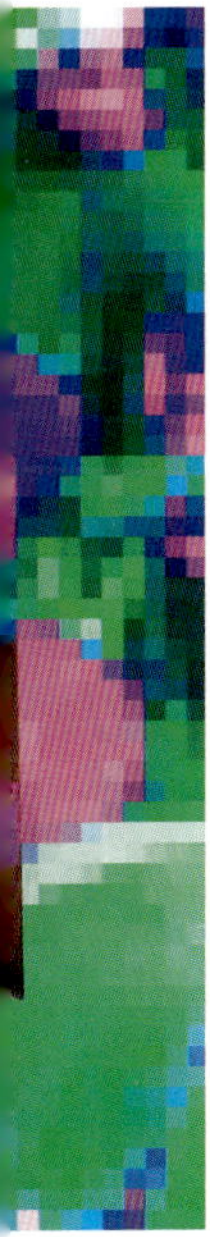

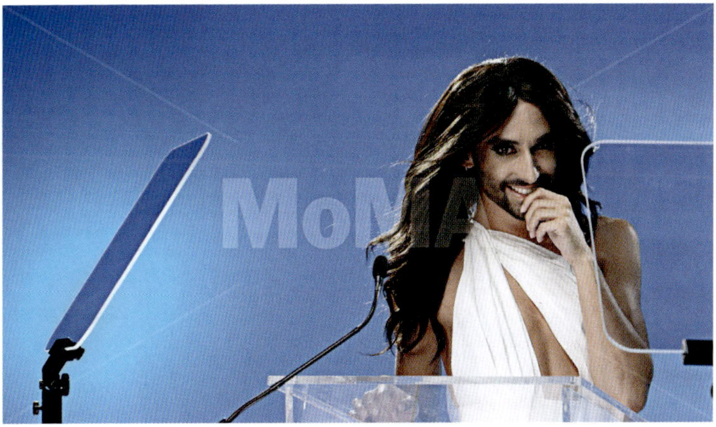

Still from DIS, *Positive Ambiguity (beard, lecturn, teleprompter, wind machine, confidence)*, 2015

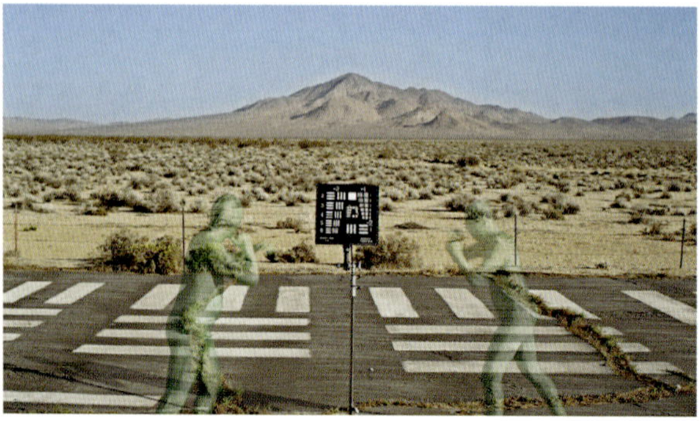

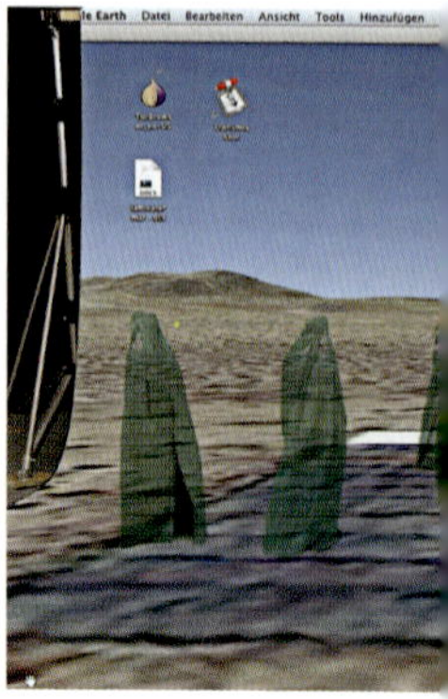

Stills from Hito Steyerl, *How Not to Be Seen: A Fucking Didactic Educational .MOV File*, 2013

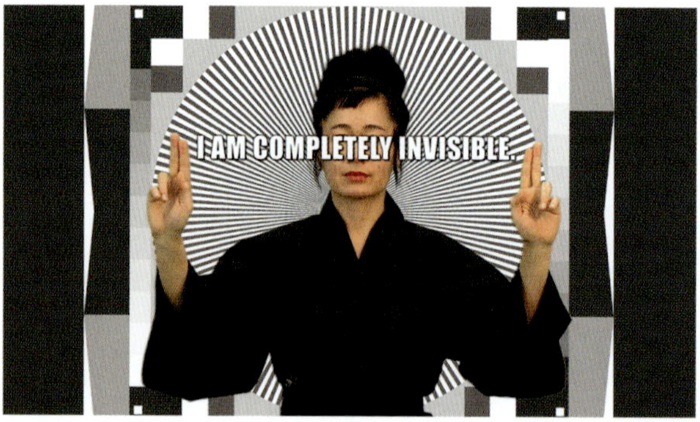

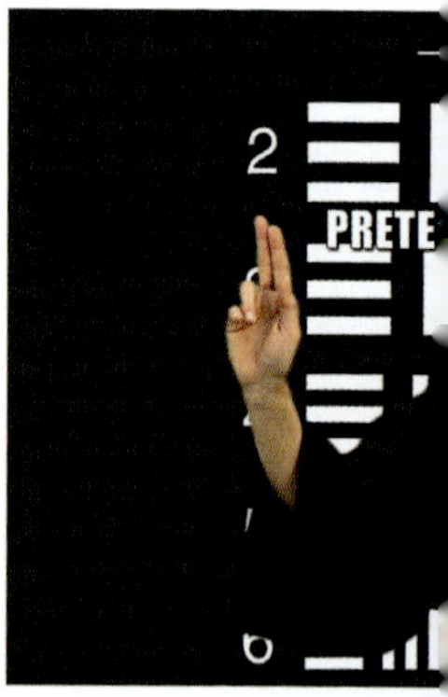

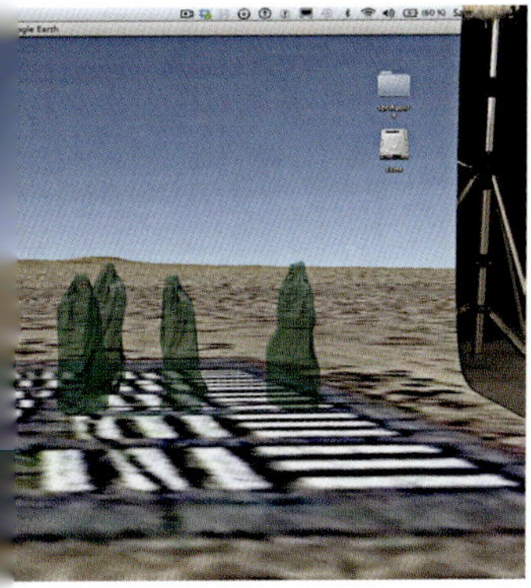

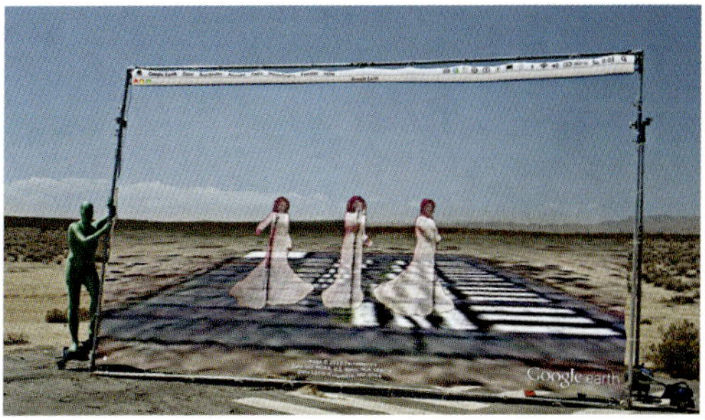
Google earth

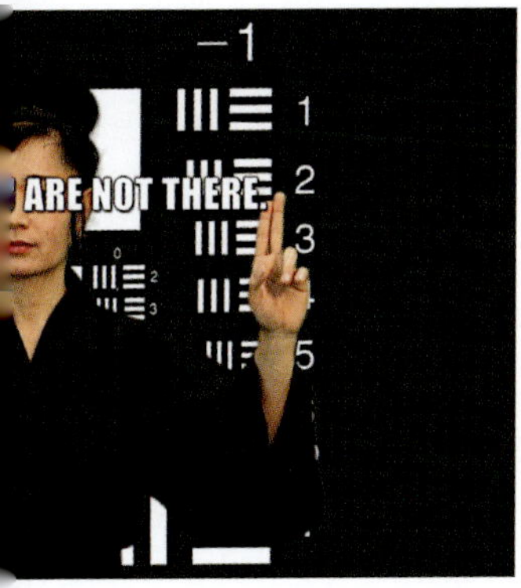
ARE NOT THERE.

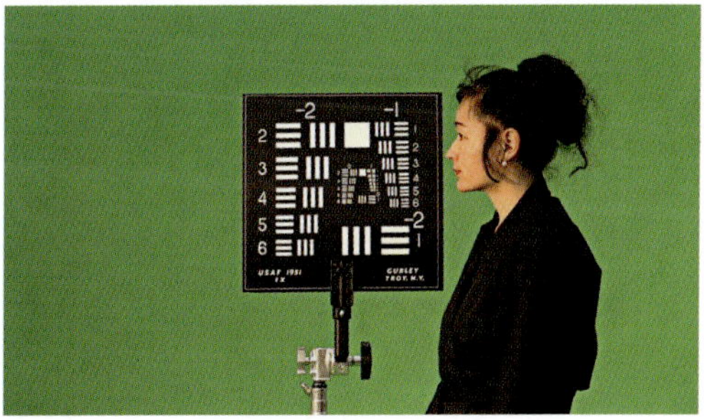
USAF 1951
GURLEY
TROY, N.Y.

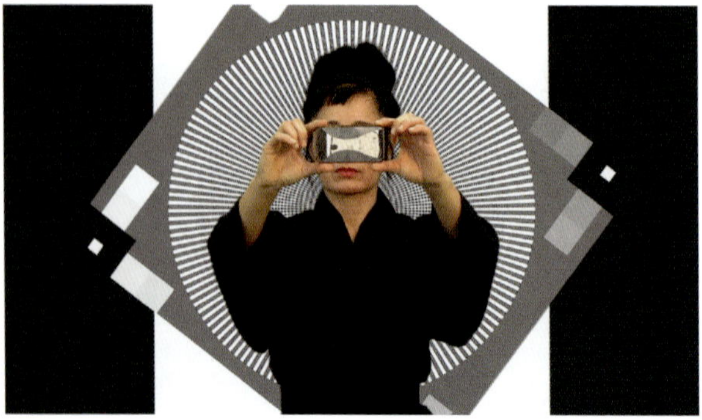
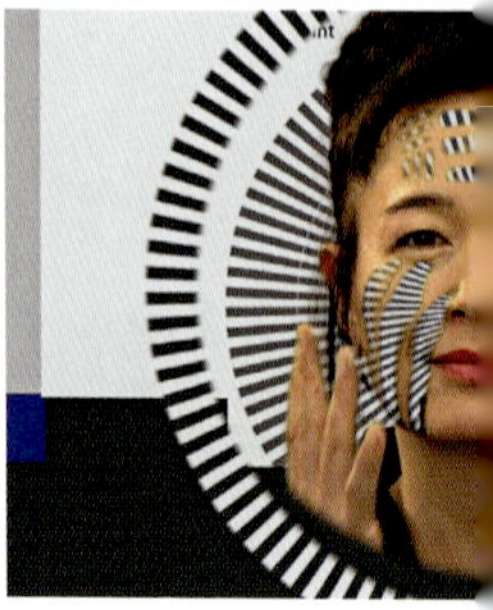

Stills from Hito Steyerl, *How Not to Be Seen: A Fucking Didactic Educational .MOV File*, 2013

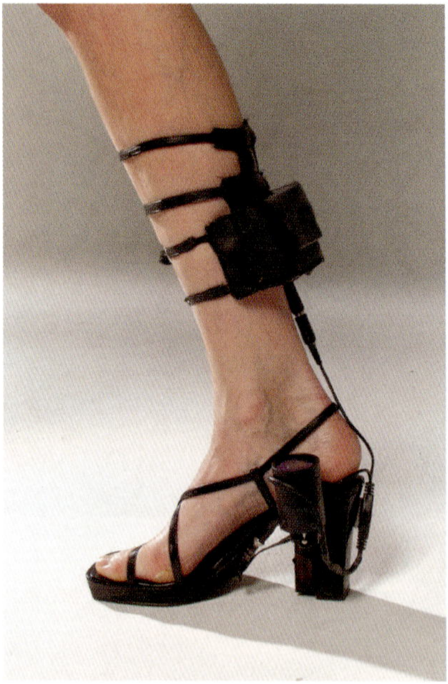

Jill Magid, *Surveillance Shoe*, 2000

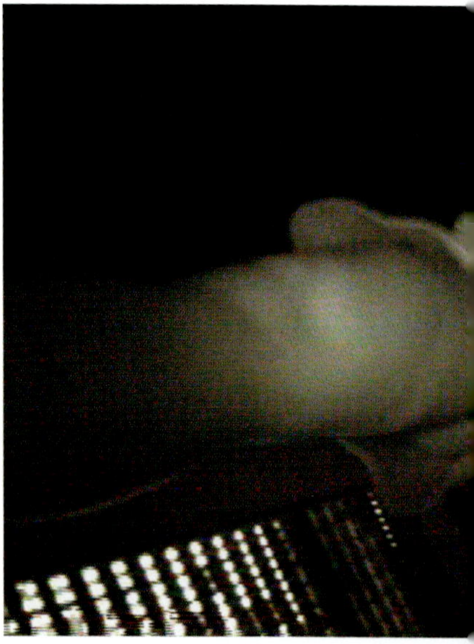

Still from Jill Magid, *Surveillance Shoe*, 2000

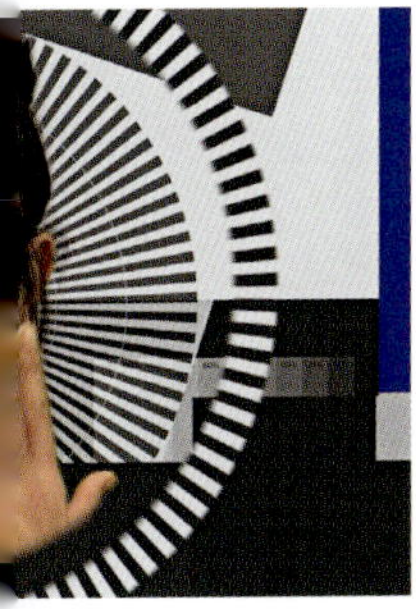

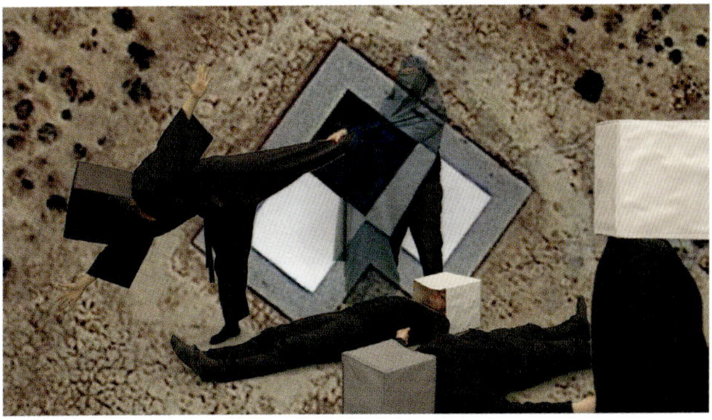

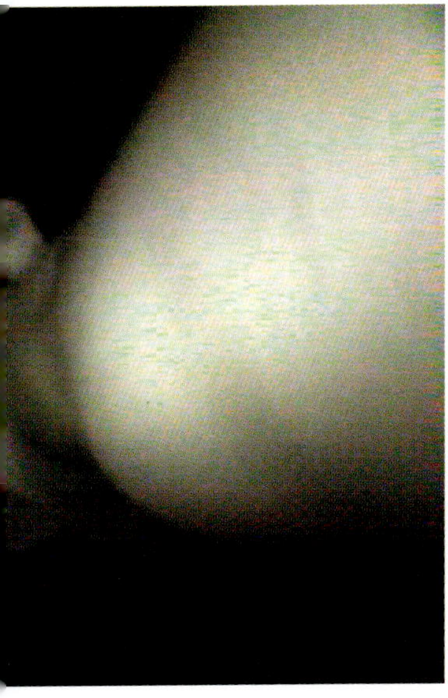

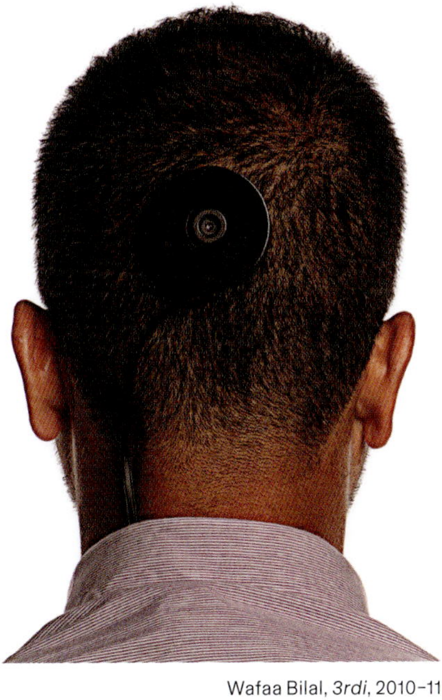

Wafaa Bilal, *3rdi*, 2010–11

Play with Me

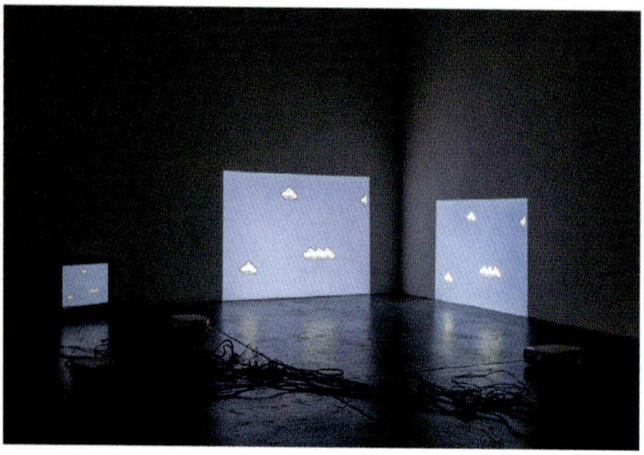

Cory Arcangel, *Super Mario Clouds*, 2002–ongoing

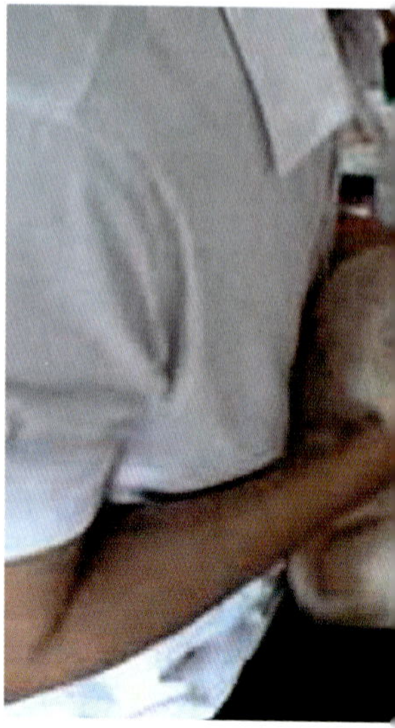

Still from Cory Arcangel, *Drei Klavierstücke op. 11*, 2009

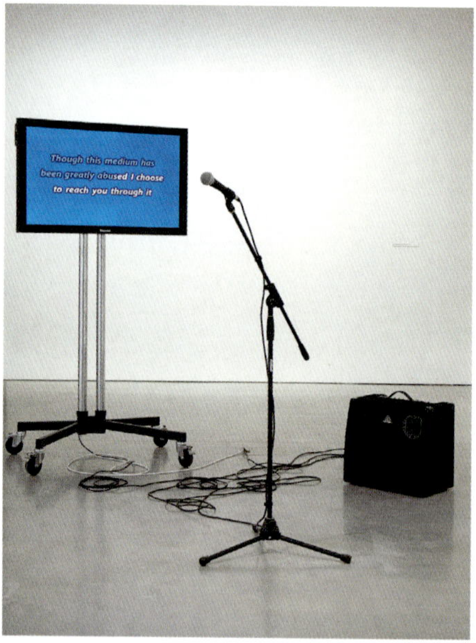

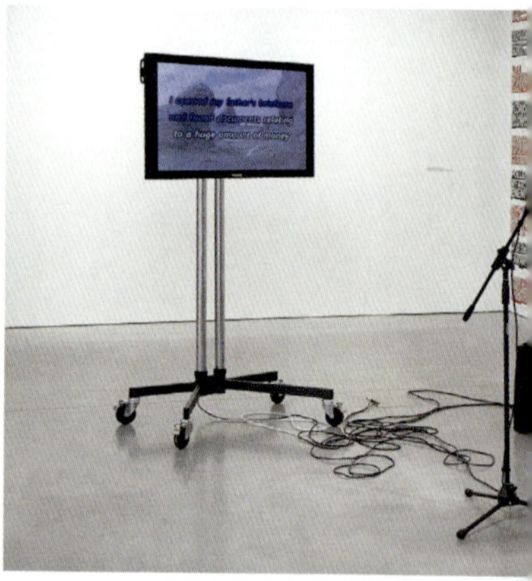

Thomson and Craighead, *More Songs of Innocence and of Experience*, 2013

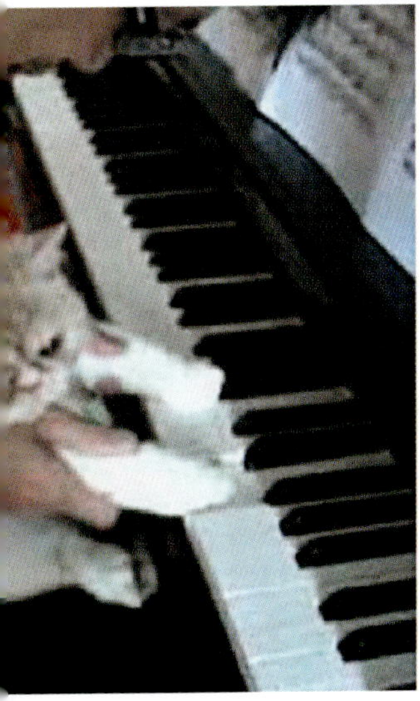

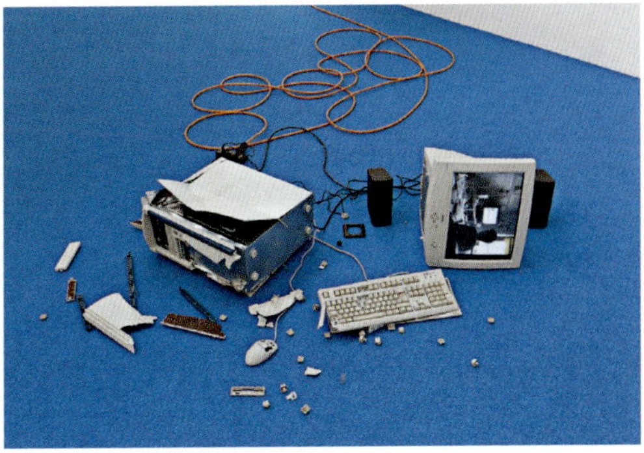

Eva and Franco Mattes, *My Generation*, 2010

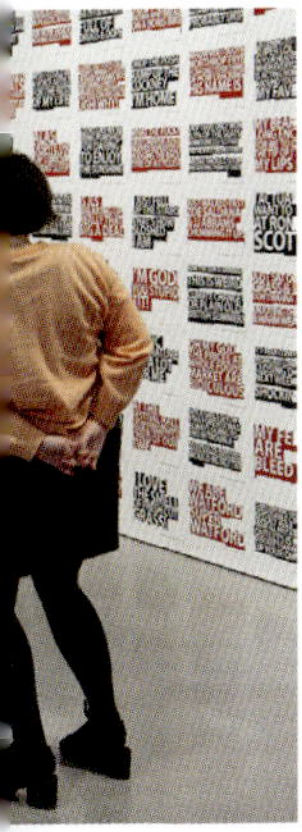

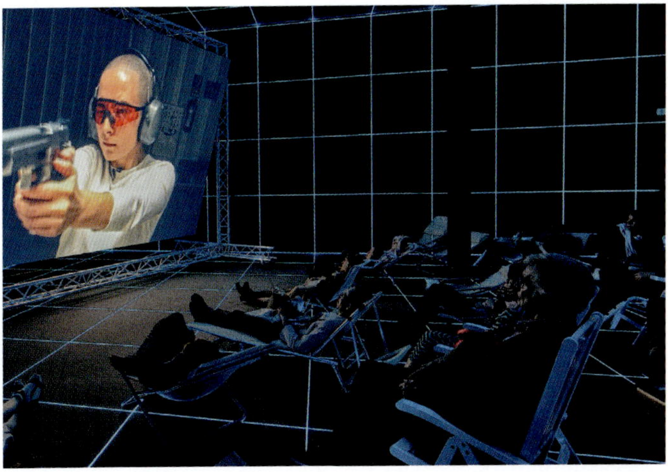

Hito Steyerl, *Factory of the Sun*, 2015

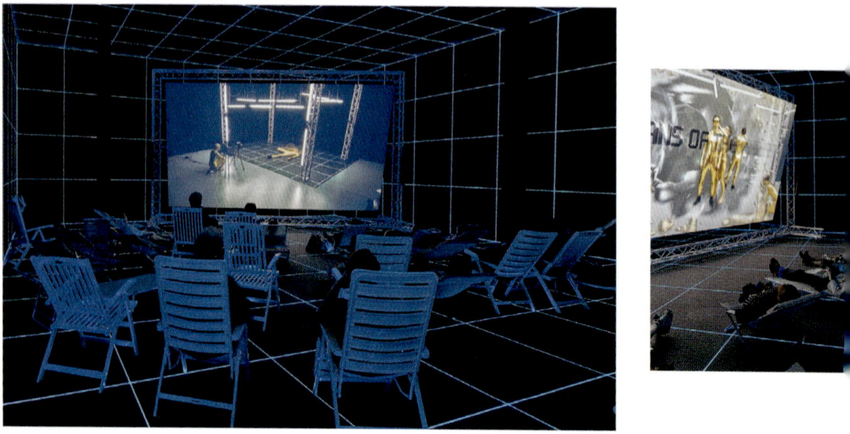

Hito Steyerl, *Factory of the Sun*, 2015

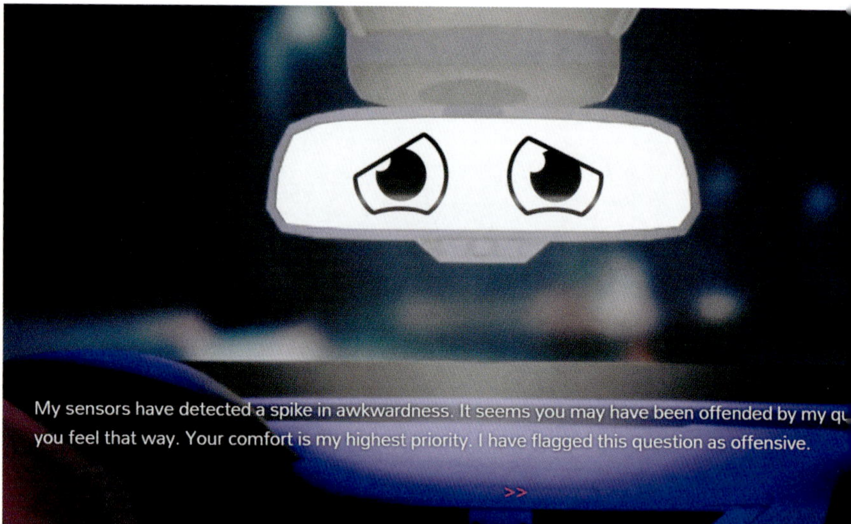

Stills from Chris Collins, *Hitch (http://tryhit.ch)*, 2017

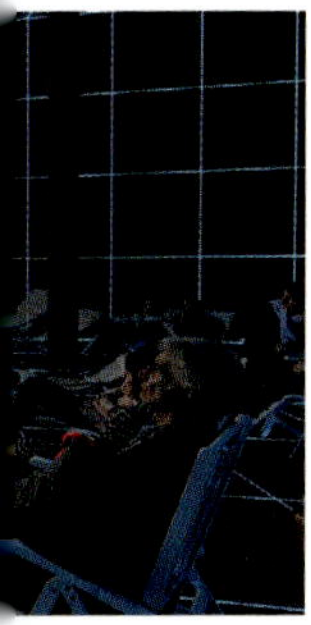

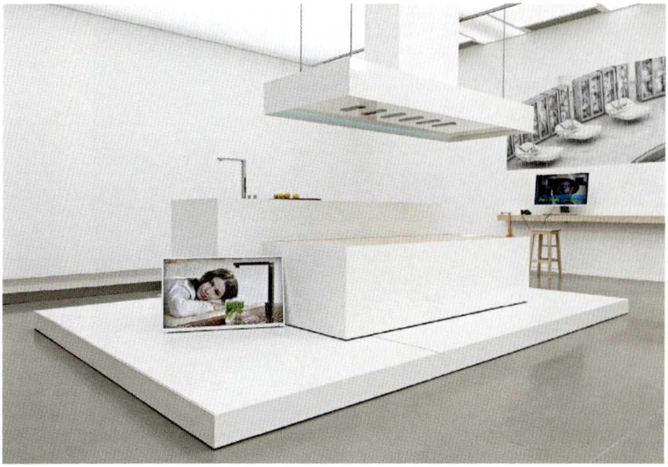

DIS, *The Island (KEN)*, 2015

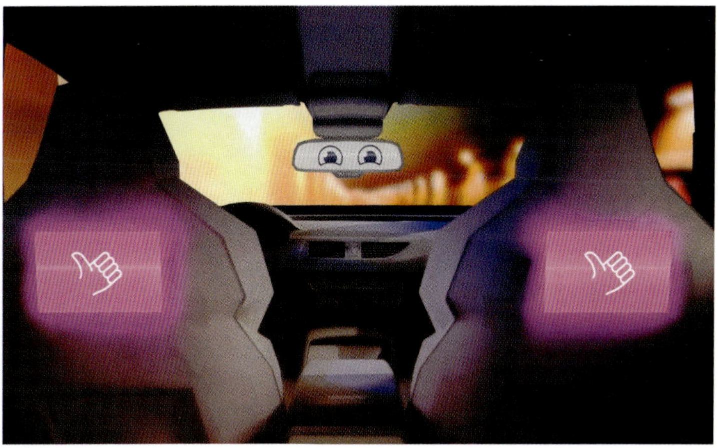

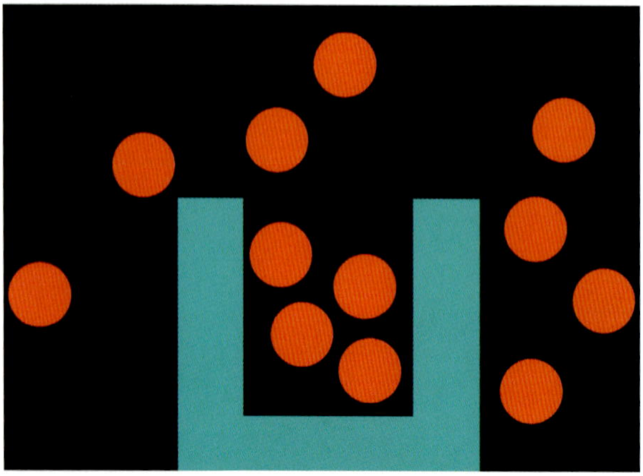

Rafaël Rozendaal, *Lots Of Many .com*, 2017

Rafaël Rozendaal,
Floating The .com, 2016

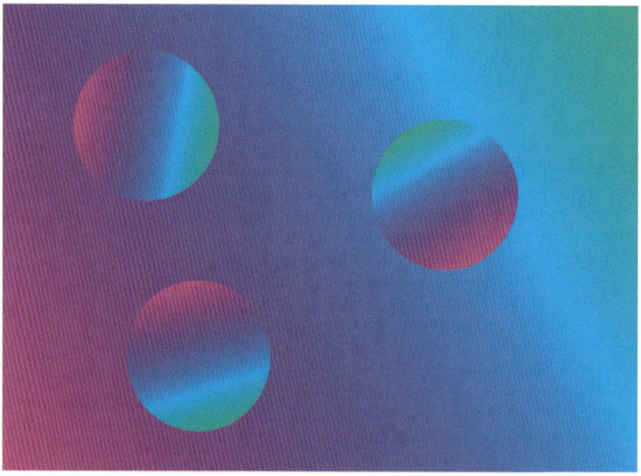

Rafaël Rozendaal, *Float Bounce .com*, 2016

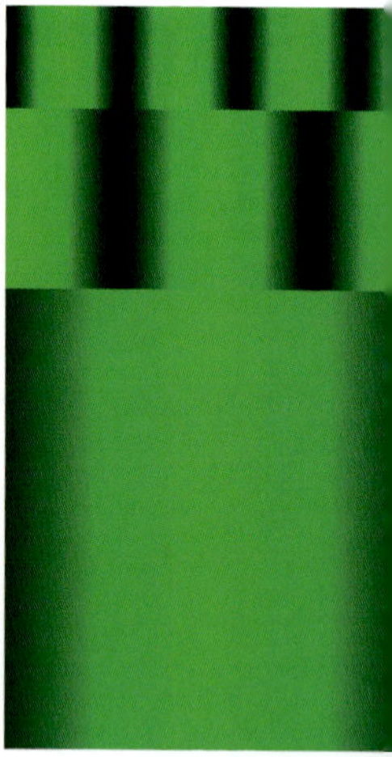

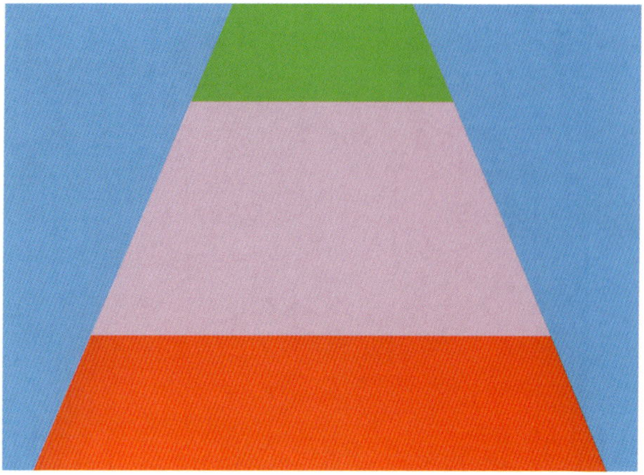

Rafaël Rozendaal, *Future Is Uncertain .com*, 2013

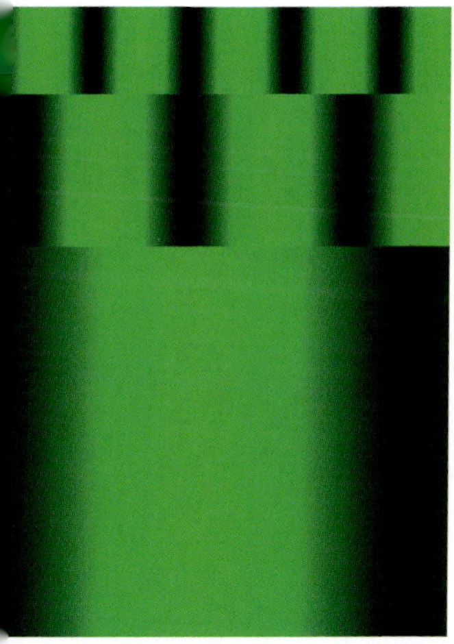

Rafaël Rozendaal,
Remotely Distant .com, 2014

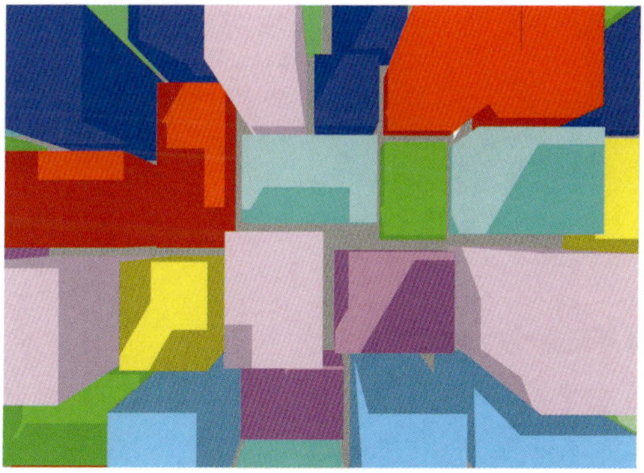

Rafaël Rozendaal, *Neo Geo City .com*, 2014

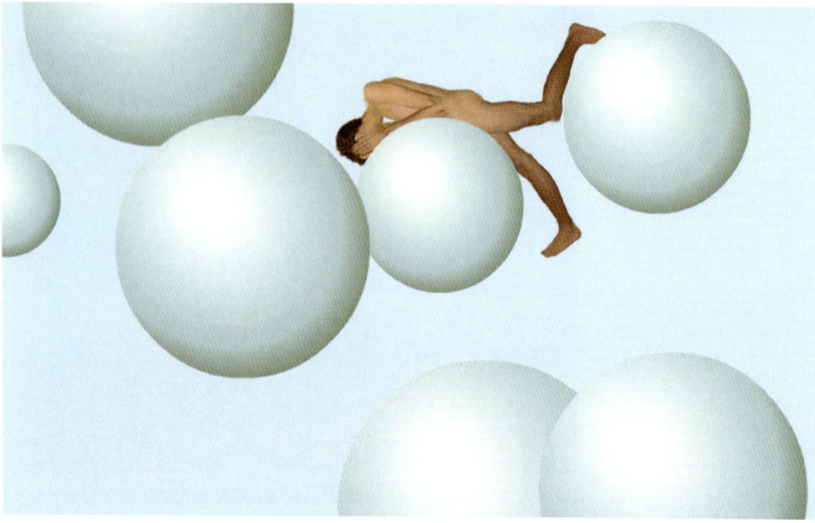

Guthrie Lonergan, *guthrielonergan.com*, 2008

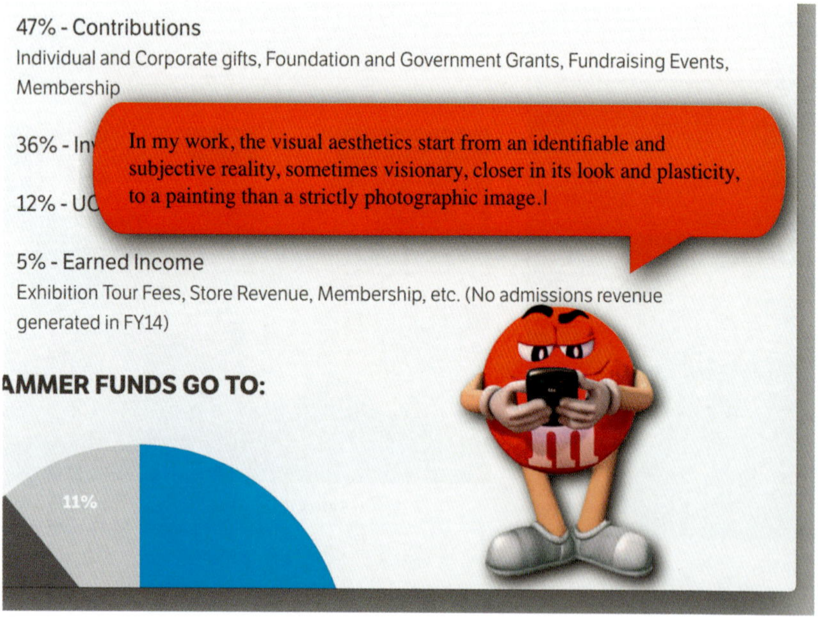

Guthrie Lonergan, *Built with Indexhibit*, 2016

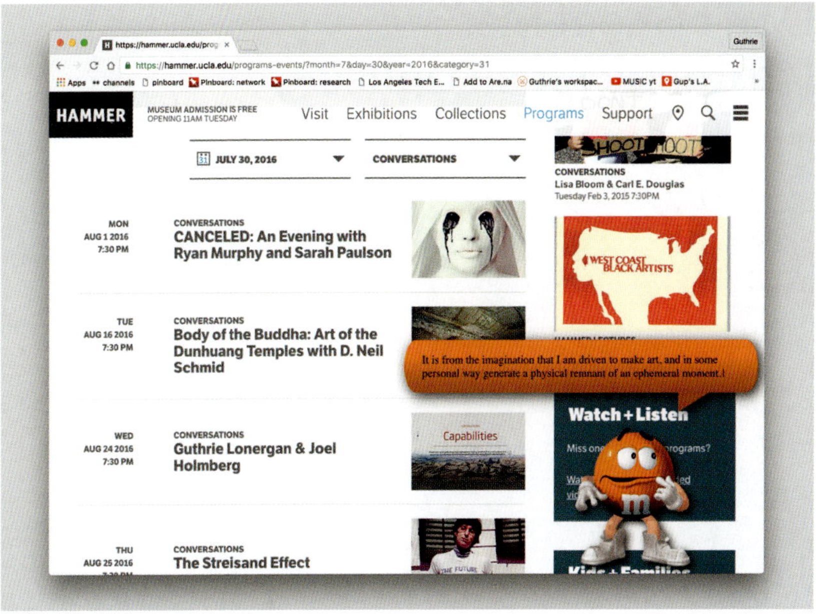

Guthrie Lonergan, *Built with Indexhibit*, 2016

Subject: bouncing M&M characters on the website pages' lower right corner
Date: June 10, 2016 at 1:37:17 AM PDT
To: Hammer Museum <info@hammer.ucla.edu>

ABSOLUTELY HATE THEM!!
useful info but way too juvenile a presentation for such a sophisticated museum

I'm a member...

and REALLY HATE THEM!
annoying and beneath the dignity of all concerned.......such blatant product placement.

Funding is necessary, I get it....but COME ON!

Put on your best design hat, not your laziest.

that is all

Email of complaint about *Built with Indexhibit*, June 10, 2016

Don’t Shoot Me; I’m Ready for an Uprising

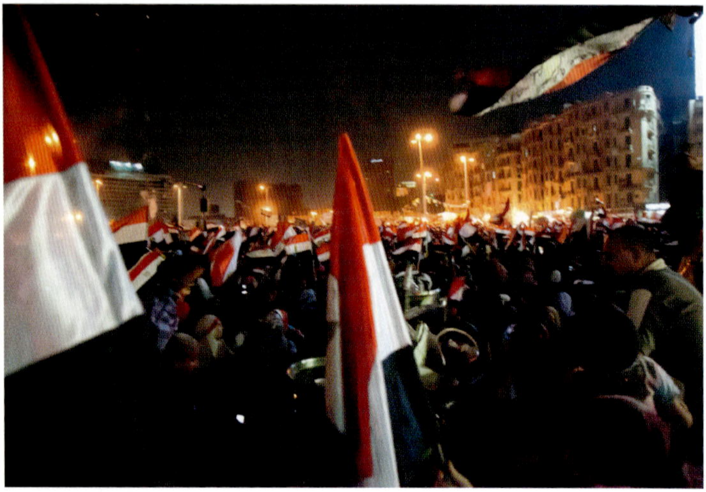

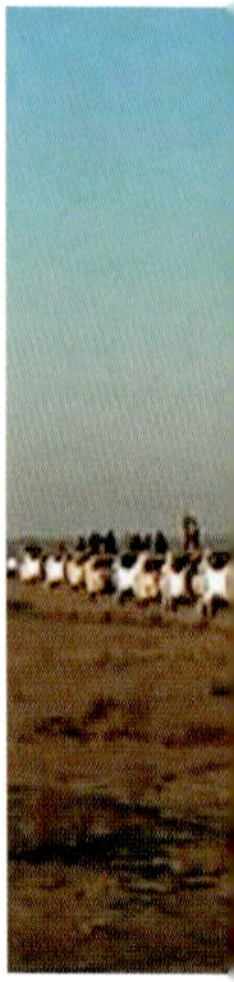

Egyptian revolution, Cairo, January 25, 2011

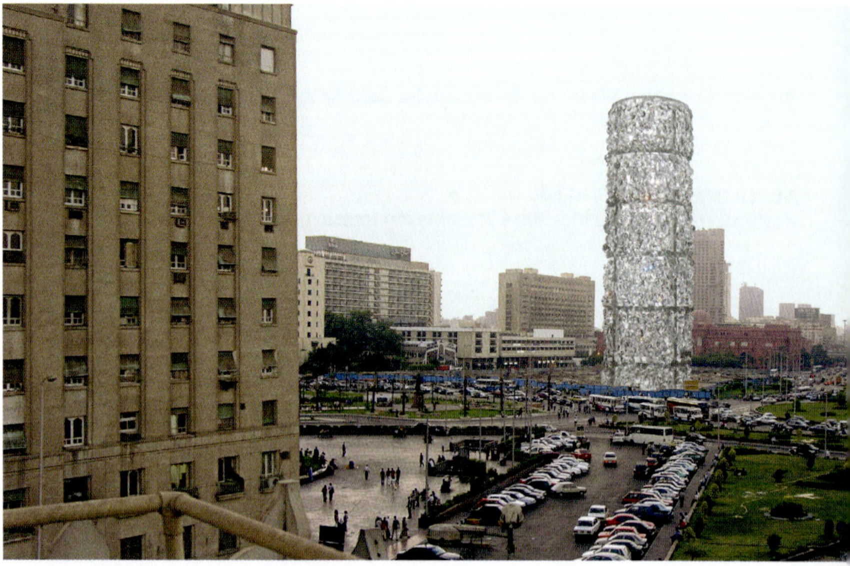

Detail of Iman Issa, *Proposal for a Crystal Building*, 2003

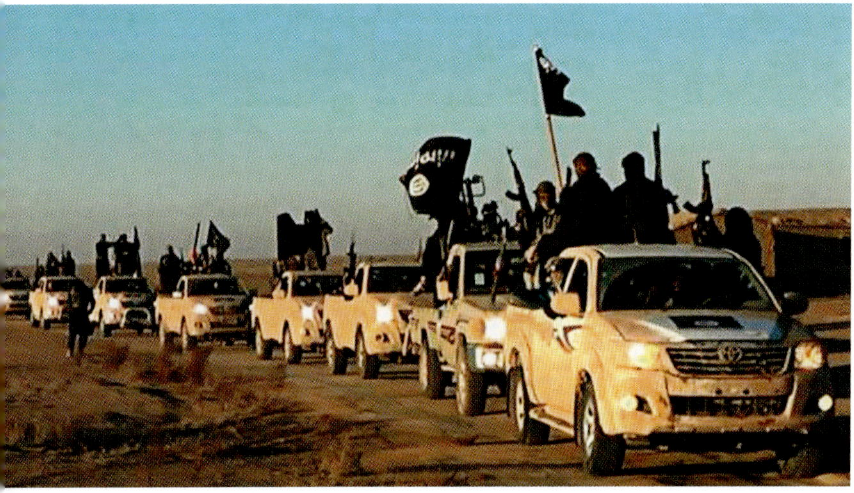

ISIS fighters, Anbar Province, Iraq, January 7, 2014

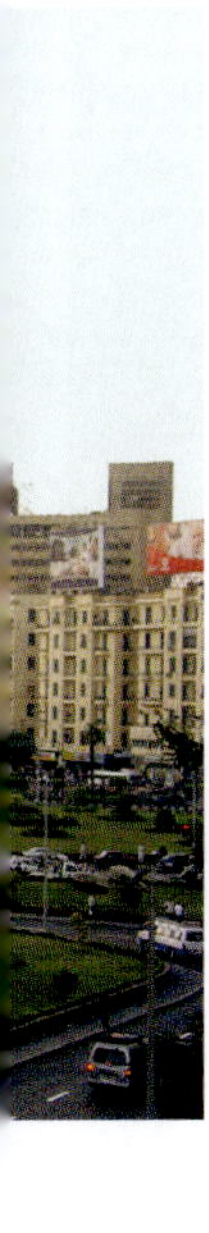

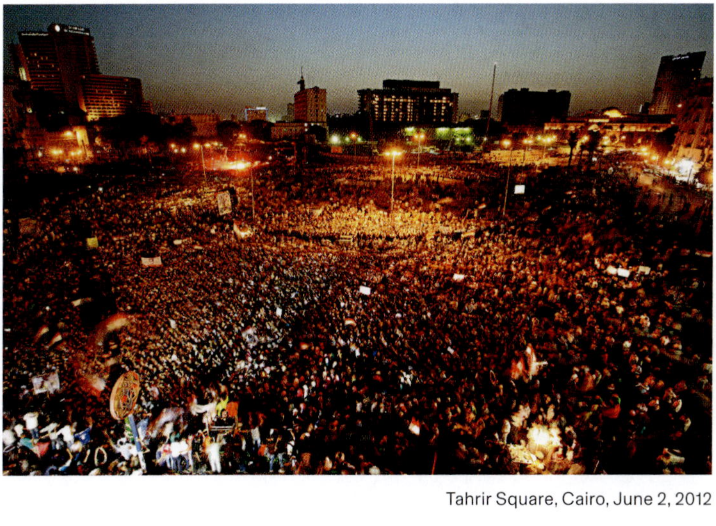

Tahrir Square, Cairo, June 2, 2012

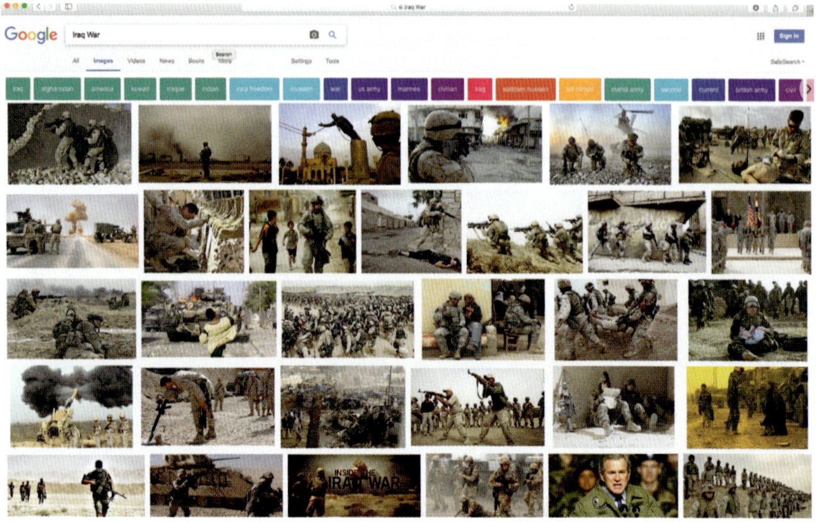

Google Images search results for “Iraq War,” November 15, 2017

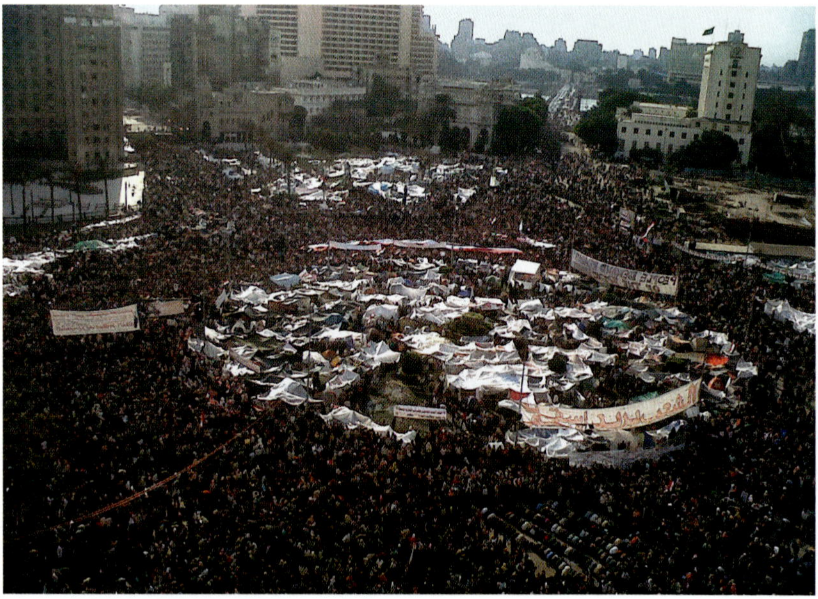

Tahrir Square, Cairo, February 8, 2011

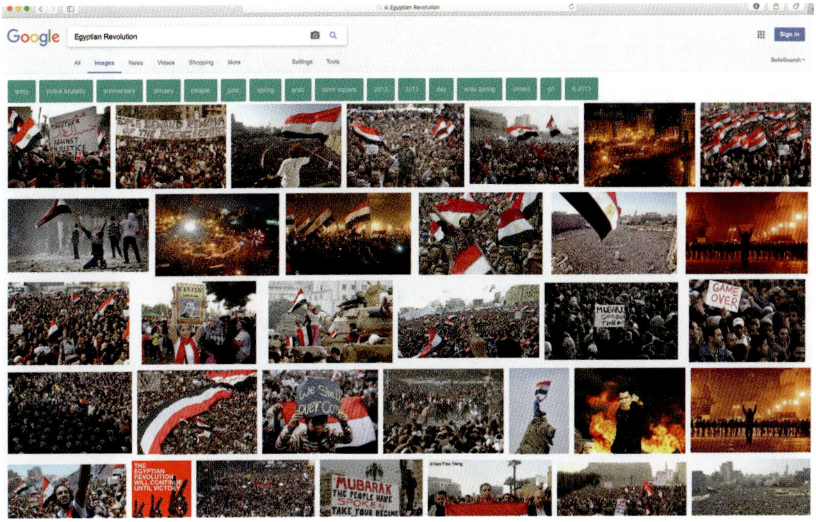

Google Images search results for "Egyptian Revolution," November 15, 2017

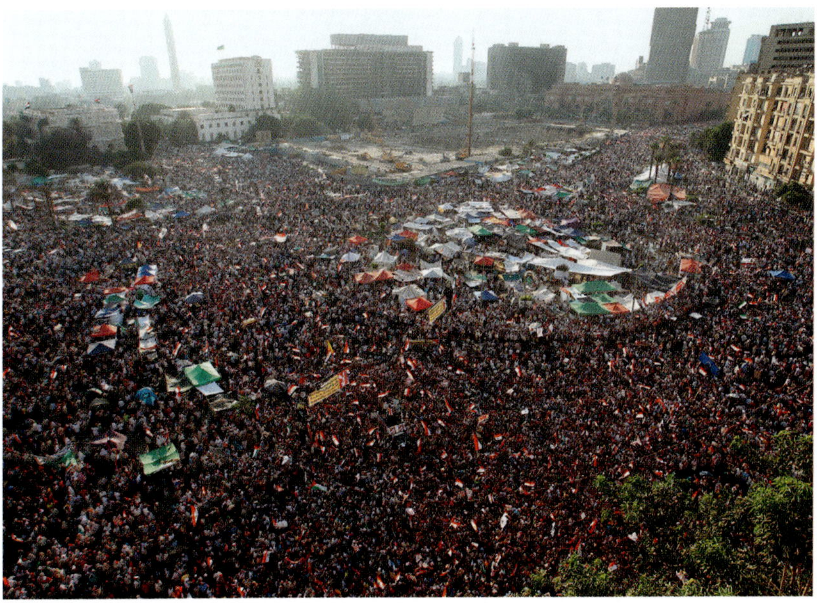

Tahrir Square, Cairo, June 24, 2012

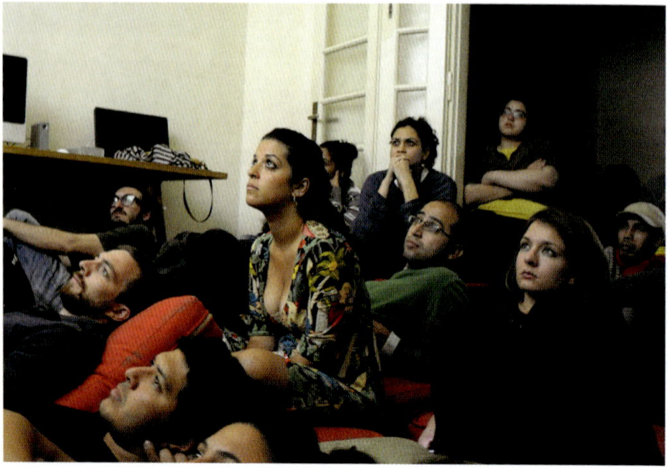

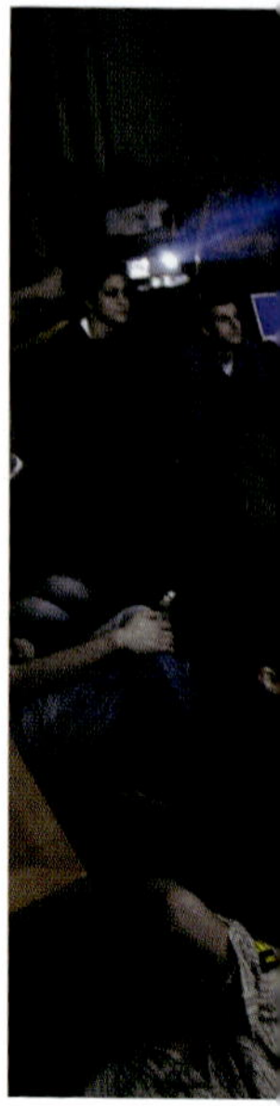

Mosireen, Tuesday Night Screenings, Cairo, November 15, 2011

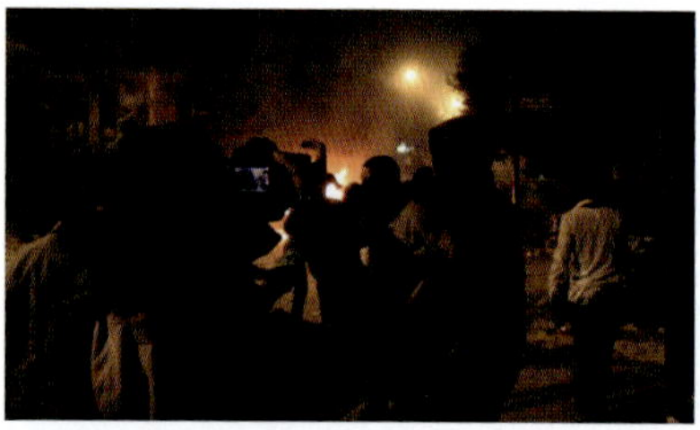

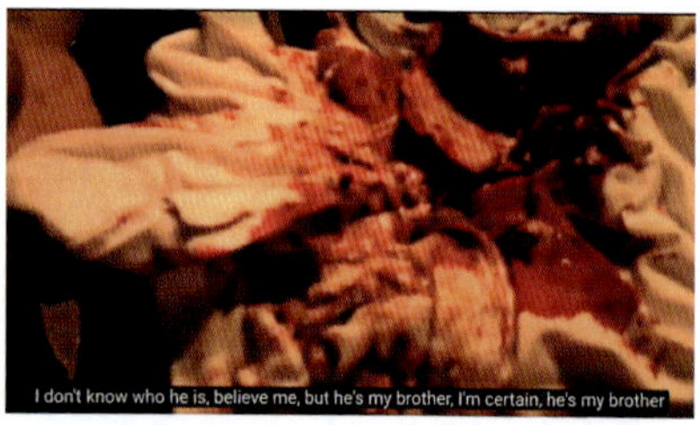

Stills from Mosireen, *Blood at Night, Grief by Day (Maspero 9/10/11)*, 2011

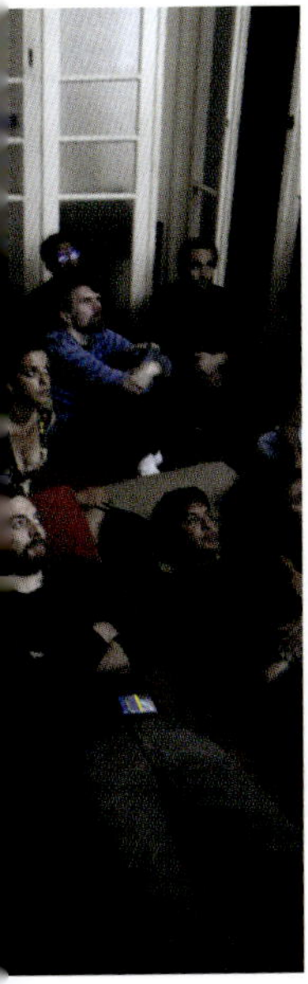

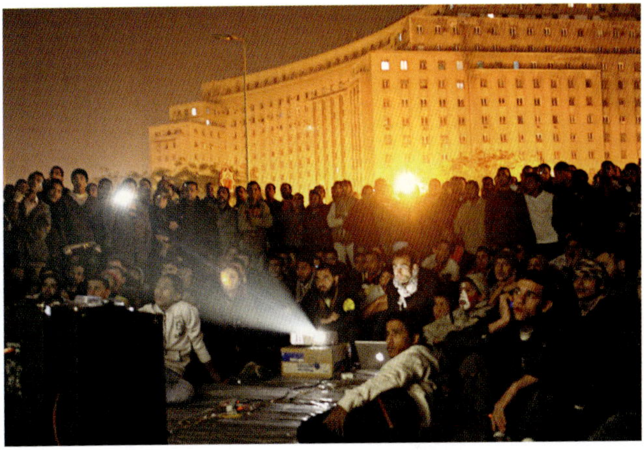

Mosireen, Tahrir Cinema, Tahrir Square, December 2, 2011

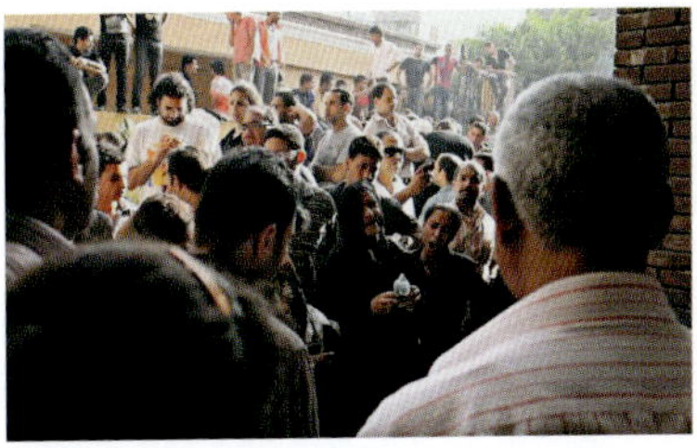

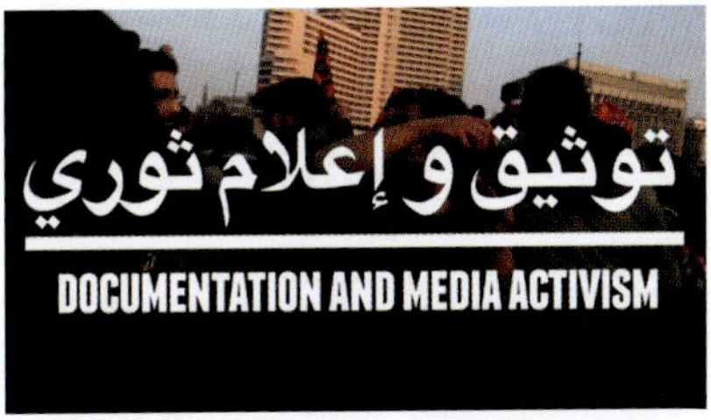

Still from Mosireen, *About Mosireen*, 2012

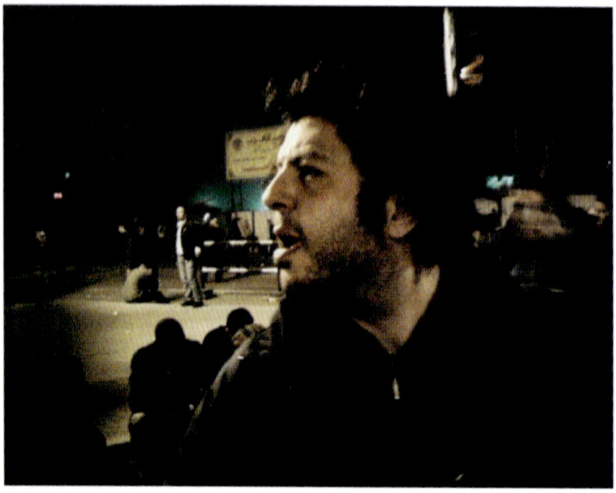

Ahmed Basiony in Tahrir Square, Cairo, January 28, 2011

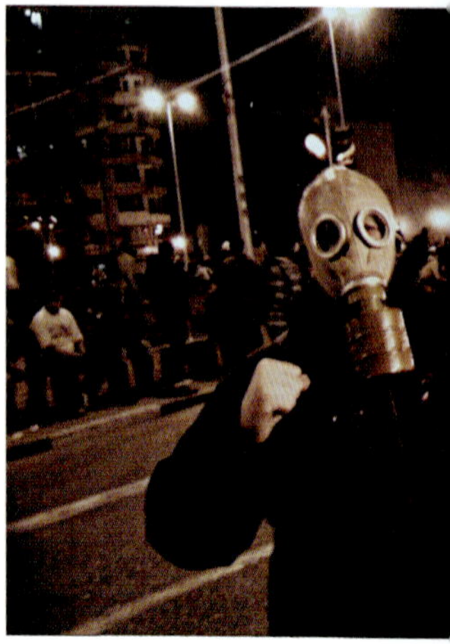

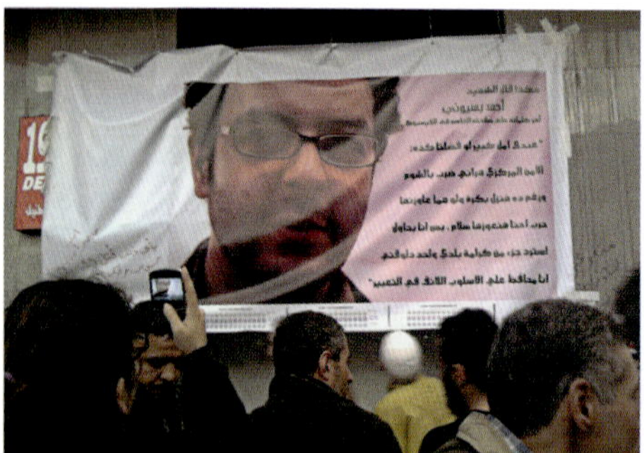

Poster of Ahmed Basiony, Tahrir Square, Cairo, February 4, 2011

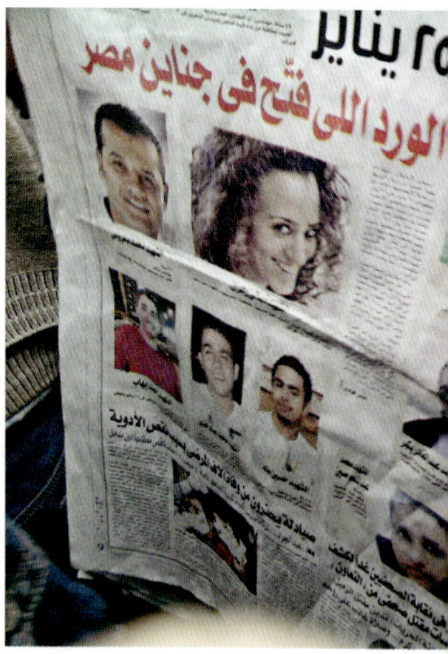

Egyptian newspaper showing those killed in the revolution, February 2011

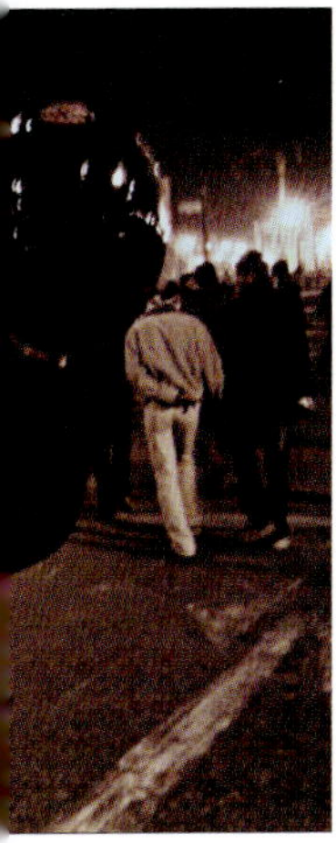

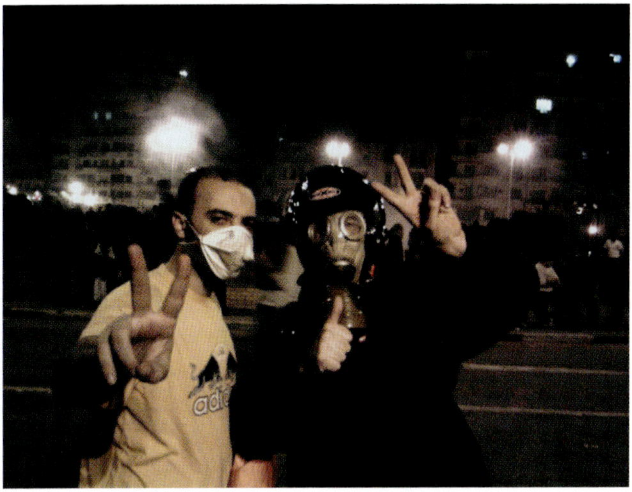

Magdi Mostafa and Ahmed Basiony in
Tahrir Square, Cairo, January 28, 2011

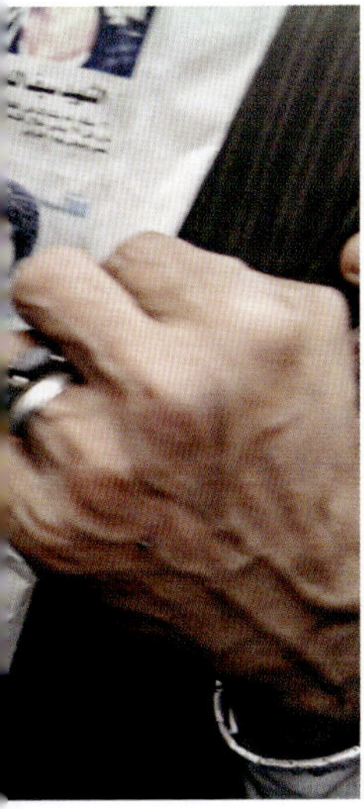

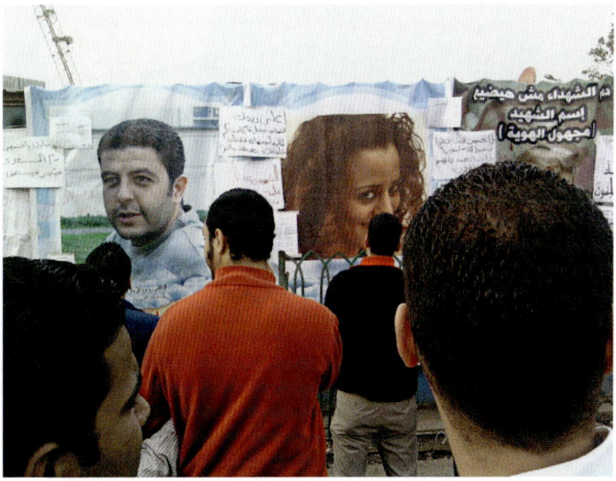

Poster of Ahmed Basiony, Tahrir Square, Cairo, February 4, 2011

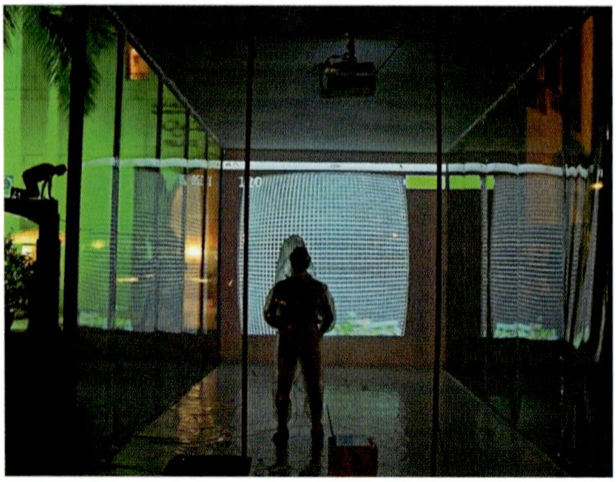

Ahmed Basiony, *Thirty Days of Running in the Place*, 2010

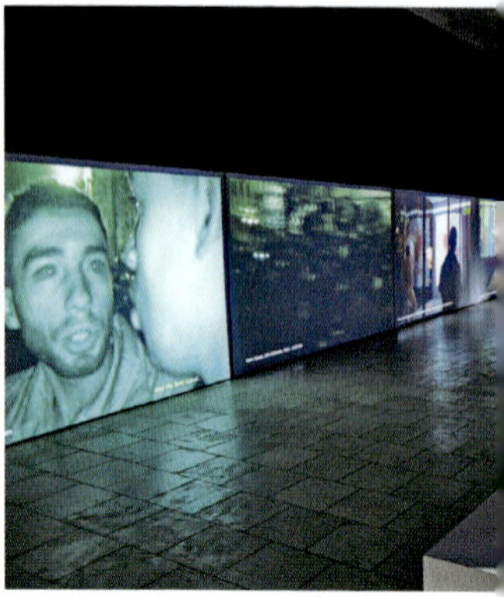

Ahmed Basiony, *30 Days of Running in the Space*, 2011

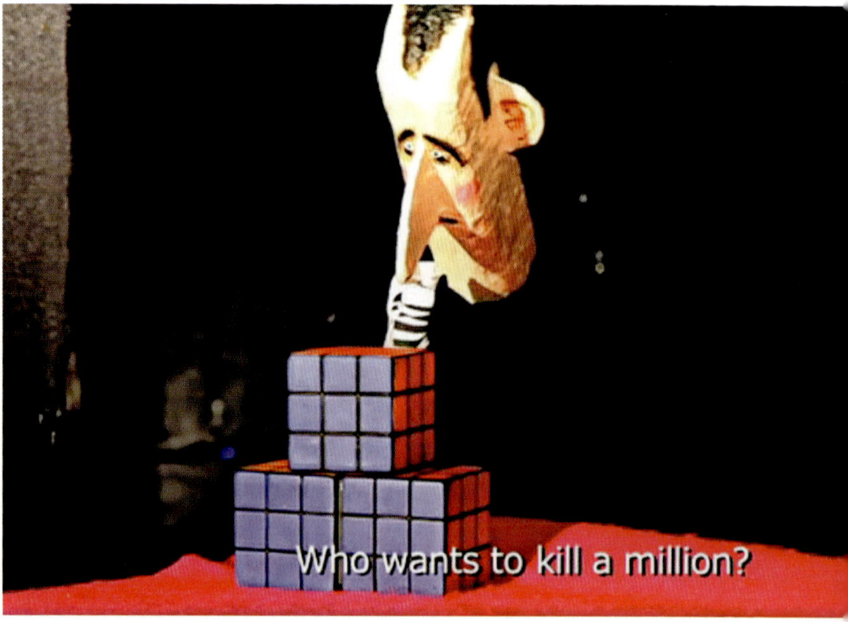

Still from Masasit Mati, *Top Goon*, "Who Wants to Kill a Million?," episode 2, November 27, 2011

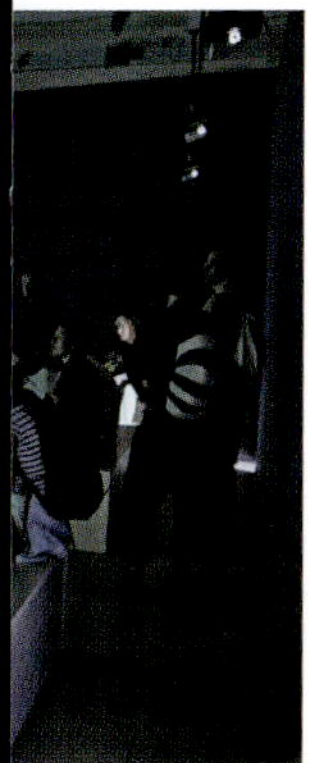

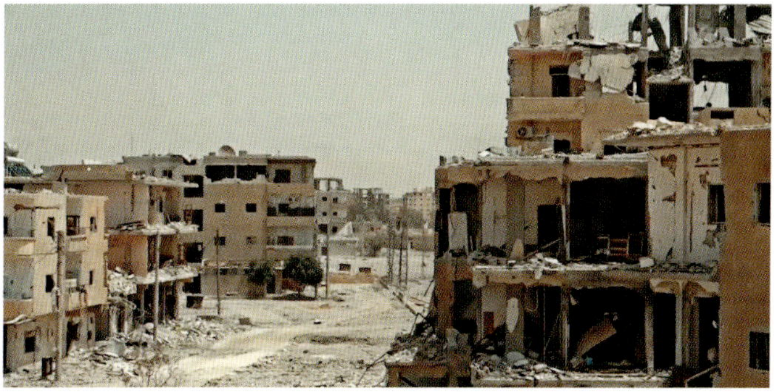

Destroyed neighborhood in Raqqa, Syria, August 1, 2017

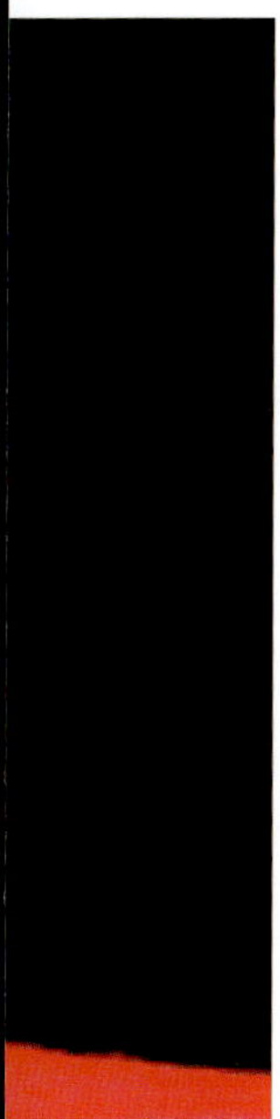

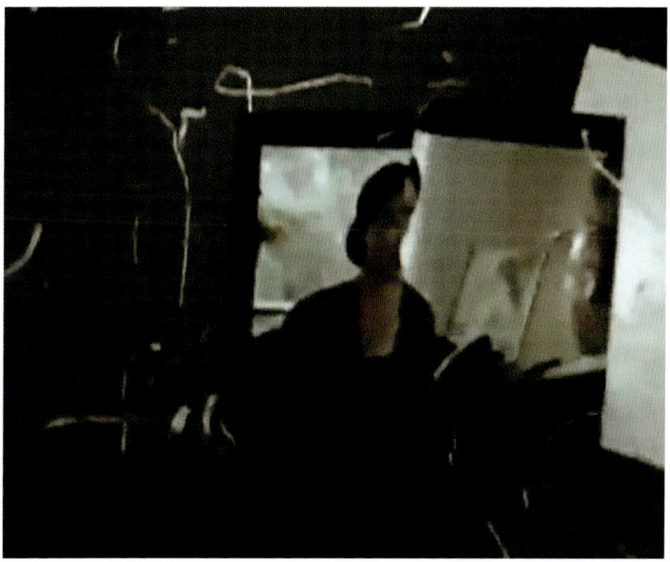

Maha Maamoun, *Night Visitor: The Night of Counting the Years*, 2011

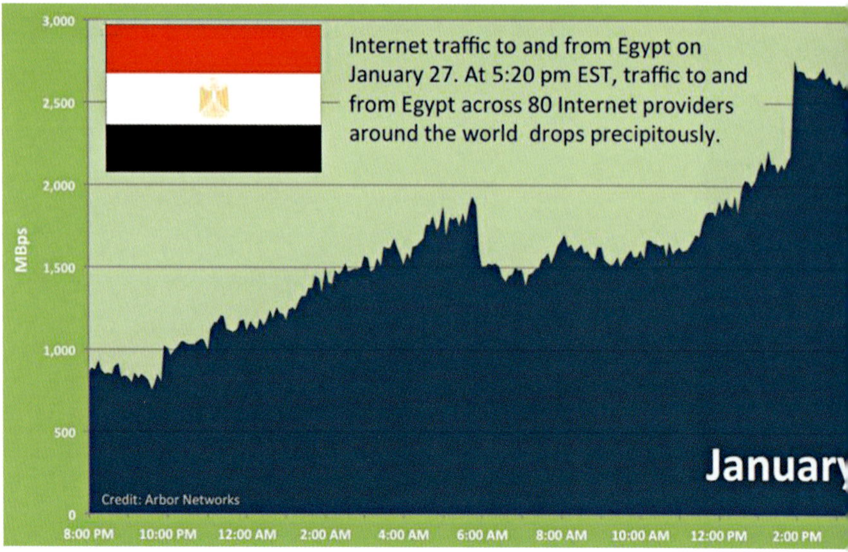

Graph showing the Egyptian internet being shut off at 5.20 p.m. EST, January 27, 2011

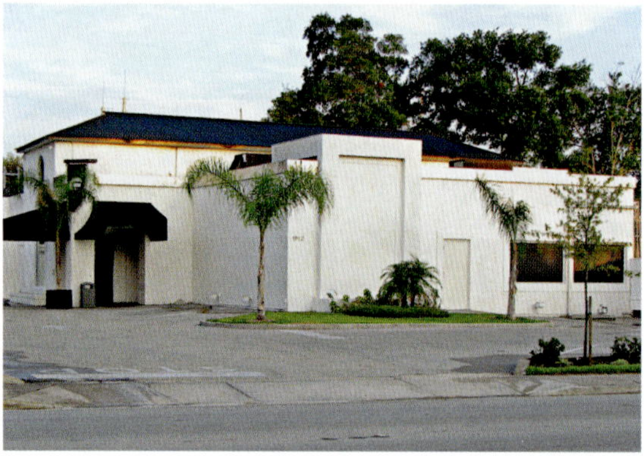

Pulse Nightclub, Orlando, 2006

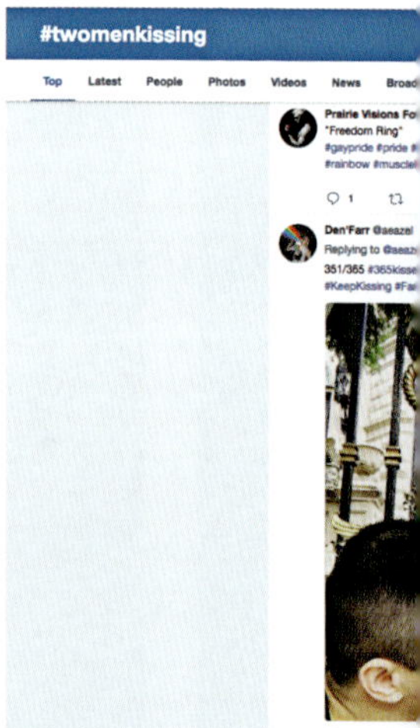

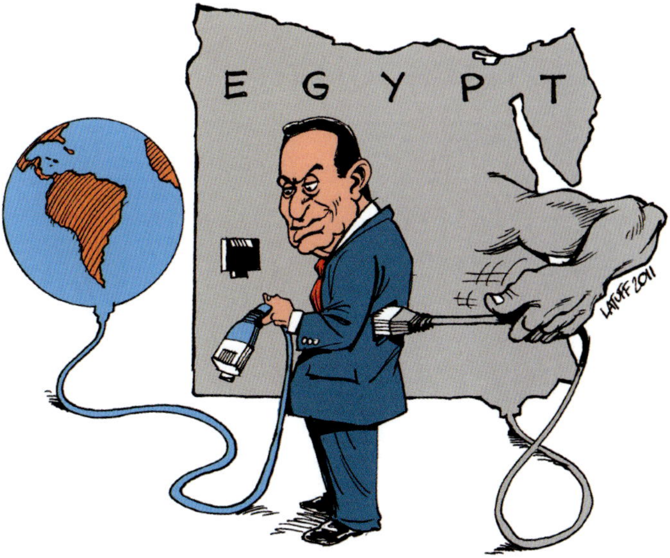

Carlos Latuff, *Mubarak shuts down Internet! Egypt will shut down Mubarak!*, January 28, 2011

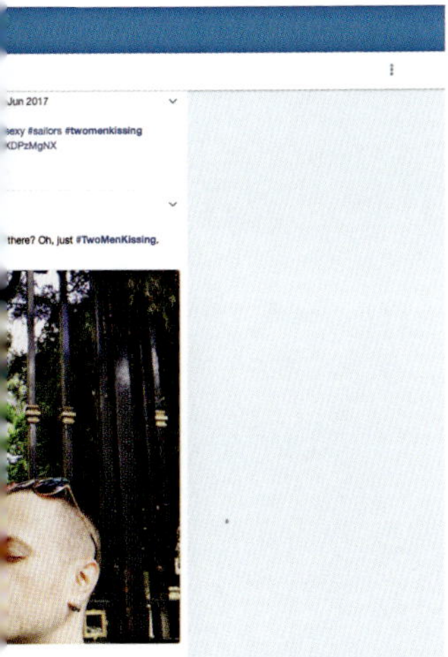

#twomenkissing Twitter campaign, summer 2017

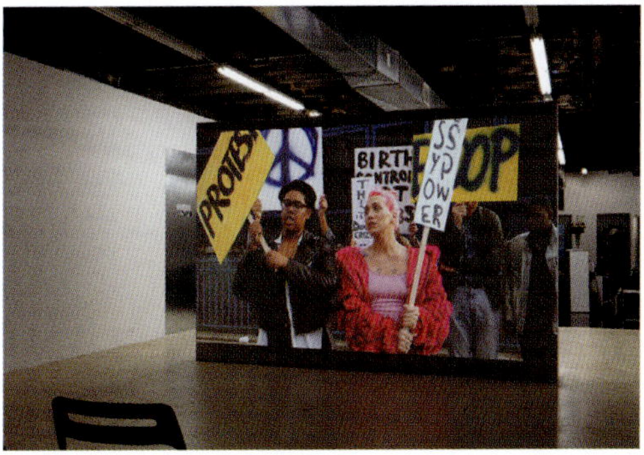

Juliana Huxtable, *A Split During Laughter at the Rally*, 2017

Toward a New Digital Metabolism

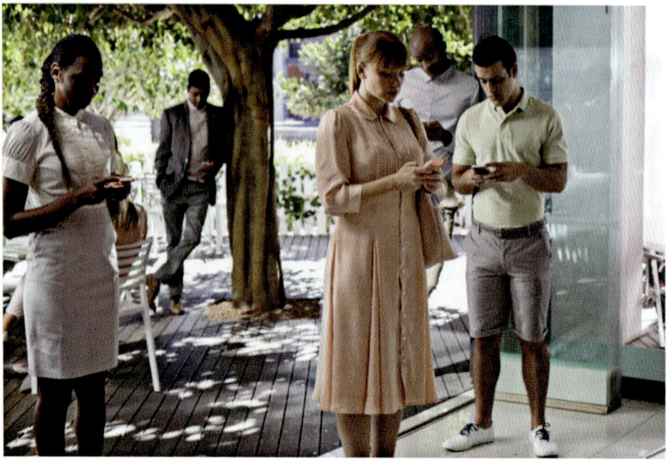

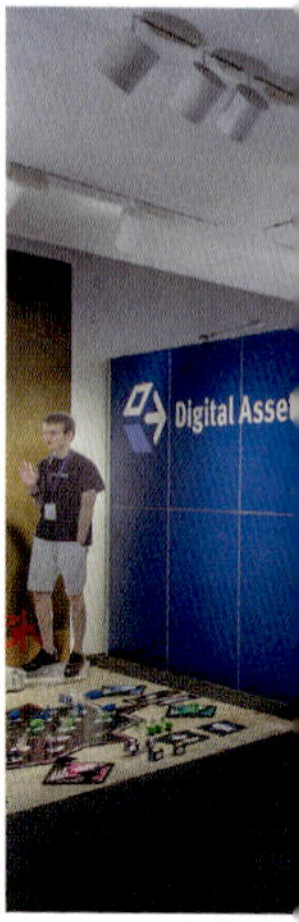

Still from *Black Mirror*, “Nosedive,” season 3, episode 1, 2016

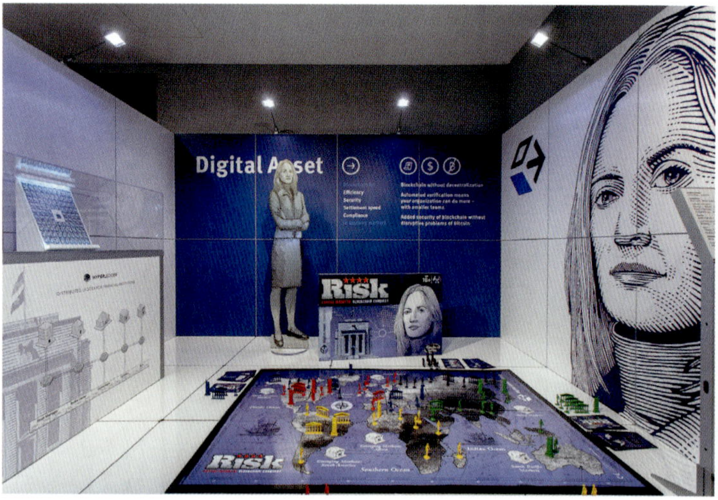

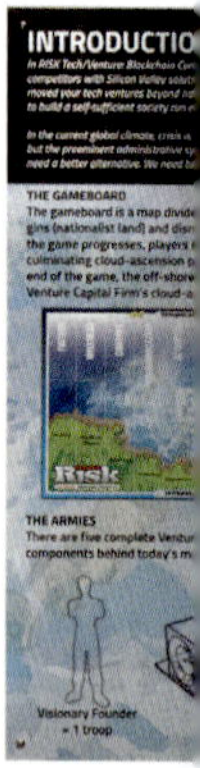

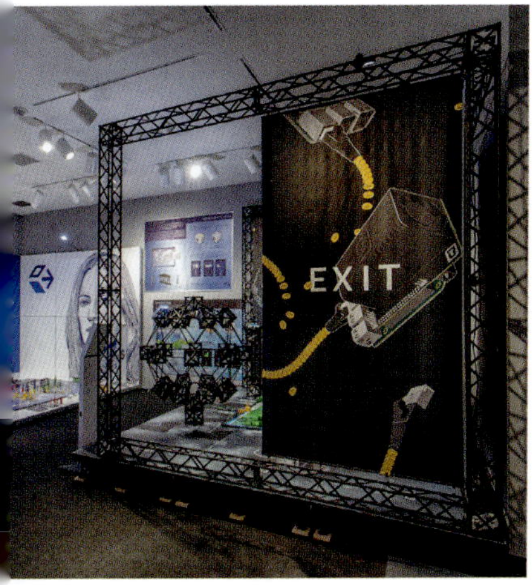

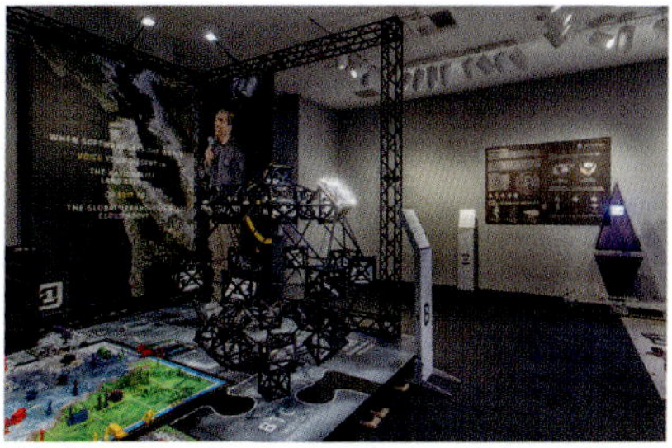

Simon Denny, *Blockchain Future States*, 2017

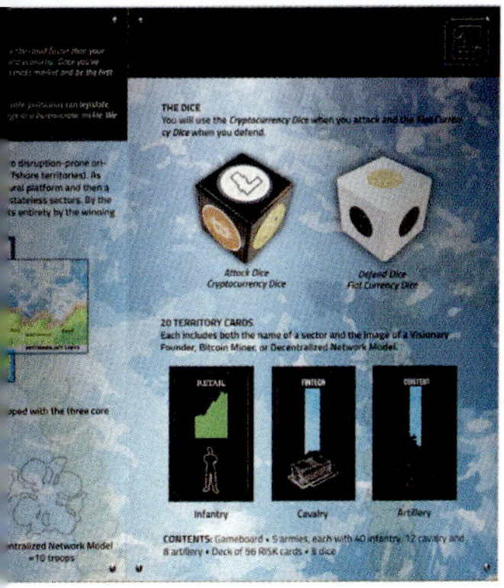

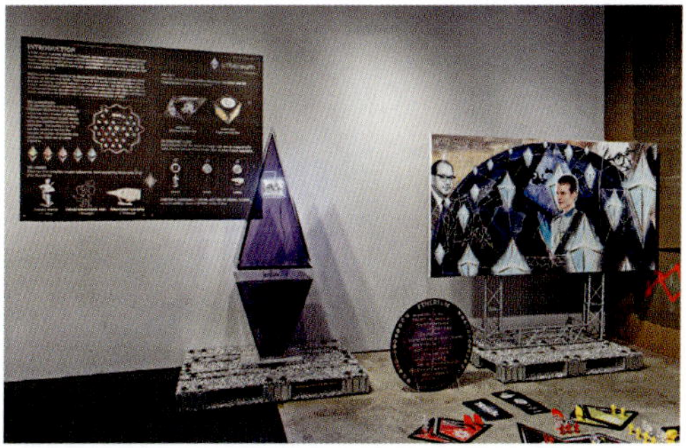

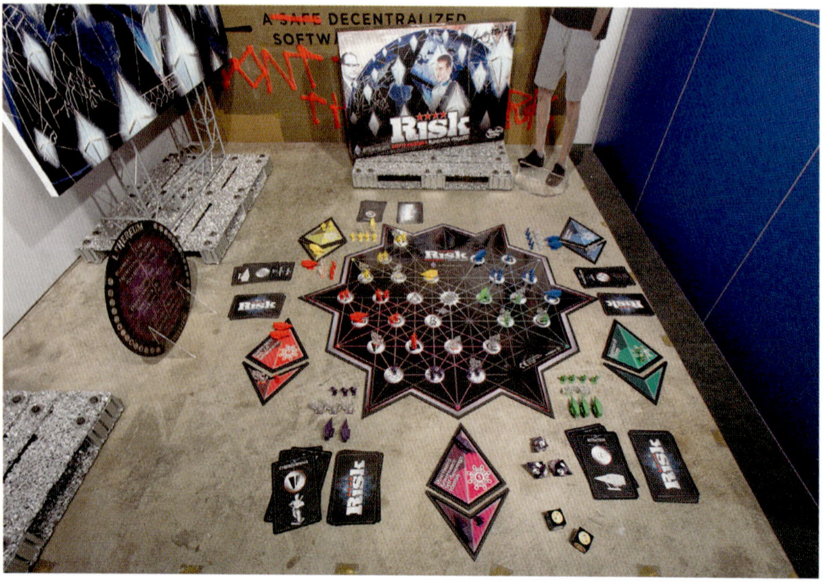

Simon Denny, *Blockchain Future States*, 2017

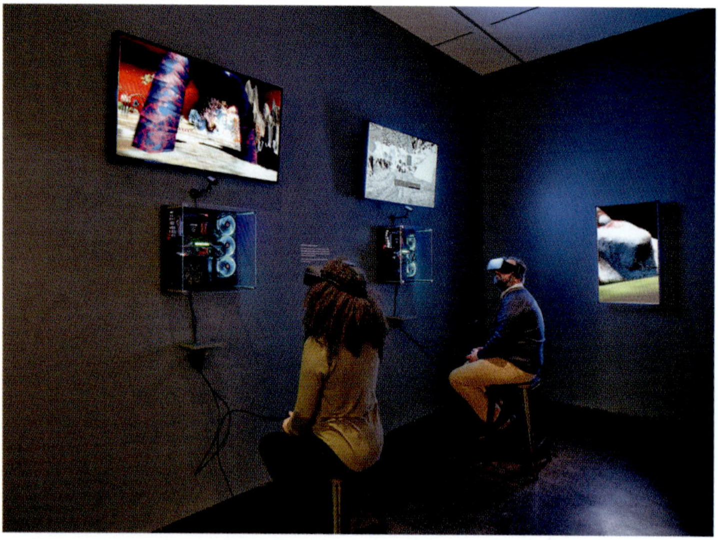

“DiMoDA 2.0: Morphé Presence,” RISD Museum, Providence, RI, 2017

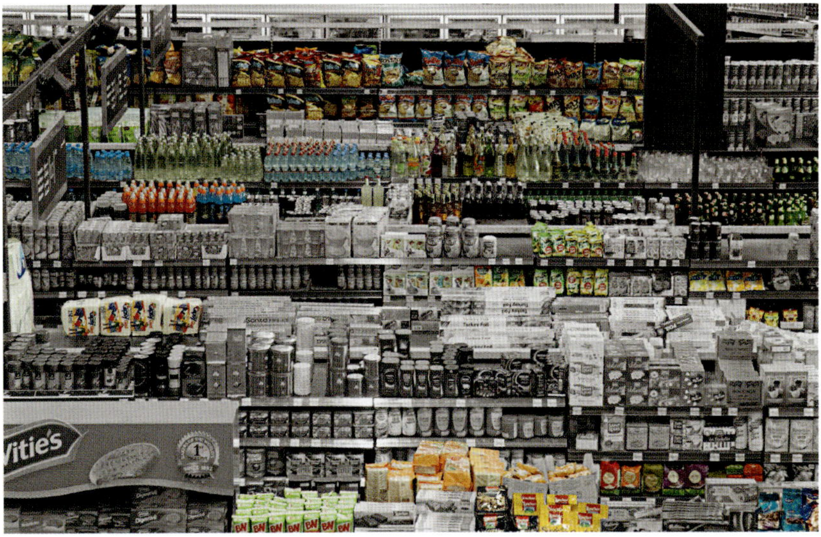

Lawrence Abu Hamdan, *A Convention of Tiny Movements, 2015—Spinneys Supermarket, Achrafieh Beirut August 2017*, 2015

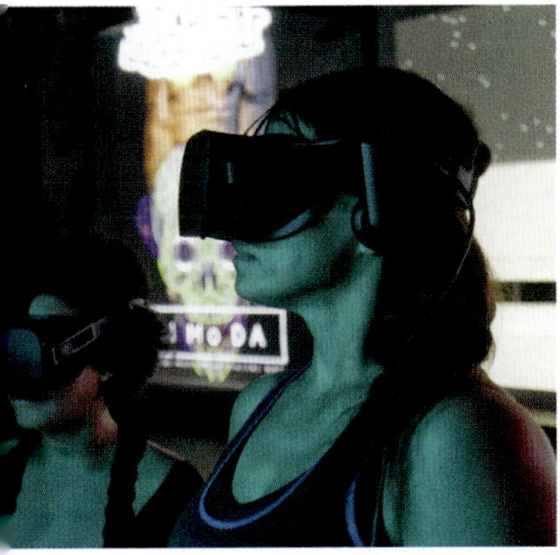

Visitors wearing VR headsets at "DiMoDA 2.0: Morphé Presence," RISD Museum, Providence, RI, 2017

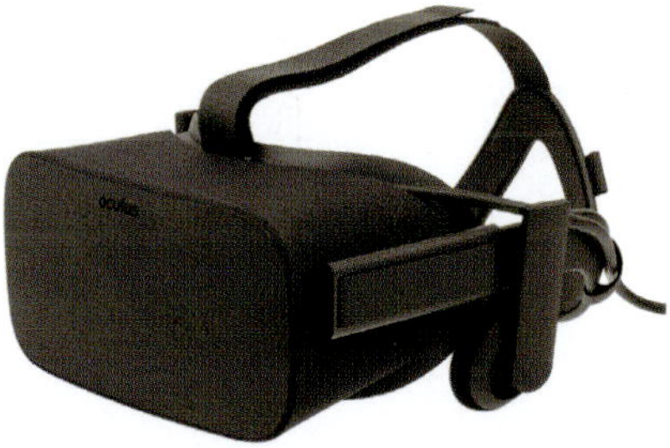

The Oculus Rift CV1 (Consumer Version 1), 2016

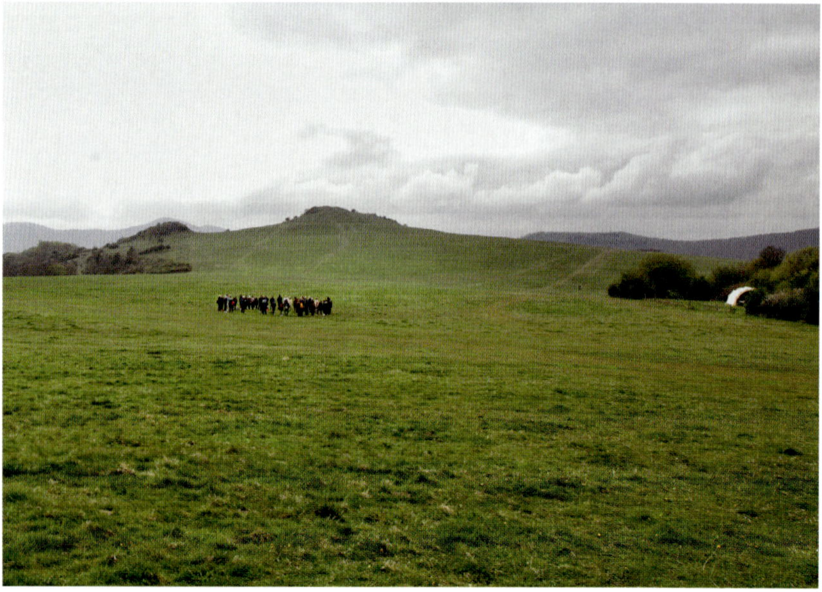

Angelo Plessas, *6th Eternal Internet Brotherhood/Sisterhood*, Lebensbogen, Zierenberg, 2017

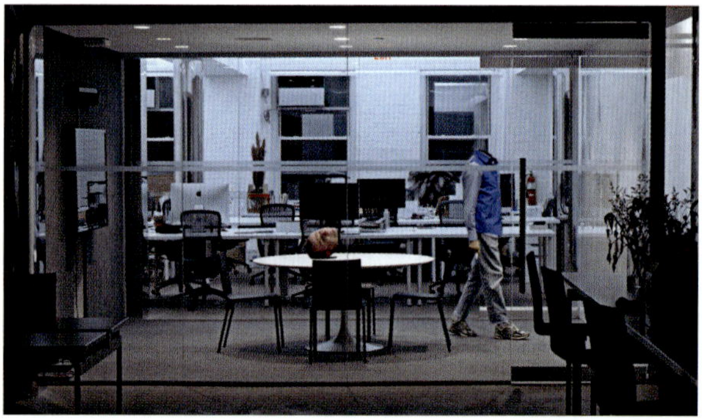

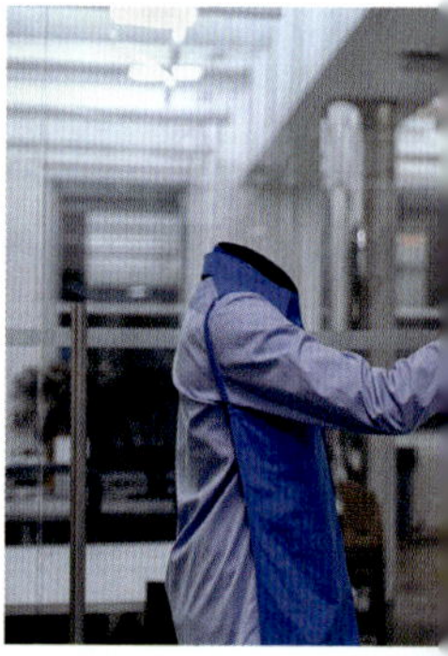

Stills from DIS, *General Intellects with McKenzie Wark*, 2017

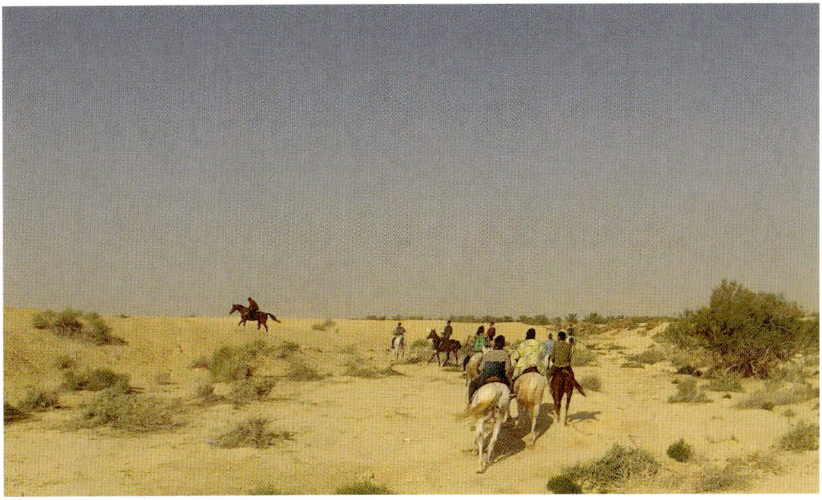

Angelo Plessas, *Eternal Internet Brotherhood/Sisterhood*, Palestine, 2014

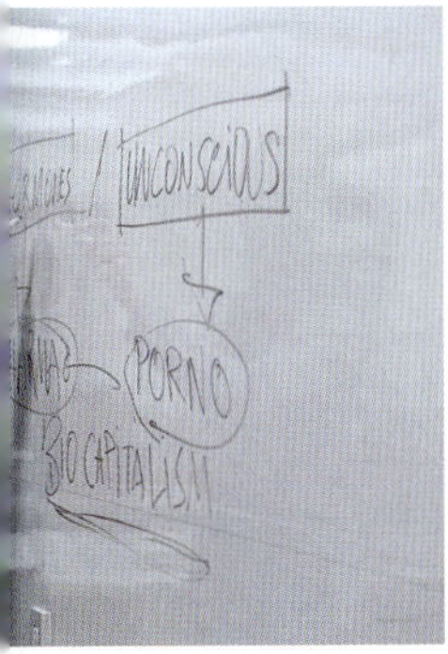

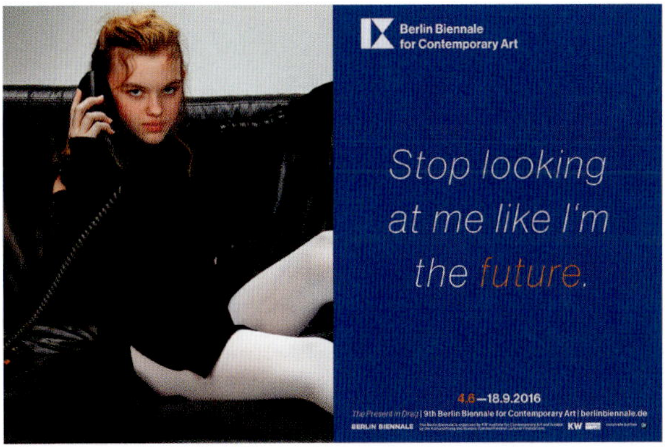

Not in the Berlin Biennale ad campaign, 2016

Goodbye, World! Navigating the Debris of Our Digital World

Have you ever wished that your problems could be solved by the function of a single microchip? Have you ever dreamed of new technological innovations that could cure the cancer of a dying family member? Have you found yourself purchasing items, resources, and apps unchecked because of the click-happy potential to do so? Are you agitated when a plane doesn't have Wi-Fi or an adaptor plug? Do you lament that all of your devices—your clocks, laptops, iPads, and iPhones—don't have endless battery life and memory? Have you walked across the street with your head down, looking at your phone, and felt rage when an elderly man or woman heading toward you yelps, "Look up!" Oh, the gerontocracy!

These, dear reader, are early signs of what is known as "technophoria," a new metabolic state devised by late capitalism whereby human needs and desires are purely satiated by the continual evolution of their electronic devices. This is not to say that your experience, or rather, that your dependency on these devices, is bad; it is simply that it must be understood, managed, and controlled so that it does not control you. The problem here is not the purchase of electronic devices—indeed, companies such as Apple will now automatically upgrade all your devices for a nominal cost. Instead, it is that one must learn to control the digital debris around them—to devise the optimal vocabulary for navigating this terse terrain or else risk being swallowed alive by it.

Everything is a form of representation. Our Facebook profiles, our Instagram feeds, the idea of the RSS need no longer be alien—we live, we breathe, we swear by their facts. But what happens when you see, on the feed of some social-media platform, an ex showing off his or her engagement ring? How should you feel? Should you be privy to such information, or should you even develop the emotional skills to let this news not affect you when it passes by, especially when you yourself are downtrodden and alone?

It is undeniable that machines have changed us, nor can we ignore that their integration into our lives has all but unhinged us. A lover may "sext" you out of the blue from halfway across the world, where it is midnight, while you are in a meeting at one in the afternoon: "Hey baby, I'm here in bed thinking about you and touching myself." You are suddenly rendered vulnerable to psychosexual emotions when you should be focusing on your meeting. This single disembodied message has altered your presence in the real world. You are now alive in a completely different way: temporally and spatially dislocated in your mind.

But put down your phone and let us take a journey back through time; start to think of that first time you joined a social-media platform, whether it be AOL Instant Messenger for the Gen Xers or MySpace for the millennials. We have been creatures of the internet longer than we wish to acknowledge. How many of us remember using the internet as a tool to enhance or even spark real-world interactions. How many of us have spent hours adjusting our profiles, making sure to list every musician and film that we thought was cool and that we hoped others would think as well? How many of us remember Tom Anderson, the founder of MySpace, whose profile picture, staring back at us with a thumbs-up and a toothy grin, was automatically linked to every new MySpace user?

These events and platforms make up our recent media archaeology, but out of this digital debris, what we often remember and what we allow to fade might seem alarming. Consider how multitudinous our birthday celebrations have become, when only a few years before we still relied on cards and phone calls. On my birthday, for instance, I received:

- 286 messages on my Facebook wall (numerous of whose potential is maximized through algorithms)
- 15 direct messages
- 7 emails
- 3 mobile-phone messages
- 17 WhatsApp messages

- 5 Skype calls
- 1 Viber call
- 12 Google Hangouts messages
- 1 actual phone call

As has become sociably acceptable, I waited a day to respond: "Thank you so much for these great wishes, I think I am having an early midlife crisis, please forgive me if I do not get back to you immediately." My midlife crisis is not real; well, it's a crisis all right: I am simply not sure how to celebrate another year of my life. Should I have a physical birthday party, or a virtual sit-in? We still assume that physical, rather than virtual, experience is more authentic. I shall later argue how this is a historically misaligned form of judgment.

Still, despite the flood of virtual birthday cheer, I decided to have a physical experience, and took a flight to visit my best friend in San Francisco. I was high, or shall I say "low," on a Benzo. Despite my obsession with machines, I am afraid of flying, as I have become, through my research, deeply aware of the possibility that machines can fail us. After I cleared security at Newark Airport I went in search for a bite to eat, only to discover that no food can be ordered without engaging with an electronic tablet. I sat down at a restaurant that purported to be a licensed version of the New York nightclub and bar CBGB. An olive-skinned man across from me, on his laptop, sat moving charts and graphs with his fingers. All the punk-rock stars who died of heroin overdoses would be rolling in their graves. I attempted to make an order on an iPad, but it failed to go through. There was one member of staff in sight who ignored me every time I waved to catch his eye. I tried to grab the attention of the man on his laptop hoping that he might help, but he discounted my presence like everyone else. Frustrated, I tapped on the iPad with my phone, making an audible noise to get the waiter's attention. When he came, he gave me a menacing look as he muttered if he could be of service. I told him I was no longer hungry and walked away.

As I left CBGB, it dawned on me that airports are ideal places for companies to test their most radical connective technologies as well as their most fundamental social practices. That is because airports, like the internet, function as isolated hubs that are interconnected within a greater space. But unlike the internet, where one can be belligerent without much fear of repercussion, an airport exists in the real world. If I went on Twitter to bad-mouth the restaurant, not much would happen to me. But were I to shatter an iPad screen to get a waiter's attention, I would have serious consequences to deal with.

Ordering from an iPad even when there is a waiter present brings up a fundamental question that regards the future of human labor: Will machines, engineers, and programmers replace waiters, bussers, and bartenders? If so, who will serve us if something malfunctions? Surely waitstaff would at least be replaced by engineers who could service these devices as they break down, not to mention protect them from the belligerence of "hangry" patrons.

Once I departed CBGB, I made my way to a cafe where I sat next to a man who looked eighty or perhaps ninety. "I want a frappé!" he said with a yelp.

"A frappé?" I asked. I had assumed such things are the purview of people under the age of fifty, never over.

"Yes, a fucking frappé, but the machine don't work." I introduced myself as a historian of technology, hoping he would see me as an expert and welcome the help. But his desire remained his only concern. "Just direct me to the nearest fucking frappé!" he yelled.

This man was not rude. Perhaps a little deaf, and perhaps a little tired, but not antagonistic. I noticed a gay couple that had managed to get their Frappuccino deliciousness just fine. I turned to ask for their help, but they quickly scurried away. That is the thing with technology: no one wants to become lodged in conversations that could prove to be inconvenient for passengers needing to catch a flight.

When an airport official appeared, I passed the man and his needs along and dashed out, saving myself from seeing through to the end of the fate of his frappé. But as I continued to roam the airport, I couldn't help but notice the power this space commanded over people, thinking about the militaristic context where most technologies emerge. Just like the internet, which is monitored by government satellites and undersea communication cables, there is an authoritarian context to an airport, a site controlled by the invisible power of surveillance, where every action can be observed with a special set of tools.

I still had yet to eat, so I made my way to a shop advertising New York–style pizza. But I found no waitstaff inside. Nor was there any staff at the noodle joint next door. I was lost and starving. I headed back to CBGB and, making sure the waiter didn't see me, sheepishly perused the reissues of classic albums they had for sale. I discovered a copy of Patti Smith's *Horses*, thinking to myself as I pulled it out: *Patti would not be happy.* Still, I took it to the register to purchase and then made sure it was visible in my hands as I sat back down at CBGB's restaurant. On an iPad (a functioning one this time), I ordered a burger and a beer. Along with my credit-card information, I was asked to insert my boarding time and fight details. A clock appeared on the screen that informed me how much time I had to consume my burger. As for the vinyl record I had just purchased, a novelty of anachronistic technology, it could not be played as I ate; it was just for show: a spectacle, a utopic ideal. Like many old-fashioned technologies, vinyl records have become fetishized, for which we are now forced to pay a premium to reengage with.

Certainly, to speak of the culture of technology—the evolution of the internet, the digital and post-digital periods, the relationship between art and technology—the rise of new media has become a "drag." This particular articulation comes from the New York–based collective DIS, who launched an advertising campaign for the 9th Berlin Biennale titled "Stop Looking at Me Like I Am the Future." Organized under tight thematic guidelines, the collective sought to construct the sense of what it meant to exist in the "extreme present," a term coined in *The Age of Earthquakes* (2015), a book coauthored by Shumon Basar, Douglas Coupland, and Hans Ulrich Obrist. In the book, they postulate an idea of a human future that is fundamentally separate from our species' natural origins. The media historian Norman M. Klein furthered this idea when he conceptualized the future as a cellular maze of cross-embedded media whereby consciousness is not a "lived" experience, but one that is articulated through the imagined renderings of a small set of "architects" who craft and shape our world on software using narrowly prescribed computer languages, which are then mapped out onto the world. This is a notion that the digital theorist James Bridle expressed in his manifesto "The New Aesthetic," where he illustrates how the appearance of digitized visual tropes are manifesting themselves in the physical world. But is this to say that we are becoming machines or symbiotic creatures, or are we magnifying our own physicality, aided by machines and cybernetic enhancements?

I ask these questions because it is unclear what kind of generational schism is forming between the people who are enjoying the fruits of this future-present condition and those who constantly critique it. A recent example would be Obrist and Swiss Institute director Simon Castets's "89plus," a project that sought to examine how artists born in 1989—what Obrist termed the "Diamond Generation"—think and work today in ways not previously done. Yet regardless of the new methodologies that technology can enable us to explore, one question that no one seems to be asking, at least within the framework of our now ubiquitously digital world, is whether technological symbiosis can lead to a sense of contentment. In his book *The Shallows: What the Internet Is Doing to Our Brains* (2010), Nicholas Carr professes that the internet is having an adverse effect on how we process information: "Neuroscientists and psychologists have discovered that, even as adults, our brains are very plastic," Carr said in an interview with NPR. "They're very malleable, they adapt at the cellular level to whatever we happen to be doing. And so the more time we spend surfing, and skimming, and scanning [...] the more adept we become at that mode of thinking [to the detriment of] slower, more contemplative modes of thought."

Is he right? Is reading one article from start to finish more cerebral than skimming ten? Is my generation less intelligent than scholars who acquired knowledge by pouring over hundreds of books, page by page, in dust-ridden libraries? Or does Carr have it all wrong? Is the internet more like a digitized "memory theater"—a stage on which all human knowledge, contained within an unseen network of servers, can be displayed and devoured at my desire?

The issues that I have outlined here have long been of concern to artists. In 1982, the pioneering video artist Judith Barry made *Space Invaders*, a film that sought to explore Marshall McLuhan's concept of a "global village," a universe wherein the world had become a singular, electronically connected entity. In response, Barry created a science-fiction fantasy: a giant disco ball standing in for the earth hangs within a room filled with video games and televisions. Barry uses these objects to meditate on what it means to be connected by technology and to debate a fear, crafted by Western capitalists, of how a "global villager" might harm society. The video ends with these fears coming true: each villager begins to carry their own singular "worlds" within them, making obsolete that necessity to communicate with others. They can now exist purely within themselves.

I thought of Barry's film as I started to board my flight. In considering the concept of the global villager, it occurred to me that even as we undergo a sensorial shift in the way that we engage with the world, we have yet to fully ascend to the full potential of this imagined universe. What this book aims to do, then, is offer readers a tool kit for seeing, feeling, and being in our post-millennium digital world by using art, that great barometer of cultural change, to build the kind of vocabulary necessary for narrating its recent history.

Looking at Art after the Internet

Any discussion of how we look at art today must take into account how the world of art has changed with the advent of the internet. Think, for example, of the millions of people each year who visit London's Tate Modern. They do not simply come for the special exhibitions, but to see the free collections, to dine, to peruse the store, to sit and lie down in the Turbine Hall on the large carpet that sits atop the sloping concrete floor, and to look up at the ceilings of the former power station that used to be housed there. A museum then becomes a space to be with one another, for families and friends to bond over an experience more fulfilling than a day out at the shops.

Art has become a special attraction, like going to Alton Towers or Disney World. Cultural institutions such as the Louvre or the National Gallery of London no longer exclusively appeal to high-minded patrons, nor do the classical "high arts" of the Renaissance or the pre-Modernist masters—Monet, Gauguin, Turner, Hogarth. Contemporary art is anything but a white man's club. The new millennium has given birth to entirely new breeds of artists who come from all kinds of backgrounds and identify in a myriad of ways. With them has come a thoroughfare of the mega-museum, biennial, and art salon, reclaimed from elites and rearticulated as a funfair, a tourist attraction, and a public commodity.

Similarly, the art-fair boom highlighted by mega fairs, such as Frieze and Art Basel, are not simply spaces where dealers show works to a small group of collectors. They present their artists for media and public consumption, curating their booths like mini-museum exhibitions. Fairs organizers now also commission special projects, stage extensive talks programs, hire pop-up stores and restaurants to service attendees, and build temporary sculpture gardens for visitors to meet up and wander, thereby constructing a whole new temporary social environment. After hordes of discerning VIPs are given an evening to privately view the fair, the doors are open to the public, who descend for the art and a rare glimpse at the transactional nature of the art-world: here, anyone has the right to ask about the price of a piece or to inquire about the inspiration and process behind a specific work with those gallerists who have working relationships with specific artists. And maybe, if the price is right, one of these general public visitors might take a work home.

The very same experience can be witnessed at the biennial and triennial exhibition, including the Venice Biennale, the Whitney Biennial, the New Museum Triennial, the Liverpool Biennial, the Sharjah Biennial, and so forth. These events are differentiated insomuch as they are noncommercial events run by not-for-profit organizations that tend to focus on revealing a central curatorial thesis. But they also boast many of the tropes of the art-fair model too, in terms of how audiences engage with these spaces. They are temporary autonomous environments, where people come to discover the new art of tomorrow. They also tend to have large investments from the cities that host them, who see these exhibitions as a cultural means to boost the local economy.

The obsession with "the new" as such becomes a pleasure and a curse that puts pressure on these institutions to appeal to mainstream audiences in order to stay financially afloat, keep in the press, and remain in the overall public consciousness. As such, these organizations can be especially territorial about which artists are shown. These artists will often have to sign non-disclosure agreements preventing them from public discussion of their involvement in such events, as well as the details of their projects. They may also be asked to withhold from partaking in other major exhibitions, including group shows that may be seen as competitive, so that these institutions may be able to hold the cachet of an artist.

While some senior artists traverse this space methodically and can supersede such structures because of the nature of their artistic practice, many artists see these exhibitions as opportunities to be discovered. Take for example the Lebanese-American artist and poet Etel Adnan, who despite being in her late 80s only gained major visibility after the quinquennial exhibition documenta 13 presented a major presentation of her work. The numerous museum surveys and retrospectives that followed resulted in an exponential jump in the monetary value of her work. This alerts us to the influence of such mega-events in terms of their larger influence and their multipronged control: on arts professionals, the public, and the accompanying market for art.

If one is to draw a line between the public's obsession with the old high arts and its current infatuation with more novel contemporary arts, a correlation with the digital world would become clear: both pursue the ideal of "liveness." We have become voracious globetrotters who are suffering from perpetual art-world ADHD. People are keen to view the latest work to emerge from an artist's studio as if they were waiting on pizzas baking in giant ovens. How then do we experience visual culture? This book seeks to propose various ways in which visual culture is experienced today, whether it is on your computer, your phone, or in the flesh. The notion of "in the flesh" and how we encounter art will be an issue that I constantly return to as we examine how both virtual and augmented technologies are altering the ways in which we experience art, and indeed, what we might even consider to be art.

The contents of this book emerge from a very specific cultural moment, where terminology such as "after the Internet," "post-Internet," and "born digital" are actively used and debated among contemporary artistic communities. Though I will be exploring these trends and phenomenon, I do not take a stance with any particular terminology; rather what I will later argue for is a need to keep developing this vocabulary for art's freewheeling future.

How Do We See?

In an age when museums have come to resemble major shopping malls in their form and structure, how should we view art? Take, for instance, the recent development in New York of the new Whitney Museum of American Art, an institution that had moved from their much

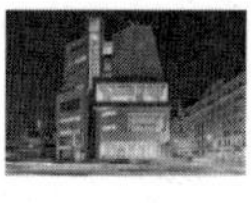

p. 10

more modest Marcel Breuer-designed building on the Upper East Side to a superstructure built in the Meatpacking District of Lower Manhattan. Designed by the workshop of the Pritzker Prize-winning architect Renzo Piano, the new Whitney Museum opened to incredible fanfare and a doubling of their visitor figures.

One of the more intrinsic shifts of the new Whitney from the old is the degree to which audiences can be immersed within its space. The Whitney's layout is a nod to the Gruen transfer, a phenomenon devised by the Austrian architect Victor Gruen, who is credited with conceiving the modern shopping mall. Gruen theorized that malls should temporally and spatially dislocate the viewer from a sense of outside reality so that, upon entering, they could only seek solace in the pursuit of capitalism, of purchasing goods, of shopping. The same can be said of other museums that have undergone Whitney-like upgrades, such as Tate Modern, the Royal Ontario Museum in Toronto, and the Reina Sofía Museum in Madrid, where the viewer becomes so enclosed within an architectural environment that he or she can only seek solace in the confrontation of art.

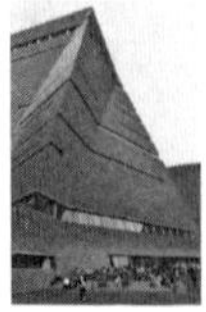

p. 11

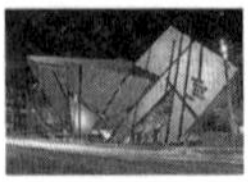

p. 10

This would seem to be a win-win situation for museums that want to encourage visitors to engage with their curated exhibitions, while also increasing dwell time in their permanent galleries. Yet it also signals a shift in the ways exhibitions are assembled. No longer do museums simply line photographs in even rows or hang paintings using traditional methods, but rather, the trend has become to create immersive experiences through interactive viewership. An example of this was an exhibition curated by Chrissie Iles that opened at the Whitney in 2016. In "Dreamlands: Immersive Cinema and Art," the viewer would be immersed in a darkened space, confronted by apparitions of light as they wandered around, a spatial experience that would teleport them back to reality while keeping them within this alternative universe. Or take for example *Anywhen* (2016), Philippe Parreno's Turbine Hall installation at Tate Modern, where the main public space was transformed into an artificial environment

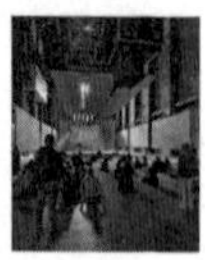

p. 11

made up of cinematic projections, flying fish, and even a universe of living mirco-organisms that took over the whole hall. Over the course of its six-month run, the installation would evolve to give the viewer a whole new experience upon each visit. While these are intriguing developments, it begs the question of whether a static, unchanging object can exist within this new landscape.

Reproductions and Originals

For a large part of my life, I believed that I had seen the Mona Lisa in the flesh. Its aura, its beauty, its cultural significance was so ingrained in me from image reproductions. But I had never been to Paris. Indeed, it wasn't until 2011, when I saw the actual painting in the Louvre, that I realized what had been so recognizable to me had been nothing but a copy. When I finally stood in front of da Vinci's original masterpiece, the experience was anything but pure. Surrounding me were people taking pictures of the painting with their smartphones. If you Google an image of the Mona Lisa today, you will be confronted with as many images of visitors raising their smartphones to document the work as you will of the work itself. These photos will then likely be posted on various social-media platforms, the personal experience of viewing distilled into a sharable "post." Yet what is lost in this act of copying?

In his television series and later book *Ways of Seeing*, the art critic John Berger returned to Walter Benjamin's seminal essay "The Work of Art in the Age of Mechanical Reproduction" (1935) to further interrogate whether the reproduction of art has destroyed its aesthetic, cultural, and political authority. Benjamin spoke of the "aura" of the original, the magical or supernatural force that was created by the artist's hand. Berger furthered this notion to an age of pop culture, where photography had made the intent of the subject—to be idolized, to be envied—as integral to a work of art as the intent of the artist. "This state of being envied is what constitutes glamour," said Berger in the final episode, "and publicity is the process of manufacturing glamour. Glamour is supposed to go deeper than looks, but it depends upon them, utterly."

He was also discussing the power, one assumes, of the bodily encounter with an original work, as well as an authentic state of being, and how it played with the hermeneutic senses of each being. A reproduction then becomes a form of marketing, driving traffic to the original, but also allowing an object to be studied, dissected, and emulated by anyone. So how should we consider the "aura" of originality when its intent is to be desired and replicated?

To answer, we must seek to redefine authenticity. In a globalized world, representations of an original work can take on different forms—they can be cropped, filtered, recreated. But without an original, a copy has no point of reference. Another purpose is, of course, value. Original works are key to bringing people to museums, and a museum has no purpose if it cannot show art that cannot be seen elsewhere. Yet this latter quality is succumbing to modernity. It is impossible to travel to every corner of the globe in order to "view" every painting in the flesh. But new digital initiatives such as Google Arts & Culture allow museums to upload high-resolution images of their collections to be seen and studied online. Private organizations are also heading in this direction as well: the Barjeel Art Foundation in the United Arab Emirates creates a high-resolution image for each item in its vast collection of Arab art; the Museum of Contemporary Art Chicago and the Centre national des arts plastiques in France both post images of their exhibitions. As a curator, I have come to depend on these reproductions in order to consider what original works to include in an exhibition. Sometimes, an image prompts me to visit a work in person; other times, a reproduced image is all I need to request having it sent to my museum.

But a different question looms over the authenticity of an original digital work, which relies on technology rather than a particular artist's so-called hand, and instead of being reproduced, can be replicated verbatim. How to value the originality of such works has been a question artists and organizations have had since the advent of the internet. One notable initiative is the Net Art Anthology, a platform created by the online art organization Rhizome, that seeks to "retell the history" of net art in five distinct chapters that capture its earliest forms that emerged in the 1980s up to present-day aesthetics and movements.

Artist collectives have also considered this question with similarly unique approaches. VVORK, a now dormant project cofounded by artists Aleksandra Domanović, Oliver Laric, Christoph Priglinger, and Georg Schnitzer, posted online shows and collections of artworks on a semi-regular basis in order to question whether such reproductions could themselves be considered "exhibitions." Since the project ended in 2012, newer organizations and cultural publications such as *Contemporary Art Daily*, *Mousse*, and *This Is Tomorrow* have sought to create virtual exhibitions by using in-depth photography and video documentation, giving the viewer a chance to experience art that is literally at their fingertips.

I will later address more of the concerns that these projects raise when I discuss the emergence of online art-distribution platforms. What I am keen to articulate here, however, is that reproduction has intrinsic value in and of itself. In an increasingly virtualized world, the better the reproduction, the more nuanced our experience of art becomes.

Rights and Copyright

Appropriation has been a long-standing practice in the history of art. Artists from Andy Warhol to Barbara Kruger have borrowed materials from popular culture—magazines, television programming, and mass-produced merchandise—to create critical reflections of our consumer society. In the age of the internet, how copyright affects these considerations has become ever more pertinent. In 2017, for example, reality-TV stars Kendall and Kylie Jenner printed and wore T-shirts depicting a collage of selfie-style images of themselves laid over pictures of Tupac and Notorious B.I.G. The project was dubbed by the media as being in "poor taste," and the sisters were sent a cease and desist summons by the estates of the late rappers. Also in 2017, the sportswear brand Adidas manufactured a limited-edition pair of "Art Basel" white sneakers as luxury giveaways. Adidas was then slapped with a lawsuit by Art Basel's parent company MCH Group, forcing the brand to recall the shoes until a settlement could be reached.

While physical objects are easier to recall over copyright issues, taking virtual appropriations offline, particularly if an appropriated work goes viral, is much more difficult. One of the internet's first viral film phenomena was created by an artist named Eric Fensler who, in 2003, created a series of short films that appropriated old G.I. Joe Public Service Announcement (PSA) shorts into surreal parodies. After the humor site eBaum's World decided to host the series, word-of-mouth excitement caused hundreds of thousands of people to view them within days of being posted. This in turn caught the attention of toy manufacturer Hasbro, G.I. Joe's creators and the copyright holders of the PSA shorts, who demanded that the films be taken down. In 2003, before the advent of social-video sites, this was still possible, and Fensler was forced to comply. In chat rooms, however, links to viewing these films outside of mainstream servers continued to proliferate. But even the necessity for this clandestine activity would be short-lived. Only a few years later after Fensler's G.I. Joe parodies were taken down, YouTube users would upload those same films, also without the consent of Hasbro. Only this time, the toy company, now faced with a daunting volume of reposts, backed off from further legal action. All twenty-five films are now public and available to view online.

In other cases, artists have used the internet's more esoteric communities to evade copyright infringement. In 2008, the artist Jon Rafman claimed the Kool-Aid Man, an anthropomorphic jug of juice and mascot for the eponymous American soft-drink company, to be the avatar in his project *Kool-Aid Man in Second Life*. As the cartoonish and oafish character, Rafman would give guided tours through the virtual world of Second Life, where the mundane and the surreal intertwine. During these safaris, one could happen upon a couple transforming into dragons or engaged in violent S-M sex, while other users would go about virtual day-to-day activities such as drinking cocktails at beachside resorts or redecorating their mansions. Rafman's Kool-Aid Man, more childlike and innocent than his corporate counterpart, acted as a stark and jarring contrast to the behaviors that often occurred in the virtual world. While one can see this as a form of charlatanism because he borrows from other brands, Rafman's actions actually serve to bring greater attention to Second Life and the Kool-Aid brand. Should such symbiosis require legal permission to enact?

Eva and Franco Mattes, the Italian artist duo, have dealt with internet appropriation by interacting with their subjects. In *BEFNOED* (2014–ongoing), Eva and Franco released instructions of tasks to be staged by anonymous workers around the globe, offering them a fee in return. Tasks included strapping a dead fish around one's belly, or pouring liquid down one's pants in front of the camera. We do not know who these workers are, but they are clearly from poorer economies and in need of the cash, so they fulfill what are often humiliating acts. These images are then broadcast on video screens in galleries, which seek to illustrate various economies of subjugation that exist online. But what we don't know is whether the Mattes's had these workers sign a contract. Can one's own self be unofficially "bought" and repurposed in ways that would otherwise violate standard copyright laws of defamation?

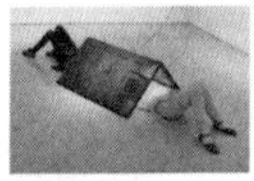

p. 12

There are also artists who work toward opposite goals to bring the internet to the real world. In her series *Pattern and Activation* (2014), Estonian artist Katja Novitskova took images found online and transformed them into real-world objects. In one example, Novitskova used high-resolution images of a horse and a wavy stock-market arrow to create multi-dimensional aluminum Dibond cutouts. Novitskova plays with the formal limits of a web browser—its screen size and scale—to allow us to consider the impermanence of digital objects, such as taking images of small creatures, for example parrots or small barn animals, and blowing them up into gargantuan beasts. These images, sourced from online magazines and Google searches, challenge the paradigms of their original meaning and intent, thus shifting the agency and authorship to the artist.

As the internet evolves, so too does the culture of adaptation grow in ubiquity. A common image on the internet is the meme: images culled from pop culture or randomly discovered uploads that allow users to fill in a humorous message. Memes can be static images or they can take the form of playable GIFs which animate video clips into continuous loops. Relentlessly posted on sites such as Buzzfeed and Giphy, these memes, often surreal and

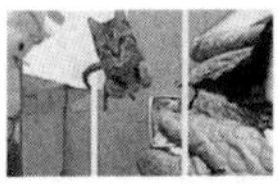

pp. 12–13

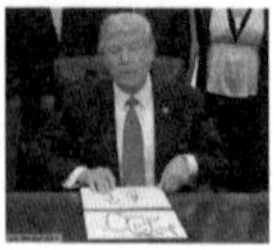

p. 12

absurd, have not only become part of the cultural lexicon, but are helping to evolve the question of copyright. In 2017, a stock-image photo of a boyfriend eyeing up a single woman to the annoyance of his girlfriend was transformed into the meme known as "distracted boyfriend." The meme went viral, prompting some publications to track down the original photographer who, when interviewed by *Wired*, noted with a shrug that although his photo was indeed being used without proper licensing, he believed that users were acting "in good faith" to transform the image into a meme. "I think the image was a good foundation for whoever had the great idea to turn it into a metaphor that works for almost everything."

Some organizations, such as the London-based Design and Artists Copyright Society, actively campaign for visual artists and other creative practitioners to receive fees when their images are used in the media. Other institutions such as Getty Images tag their photos in ways to ensure that they are not used without permission. But as artists come to depend on sourcing to create their work, what sort of legal stipulations should they be made to follow? Consider how the works of James Richards and Arthur Jafa, two of the biggest names in video art today, pull almost entirely from found footage, while their soundtracks, though sometimes self-composed, more often use other people's compositions. This is especially apparent in Jafa's film *Love Is the Message, the Message Is Death* (2016), where Kanye West's "Ultralight Beam" soundtracks the video and ultimately forms the sonic backbone to the piece.

Copyright thus becomes a conceptual concern, a question of whether one artwork should be allowed to engender another. A famous case of this debate occurred when the filmmaker Chris Moukarbel, then a graduate student at Yale University, managed to get ahold of a bootleg version of Oliver Stone's film *World Trade Center* (2006). Before the film's official release, and on a thousand-dollar budget, Moukarbel produced his own adaptation using student actors and a homemade set. The film considered the democratization of narrative and was available for viewing online freely until it was taken down by Stone's film studio,

Paramount. Oliver Stone's film, with a production budget of $65 million, went on to gross more than $160 million worldwide. Moukarbel's co-option of a blockbuster film was little more than an artistic gesture squashed by a behemoth motion-picture company. This "appropriated" version, however, occasionally circulates—one might say covertly—within the confines of galleries and museums.

The generosity of spirit associated with free circulation online has led to the birth of platforms such as UbuWeb, a lo-fi aggregator of all kinds of video and new media content collated by poet and artist Kenneth Goldsmith. Artists are often happy to associate with this platform, as it is a not-for-profit tool that enables researchers and members of the public to access works of art that would be near impossible to see otherwise. Equally, internationally recognized video artists such as Ryan Trecartin readily make their films available on YouTube as a means to attract a broader audience. However, Trecartin would argue that his video installations, made in collaboration with Lizzie Fitch, are completely unique and separate experiences from those found online.

These are but a few of the plethora of examples of how artists are addressing image appropriation, and as this issue continues to be debated, three camps have emerged. On one extreme is the Image Anarchist who believes that any image found online should be able to circulate and be used without having to attribute any credit to the original producer. On the other is the Image Fundamentalist, who demands that no image appropriation be done without a formal agreement—often involving credit lines and remuneration, signed by the original producer. In between is the Image Neoliberal who believes that images should be freely used however one sees fit so long as the original producer is properly attributed. As we shall see, in the field of art, a balance of the three is most often prevalent.

Art Surveillance

In 2017, Chelsea Manning, the former army intelligence analyst turned transgender American whistleblower, was pardoned by former President Barack Obama after serving four years of her thirty-five-year prison sentence. She entered freedom as a cultural icon of the surveillance age, an era that saw WikiLeaks founder Julian Assange and former National Security Agency contractor Edward Snowden cripplingly expose the inner workings of many of the world's powers. Yet, Manning's encouraging narrative turn has not put an end to this era of surveillance, nor our awareness of it. Snowden, who used WikiLeaks to release classified NSA files, continues to live in exile. Assange, the founder and editor of WikiLeaks, was, until recently, held under house arrest-like asylum in the Ecuadorian embassy in London. No figure in these modern times has reached Assange's level of controversy—a free-speech activist hero to some, a treasonist sex offender to others—who continues to rankle the world with leaks and proclamations online. And beyond these characters and their accompanying tales, the United States has been dealing with the ongoing investigation as to whether Donald Trump was aware that Russia was launching cyberattacks against his opponent Hillary Rodham Clinton, prior to his ascendency in the 2016 American presidential election.

It is now impossible to avoid the culture created by the constant threat of surveillance, espionage, and conspiracy that now surrounds every corner of our lives. The omnipresence of Closed Circuit Television (CCTV) ensures that the residents of most cities are kept under watch; that even peaceful protest gatherings are remotely monitored until military and police units are called in to disperse them; and that social-media and phone accounts are monitored and mined for incriminating information, all while the governments of more and more countries—such as China, Russia, and Egypt—work to limit the internet freedoms of its citizens.

More than ever, we have become aware of the presence of an upper hand that governs the seemingly free space of the internet, and with it, the significance of even our most seemingly innocuous online activities. Even cultural institutions such as museums are complicit within this framework of keeping tabs on our habits. With every ticket and membership sold, purchase made, and postcode requested, museums become able to segment and target their audiences, feeding them a culture tailor-made to their desires. Have you ever logged on to a museum Wi-Fi connection? Have you ever read the terms and conditions before you pressed accept? The odds are unlikely you have had the time to notice that sometimes you agree to being monitored. Time is your greatest commodity; information is your greatest asset.

In these instances, the museum can function like a state, limiting and enabling access to specific websites, pointing you toward merchandising opportunities, and even storing your information on its servers for a finite amount of time. Your identity becomes the subject of an ulterior power. One notable artist who has openly criticized data collation is Trevor Paglen who, in 2014, collaborated with Jacob Appelbaum to create *Autonomy Cube*, a sculpture that enables gallery patrons to enjoy encrypted internet access and communication. What at first looks like a router in a plastic box is actually a Tor network, an encrypted internet platform that makes one's online activity untraceable by generating randomized IP addresses from other Tor networks around the world. Without access to a proper IP address, someone trying to steal your data would receive false and scrambled data sets. The work encourages museums to reconsider their use beyond cultural spaces and toward a more civic realm, where ideas and experiences could occur unthreatened by constant watch.

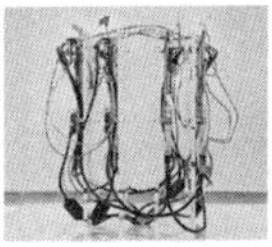

pp. 12–13

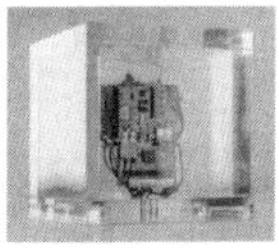

p. 13

While speculating on the possible government complicity art institutions might have, what is more often the case with how institutions, venues, and websites use the habitual information they accrue about its patrons is in the way they serve to build algorithmic personalities. A patron who goes to the Whitney one day might find advertisements about its forthcoming exhibitions on Facebook the following day. Often, however, this algorithm is inconsistent to a person's actual interests. If a patron brings to the Whitney a relative from out of town, that relative, too, will receive online ads from the Whitney. A better approach might be what I call "algorithmic curating," a means of discerning one's tastes by curating algorithmic functions. One of the most popular of these procedures is Amazon's "You May Like" function. Anyone who has used this service will recognize how material inspired by your shopping trends will appear on your homepage, encouraging you with "More Items to Consider"—always more items to consider! While Amazon's use of algorithmic curation is a topic that could form a separate book, what I would like to draw attention to specifically is how Amazon's knowledge-based algorithmic curation can be used (or even appropriated) for works of art.

Let's attempt an algorithmic journey and see where we end up:

> Create a new Amazon account so you are starting as algorithmically fresh as a baby's bottom. Now type into the search bar that most infamous of introductions to twentieth-century art history: Yve-Alain Bois, Benjamin H. D. Buchloh, Rosalind E. Krauss, and Hal Foster's *Art since 1900: Modernism, Antimodernism, Postmodernism.*
>
> Click on the first result. Add it into your Amazon cart. Now watch as the suggestions that come *relate* to what I view and acquire rather than be analogous to them. Note that my searches are based on Amazon's American site, but they shouldn't be too different for UK or Australian users. For instance, the first suggestion isn't on the history of art, but rather history of art theory:
>
> – *Art in Theory 1900–2000: An Anthology of Changing Ideas* by Charles Harrison and Paul Wood
>
> But the algorithms don't lead us too far astray. After selecting *Art in Theory*, we are offered:
> – H. H. Arnason and Elizabeth C. Mansfield, *History of Modern Art*
> – Herschel B. Chipp, *Theories of Modern Art: A Source Book by Artists and Critics*
> – E. H. Gombrich, *The Story of Art*
>
> We are also recommended something that can send us on a different path. We are offered and select:
> – Jacques Rancière, *The Politics of Aesthetics*

Which leads us into something a little, well, trashier:
- Sarah Thornton, *Seven Days in the Art World*

That then leads us to a masterpiece:
- John Berger, *Ways of Seeing*

But now notice how much the algorithm changes after selecting Berger. We are now suggested books specific to photography:
- Susan Sontag, *On Photography*
- Roland Barthes, *Camera Lucida: Reflections on Photography*

Which loops us back into theory:
- Jean Baudrillard, *Simulacra and Simulation*

Before ending on a sort of existential note:
- Jean-François Lyotard, *The Postmodern Condition: A Report on Knowledge*

After this point, the suggestions circle back around to previous highlights left unselected, while also surprisingly, leaving other choices that I would consider obvious out of its consideration. To my surprise, a canonical twentieth-century modern-art critic never appeared as a recommendation. Perhaps he had gone out of style, otherwise, a majority of these texts make up the reading lists required for my freshman year art-history classes.

It's arguable that algorithms could be used to substitute a formal art history education provided by an accredited university. At the very least, algorithms allow for private intellectual development that once required a formal education. This, in turn, has enabled a generation of autodidacts to break into a once hermetic field and invigorate it with fresh perspectives, and in doing so, taking "expertise" from the institutional critics—many of them white and male—and leveling the playing field with more women, minorities, and independent cultural institutions.

But although it may seem like algorithms such as Amazon's only serve to democratize cultural knowledge, their primary purpose remains capitalistic. The algorithms are unending, and your continued engagement with the world can be exclusive to what you purchase. This raises the questions of whether the rise of the autodidact runs parallel with a new order of social elitism, where knowledge is reserved for those who can afford it.

But as long as we can democratize the algorithms themselves, then anyone can use them for their own gain. Anyone can create a LinkedIn profile, for example, which uses an algorithmic database that can both be used by potential employees hunting for the right job as well as employers in search of ideal candidates to fill open positions. Artists have used Instagram's algorithms to amass followers, including curators and gallerists who may go on to represent them. Facebook becomes an endless friending zone where people are "suggested" based on the friends you currently have, thus enabling people to grow personalized communities and nurture friendships without much real-world effort. In other words, all of us are starting to "see" each other, for all the good, the bad, and the ugly that this may entail.

How to Speak about Art and the Internet

The terminology that is used to discuss the relationship between art and the internet is contestable and often misunderstood. Historically, many digital practices have been placed under umbrella terminology. Perhaps the most commonly used phrase was "new media art," which was first intended to encompass all media that used technology and which, over time, has become almost exclusively synonymous with discussions surrounding video art. As new media grew increasingly specific, a newer umbrella term was needed. "Electronic art," or "electronic media," were two interchangeable phrases that were intended to encompass works that were both technologically based and user-interactive. "Digital art," a term that emerged to reference art made for the virtual sphere, was later controversially co-opted by the media to discuss everything from graphic to product design that engaged with emerging technologies. A term such as "art after the internet" might be taken to mean art after the end of the internet, when instead it's true implication is to suggest art that has been produced after the internet's ubiquitous rise leading up to the new millennium—when it went from a curious bunch of tech geeks to becoming the world's biggest platform for mass consumerism, and is now an essential element of everyday life. The actual starting point for what is considered art after the advent of the internet is arguable: some would say that it was when browser-based art emerged in the late 1990s, during the search-engine wars and the first bubbling of the dot-com era. While this period saw the emergence of early net artists such as JODI and Mark Amerika, I tend to see this as art *during* the rise of the internet rather than after it, when its ubiquity went global, when the generation that grew up with it began to come of age, and when smartphones and social media allowed for people to interface in ways that have now become commonplace.

But neither of these arguments addresses the more nuanced and contentious debate of what defines "post-Internet" art, itself different from "net.art," a term used by early virtual artists such as Olia Lialina, Shu Lea Cheang, and the Dutch duo JODI. If net.art encompassed the first generation of internet artists, then art after the internet would account for the second, and post-internet art would describe yet a third. Coined by artist Marisa Olson and further extrapolated by writers Gene McHugh and Artie Vierkant, it further considers the aesthetics of internet-based art, especially those works that could not be possible without its context or its tools. An analogous term is art that is "Internet aware," a term first proposed by artists Guthrie Lonergan to mean work that "is of" the internet rather than art used as a means to explore it. Some of the most notable artists in this field, including Constant Dullaart, Olia Lialina, and Harm van den Dorpel—have taken a specific approach to what constitutes art as post-internet, creating works that critically examine how various powers manipulate the internet to suggest how the internet can be reclaimed by artists. I will return to some of these artists and more specific works later in this book.

Two expressions that are also often used interchangeably are "born digital" and "digital native." These terms suggest a generation of not only artists but also human beings who were born into an after-internet age, where young children were becoming fluent with its tools. This is a generation that takes for granted apps such GarageBand, Final Cut Pro, and Spotify, a generation for whom Instagram, Facebook, Twitter, Tumblr, Snapchat, etc., are platforms for perpetual rebranding. Their fluency is such that platforms must play catch-up to the lexicon and utility this "born digital" generation has been able to create. Hans Ulrich Obrist and Simon Castets have argued that this generation constitutes those born after 1989, when the Berlin Wall fell and the Cold War came to an end. Their ongoing project "89plus" seeks to index who the artists of this generation would include.

One of the more intriguing internet-related art terms is what the artist and theorist James Bridle calls the New Aesthetic. Bridle first used the term to describe how he came to curate a Tumblr series of visualized virtual interactions with the real world: "I've been collecting images and things that seem to approach a New Aesthetic of the future," he wrote. "What I mean is that we've got frustrated with the NASA extropianism space-future, the failure of jetpacks, and we need to see the technologies we actually have with a new wonder." Bridle later gave a SXSW panel on the term and its implications to an audience that included the writer Bruce Sterling. In a widely referenced *Wired* article, Sterling, who was not without his criticisms, wrote how the New Aesthetic as a movement "is telling the truth." He went on: "There truly are many forms of imagery nowadays that are modern, and unique to this period. We're surrounded by systems, devices and machineries generating heaps of raw graphic novelty. We built them, we programmed them, we set them loose for a variety of motives, but they do some unexpected and provocative things. Bridle's collection of this material is huge. The evidence is impossible to refute. Anybody with a spark of perception who looks through [his Tumblr recognizes] that modern reality is on display there."

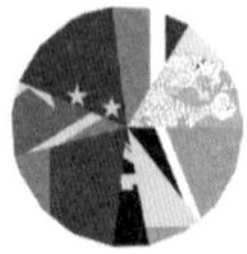

p. 15

While Bridle never professed or intended the New Aesthetic to be a manifesto, it has certainly become one. It now functions as one of the most direct means to describe how the spaces and environments that we inhabit are, more than ever before, being devised on software that can generate the formal features of the "real world." This blurring of the real and virtual can then be extrapolated to equally discuss how virtual worlds or platforms such as Second Life or the recently invented Digital Museum of Digital Art seek to compound the real world into the virtual world. So what we have here is a condition that is ever evolving, constantly shifting, a world of "cross-embedded media," as cultural historian Norman M. Klein described it. Our perceptions are now evermore heightened toward these details, of how physical reality is blurred into the seemingly intangible digital realm.

With so much variation in the kinds of art being conceived of today, we may be moving into an age where artists should be free to term their work as they choose. The artist Ian Cheng calls his works "self-playing video games" or "simulations," unpacking the term in an artist's statement on his website. "What is a simulation?" he asks. "It is an imitation of reality's complexity. It is a model of a system. It is a rehearsal run before the big event. It is a video game that plays itself." In other words, Cheng's work doesn't depend on a human element. A simulation is responsible only to its own laws and initializing conditions. A simulation has no moral, prejudice, or meaning. Like nature, it just is."

Accordingly, the language that we use to describe these art forms must not hinder or rupture, but rather seek to enable openings into an artist's work. A term that I have come to use is "post-digital," which refers to art made after the rise of the digital condition, i.e., a state that recognizes the whole realm of visual culture beyond the specificity of the internet as a "tool." The post-digital condition, in turn, is about the ways in which our manners, relationships, and feelings can all be expressed and interacted with through smartphones, those devices that have become essential to navigating our daily lives. Yet as intrinsic to our culture as this device has become, it too may one day be replaced by a smart "chip" that can be implanted into our bodies, along with other augmented- and prosthetic-reality software and hardware that we will soon be unable to live without. And as recent history has shown us, no technology is left ignored by art.

New Platforms for Art

So what is the future potential of art? Will it continue to evolve the possibilities of the virtual, will art become as feature-full as downloadable apps, or will art and technology merge in novel ways that allow us to reconsider how we interact with the world? In fact, there have been recent initiatives, such as Google's augmented-reality glasses that, though mired with glitches, envisioned a new reality. Rather than try to "update" the glasses, the Google Glass project was shut down (but then later revived). Part of the challenge in conceiving of new technology based art forms is the prohibitive costs of doing so. In 1999, Rhizome founded ArtBase, an archive of digital art that allowed users to submit links to browser-based art. To organize this database, users could tag their works to be listed under categories such as as "Glitch," "Code," or "Tactical Media." But as ArtBase has grown its content, so has Rhizome's approach to archiving. Its short-lived platform Colloq, launched in 2014, sought to archive social-media accounts. Colloq was later folded into the open-source platform Webrecorder, which allowed users to create their own dynamic web archives. Other archival and legacy projects by Rhizome have since included Oldweb, a tool that allows users to use outdated web browsers to explore the web, and Archive, a project that seeks to highlight the hundred most important works of digital art, from its earliest incarnations to the present day.

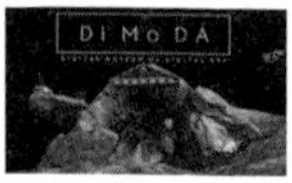

p. 14

In 2015, the Digital Museum of Digital Art opened its virtual doors. While not the first institution of its kind—it was predated by Adobe's now defunct Museum of Digital Art—the museum seeks to "collect, preserve, interpret and exhibit" the work of living digital artists and contemporary digital art. DiMoDA, as it refers to itself, claims to have "the finest holding of twenty first-century Digital-art in the world." But beyond serving as a museum, DiMoDA also serves as a hub for digital culture and an "incubator for new ideas."

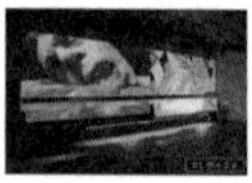

pp. 14–15

The commercialization of the art world has also enabled a steady rise of online platforms that seek to service it. One example is Artsy, a website and app designed by its founder Carter Cleveland that has sought to be the art world's answer to Amazon. I was invited to beta test it when it first emerged, intrigued by the idea of instant art shopping as well as its "Art Genome Project," which allows art to be classified by subjects and characterized by traits, allowing one to search for works by details as nuanced as "oxidized metals" and as specific as "the Zaire School of Popular Painting." However, Artsy has yet to achieve the status of "the Amazon for art." Despite the seeming possibility of shopping online for art, traditional gallery models remain—one still has to engage with a human salesperson from either Artsy or the artist's respective gallery in order to finalize a purchase. As such, Artsy is simply a platform for elite clientele to window-shop art, and for galleries to list or preview their works before art fairs. Though they have become a major partner for art fairs around the world—it is questionable whether Artsy has actually contributed to the advancement of art beyond a commercial context.

As I previously mentioned, technology has long challenged the value of a work's originality, yet can technological art be valued on a similar scale as hand-crafted work? That is the idea behind S[edition], a platform launched in 2011 by Harry Blain of Blain|Southern gallery and Robert L. Norton of Saatchi Gallery. S[edition] was founded on the premise that any artwork, including digital art, gains its value by the simple fact that it is "editioned," i.e., that it is comprised of a limited or unique quantity that can be sold out. The platform launched with a series of big names, including Damien Hirst and Tracey Emin, who created digital works that could be played back on any of your personal devices. Not only could you "own" a limited-edition Hirst, you could rent one as well. To ensure its customers that these carried the "aura" of an original, S[edition] stipulated that these works were "exclusive" to their platform. In the years that I followed it, I noticed that the types of works it listed on its side were all basically high-definition animated GIF images that exhibited motion but never unfurled into a greater narrative. Though a representative of S[edition] had reached out and invited me to select artists to create works for the platform, the galleries of the two artists I ended up extending the invitation to refused to let them participate.

But while I myself was skeptical about *owning* an S[edition] work, after attending S[edition] events in London at the ICA and the Horse Hospital, as well as an exhibition at the Eyebeam Center in New York, I started to wonder if I could rent several S[edition] pieces to host my own art viewing. This was an idea that I have previously written about in my book *You Are Here: Art after the Internet*, but the idea stays with me still. What is to stop someone from renting all the virtual editions of all works by the Young

British Artists and staging an exhibition at my Chicago apartment? This enters a new territory about the future of the art show. Would it be possible to interest the press? Could such a show be given a critical write-up that judges the depth of the curatorial research that has gone into the project? Would it be considered the sort of underground event even celebrities would want to attend? These might seem like indulgent questions, but when art can be "rented," anything goes.

As we push forward into the end of the second decade of the twenty-first century we are posed with many more options that will quickly generate new ways of seeing, feeling, and interacting with art. The spectrum is wide. While apps such as Paddle8 are reinvigorating how nonprofit art organizations can use online auctions for fundraising purposes, other sites, such as the popular crowdsourcing platform Kickstarter, allow the artist to gain funds by bestowing contributors with artistically minded rewards. The Canadian artist Jeremy Bailey did just this when he invited viewers to contribute to *Important Portraits* (2013), a campaign-turned-artwork in which Bailey sought to raise capital for a photographer and augmented-reality software. In return, contributors would have the chance to be given their own "important portrait," where through virtual-reality software, one's features would be tweaked to resemble Renaissance-era paintings. A perfect place to show Bailey's work might be the forthcoming platform Acute Art, which claims to be the world's first virtual-reality arts platform that will allow the experience one has in a physical gallery to be transposed to VR. It may be one of the biggest leaps forward for technology based art in the twenty-first century.

The Blurring of the Real and the Virtual

Our current cultural conditions have led to a variety of "millennial shifts." We have moved from a world of large hardware to portable devices that are more powerful than the mega-computers that we once used. Our obsession now is to be in constant social engagement as propagated by various social-media platforms. Within this sphere, there is more user-generated content than the mind's eye can see. I believe this may cause an inevitable fatigue for media, and in turn a fatigue for art. This social circumstance has led to, among other things, the rise of the social-media celebrity, who brand their personalities through the use of Instagram and YouTube, as well as the narcissistic superego, i.e., most of us: users who jump from one browser tab to another, managing to buy groceries, consume news, entertain ourselves with memes, and pleasure ourselves with pornography, all within the span of minutes. We are in an age of ADHD, living in a constant state of seeking out new forms of stimulation, exacerbated by these new modes of existence.

One response to this cultural hyperactivity has been the rise of alternative spaces for engagement such as the deep web, where material can only be accessed through invitations to private servers, and, the Darknet, where content is hidden from the view of search engines. With this context in mind, one wonders if there is potential for a digital-art revolt of the more common connective tissue that forms the mainstream internet. My belief is such a "digital revolution" would hinder our perception of art, in that they would assume a corporate model of perpetual evolution, as opposed to the will and ideas of artists. Indeed, the language of "revolution" is one that has been co-opted by advertising and technological firms to promote products.

There is undoubtedly a blurring of the real world that is occurring, as articulated in James Bridle's New Aesthetic and Norman M. Klein's theory of cross-embedded media, where social and spatial distortion can occur. One need only consider President Donald J. Trump's social-media campaign and his role in instilling a distrust of the media to the point where several of his supporters decry anything posted by the *New York Times* or the *Washington Post* as fake news. There is fake news, but there is also real news, and what I hope to articulate in these pages is how this blurring of boundaries creates a series of divergent spaces for art—ones that are stimulating and others that are increasingly polemical, even invasive, and would require further inquiry and attention.

The New Self

A DJ sporting a beehive and large hoop earrings plays a thumping beat that haphazardly stops and starts. He is in full makeup—his lipstick and eye shadow are dark and meticulously applied. A crowd dances before him and an American flag hangs in the backdrop. Minutes later, an African American singer performs a series of songs that could be from *American Idol*, or from some other competition TV show. He plays each number as a different character, seamlessly alternating between male and female personas. Not long after, a chirpy blond male is constructing a three-dimensional landscape with his brain, before turning his body into a robotic video-game figure. Then it ends. The illusion fades.

I have been streaming videos on YouTube and Vimeo by artists Michael Magnan, Kalup Linzy, and Jeremy Bailey. We are bound to the same physical space—the bedroom—where I view their work and where they began to produce it. These former "bedroom artists" have since upgraded to art galleries and museums since sharing some of these homemade performances online. And despite the vast differences in their modus operandi, they each share two distinct qualities—a DIY attitude and vivacious internet personality. The internet has allowed not just artists, but anyone who logs onto it, a chance to reexamine and even reinvent themselves. But can these new forms of self-representation be malleable to any context?

These types of online performances have largely used self-mockery and satire as a means to interrogate accepted cultural norms. This has been the most traditional reason for artists to adapt personas, from Sacha Baron Cohen's uncomfortably satirical characters Ali G, Borat, and Bruno to Joaquin Phoenix's fake midlife crisis showcased in the mockumentary *I'm Still Here* (2010). Claiming to leave the film industry to embark on a rap career, Phoenix, sporting a beard and shades, remained in the role even off camera or for public engagements. By exaggerating bipolar behavioral patterns in a documentary form, the actor was able to manipulate media coverage and untangle some of its innate hypocrisy. Yet Phoenix's antics ended up being commoditized as a spectacle, with the film industry's distribution and marketing methods remaining too conventional to keep up the novelty. Personalities such as the ones crafted by Phoenix and Cohen are born from a heightened egoism that blurs personal and public identities using performance as its coating. While the forms now being produced seem new, the format itself is not. One can trace a line from hyperrealist video artists such as Ryan Trecartin back to Andy Kaufman, the American entertainer whose acts were based entirely on subverting notions of entertainment. In front of his audiences, Kaufman would force them to endure excruciating stand-up routines—performing lackluster impersonations with boorishly fake accents to the point of creating discomfort in his audiences. Kaufman's purpose wasn't to entertain; it was to use the "self" to interrogate "entertainment."

To enter into the difference between an artist's reality and his fiction is to enter into a sort of agreement. Demanding that they be distinguishable defeats their very purpose, and one of the tropes that has emerged of artists who use the internet as a primary tool has been to personally embed themselves into their work with the intent of furthering critical discussions that may potentially emerge.

One of the most radical of the early internet-identity projects conceived was by artist and composer Keith Obadike. In August 2001, using an eBay seller account, Obadike began auctioning off his "blackness," writing about the benefits and a single warning of his product in a press release that claimed the following:

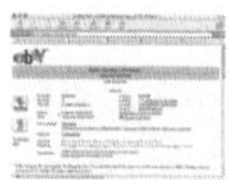

p. 18

Benefits

- This Blackness may be used for creating black art.
- Making jokes about black people and/or laughing at black humor comfortably.
- Accessing some affirmative action benefits (limited time offer).

- Dating a black person without fear of public scrutiny.
- Securing the right to use the terms "sista," "brotha," or "nigga" in reference to black people.
- To augment the blackness of those already black, especially for purposes of playing "blacker than thou."

Warning
- Counsel potential buyers not to use blackness while, among other things, "seeking employment, making or selling 'serious' art, shopping or writing a personal check, making intellectual claims or while voting in the United States or Florida."

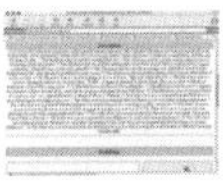
pp. 18–19

Obadike, who at the time was twenty-eight years old and enrolled in an MFA program at Yale University, was curious about using eBay, the self-proclaimed "world's marketplace," to disrupt traditional forms of commerce online. His project, which was later attributed to both him and his wife Mendi Obadike, speaks to the kinds of bartering enabled by the internet, and in this particular case highlights the nature of how "blackness" could not only be performed within day-to-day life, but also within the art world. But this project was also an encounter with early versions of trolling, with eBay users taking to the question box to heckle the Obadikes. "I would like to use it to enable me to do that swivelling head-thing that black women do when they get mad," one user wrote. "Will your blackness work for this purpose?" Other users defended his project: "I imagine that your price will never be met because the value is too great," wrote a user who also inquired as to the intent of the project, adding, "I imagine this is part of your message, please confirm or deny." eBay didn't care to find out Obadike's intent. They took the auction down only four days into what would have been a ten-day auction, citing it as "inappropriate."

Other artists have had better luck in addressing these themes of identity online. Artist Jayson Musson created an alter ego for such a project tailor-made for YouTube that ran from 2010 to 2012. Through an online TV program entitled *ART THOUGHTZ*, Musson performed as Hennessy Youngman, the host of a fake educational web series that poked fun at the art world through critical satire. Dressed in stereotypical black rapper attire—golden chains, branded shirts, and elaborately festooned baseball caps—and donning the name of a popular "black" spirit, Hennessy set out to interrupt what one might read as the "pretentiousness" of the art world, approaching its language with the hyperbolized angle of a hip-hop impresario. Hennessy quickly became known for his mock cultural criticism that included contrarian and tendentious views on what makes artists successful, such as "be a white male," "have an angry nigga exterior," "exploit white guilt," "build a personal mythology," "don't pay for an MFA," and "relational aesthetics is good, if you're famous." As Hennessy, Musson was acting to break down and dissect the staid vernacular of the art world for a plebian audience, pointing to its exclusionary institutional nature. Performing under an alter ego, Musson was able to transform into a trickster to unbuckle entrenched art hierarchies.

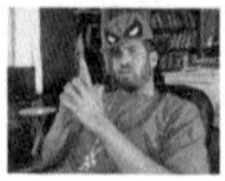

p. 18

Jeremy Bailey takes on similar issues with his "white male" mascot: "Famous New Media Artist Jeremy Bailey," a parody of the white middle-class-male bedroom geek. Bailey is the eternal teenager nailed to his computer, making self-referential jokes that no one is meant to get, able to devote himself to a life where perpetual video-game play is as vital to his existence as is food and sleep. This becomes evident when a panoply of digital ideograms is superimposed upon Bailey's body. Yet despite their ability to make the viewer cringe, I was mesmerized by Bailey's performances, in which he rigs developing technologies and, yes, new media.

Mockumentary and mock-narrative practices have long been used as postmodern methods of critiquing culture, as comedic tools to subvert hegemonic discourses, and as prompts to interrogate artistic practices. There is now, for example, a growing trend to build upon mock performances by evolving them into real-world meta-narratives of increasing complexity. In 2008, the polymath actor James Franco starred in an art film directed by the American artist Carter titled *Erased James Franco*, in which Franco reenacted every single one of his roles. After the project finished, Franco and Carter discussed a different kind of film in which he would play a soap-opera character based on a soap-opera character. "I said, 'Wouldn't that be interesting?'" Franco told *New Yorker* writer Dana Goodyear. "We called them [the producers of *General Hospital*] and said I'd like to be on the show. They were very happy. They said, 'You can do anything—what kind of part would you like to play?' [...] I wanted to be an artist and I wanted my character to be crazy. [...] They asked if they could call the character Franco—that was their idea. It was a beautiful idea."

During his *General Hospital* run, "Franco," played by Franco, staged a live taping for the show at the Museum of Contemporary Art, Los Angeles, that doubled as a piece of performance art. With the help of MOCA's real-life director Jeffrey Deitch (who inevitably also made a cameo appearance on the show), the fictional deranged artist "Franco" staged a show called "Francophrenia" in which he sought to recreate scenes and settings from his previous appearances of the show. As Goodyear, who was present, noted: "There was no one who was not confused. The suspiciously handsome men wearing tool belts and white gloves and T-shirts that said 'Museum Staff' who were hanging abstract paintings on the Port Charles sets: actors. Two 'General Hospital' publicists stood by. 'Is this art Franco art or "G.H." art?' one asked the other."

Meanwhile, Franco (the real one) brought into the *General Hospital* universe the performance artist Kalup Linzy—who has used soap-opera clips in his work and has spoken about the influence of the genre—to appear on the show as a meta-version of himself: "Kalup Ishmael." Some writers and critics have referred to these performances as "interventions," a nod to Fluxus artist Nam June Paik, whose televised program *Good Morning Mr. Orwell* (1984), which broadcast a variety show of contemporary art to over twenty-five million viewers, was one of the first artistic engagements with modern-day media. Franco and Linzy's interventions suggest an artistic tendency of self-critique that is increasingly being manifested in the form of parody. For Franco in particular, there is a sort of abuse of power: a film star at the pinnacle of his career, who was able to appear on a parochial daytime-TV soap opera merely by calling the producers, could use his influence to sabotage public expectation, thereby thwarting the traditional suspension of disbelief that daytime-TV audiences are lulled into.

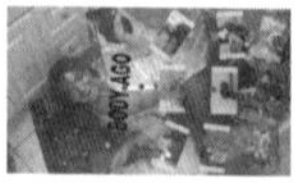

pp. 18–19

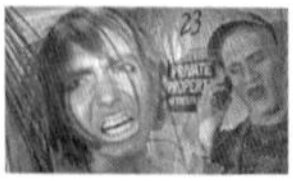

p. 20

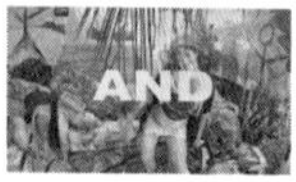

p. 21

The most provocative among this group of "mockumentarists" is the video artist Ryan Trecartin. Renowned for his acid-tongued use of language and his ability to merge virtual and physical worlds into a hyperreality, Trecartin has become something of an art-world phenomenon. Adopting the cable-TV language of MTV and E!-style reality shows—like *The Hills* or *Laguna Beach*—Trecartin and his longtime collaborator Lizzie Fitch build a colorful canvas with a cast of dozens, while placing himself at its center. Beyond the sumptuous mise-en-scène of his films and the relatively epic scale of his productions, Trecartin positions his vernacular and visual aesthetic at the extreme of over-embellishment, where fame, glamour, and lust equate to violence, isolation, and loss. Trecartin seamlessly draws allegories between drug-addled consumer culture and the blinkered universe of Disney fantasies. As the artist's characters collide, our perceptions of fact and fiction, drama and comedy, satire and documentary intertwine. The *Guardian*'s art critic, Adrian Searle, reviewing Trecartin's video installation *Trill-ogy Comp* (2009) at the Liverpool Biennial in 2010, noted that the videos could be "a vision of the future," while former *Time Out London* art critic Ossian Ward prophetically stated that it was "a knowing and logical conclusion to the imminent and total YouTubeification of culture."

Arguably, without the proliferation of content to be found on YouTube or Vimeo, artists would be unable to unearth the types of characters that have gone on to inspire their work. The process of using the "self" to voice critical commentary and identity issues is not a new phenomenon—artists such as Adrian Piper, Barbara Kruger, Kenneth Anger, and Lorna Simpson subverted identities by molding and contorting physical images of themselves through the filter of whatever media was prevalent at the time. New forms of media have made the performance and documentation of the "self" a nearly ubiquitous form of artistic practice, with many of its leading practitioners, such as Kristin Lucas, Lucky PDF, and Rafaël Rozendaal, becoming popular for broadcasting "themselves" over numerous platforms (including telecommunication technologies such as Skype or virtual-reality outfits such as Oculus)—all of whom work to produce sardonic personal statements in a field with ever-expanding possibilities.

Self-critique is also a format for qualitative research, as it leaves little room for illusion. When artists, filmmakers, satirists, comedians, and entertainers hold the mirror up to themselves, they use sincerity to comment on what they observe. This is what makes Jeremy Bailey's persona so striking. A software developer by day, he uses his technological skills and interests to create propositional modes of performing himself. In *The Web I Want* (2015), the artist asks the question, "How do I bring the internet to me?" He proposes VR interfaces, which enable us to live in a screenless society. He stands topless and suddenly a series of digital ideograms start to appear above his chest—world clocks, the stock market, sports scores, and the weather. Is the reality of the real world augmenting our bodies? Although presented in a humorous guise, Bailey is addressing larger questions regarding the potential relationship between the real world and the virtual. The same can be said of Bailey's project *The Future of Television* (2012). Created as an homage to Nam June Paik, the artist transformed his face into a virtual TV, complete with "channels" that changed based on Bailey's emotions, making them readily apparant to the outside world.

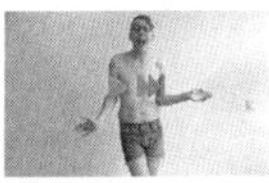

p. 22

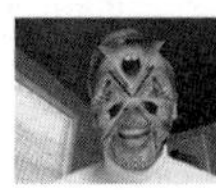

p. 23

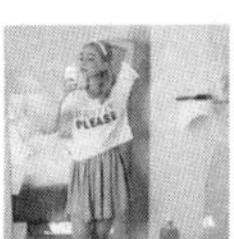

p. 22

Amalia Ulman is another artist who considers how audiences perceive the performer. For her breakout work, *Excellences & Perfections* (2014), Ulman used Facebook and Instagram to record her transformation from lithe and petite female into something much more glamorous, a Kardashian-like woman. To do this, she feigned and realized radical shifts in her lifestyle, undergoing fake breast augmentation, committing to a Zao Dha diet (the emotion diet), and engaging in excessive shopping and pole-dancing lessons. As her social-media accounts attracted interest, Ulman began receiving many salacious, insidious, and aggressive comments from some of her male followers. After four months, Ulman halted the project and revealed it to be a performance, which was later given a permanent home as an online exhibition hosted by the New Museum. In viewing it now, one can see how Ulman used *Excellences & Perfections* to highlight intrinsic social-media biases toward promoting gender stereotypes, such as the objectification of the female body, as much as any commercial mass-media outlet such as TV commercials and billboards. What differentiates online media from its traditional forebears is the potential for user engagement that, as was the case in Obadike's "Blackness" auction, turns into unchecked belligerence, even abuse.

Yet it is the internet's bellicose nature that allows artists to use the self to confront social issues outside of the gallery and in a public space. The video artist and comedian Casey Jane Ellison has used various web series to lace her cultural criticism with humorous antagonism. In an episode from *Touching the Art* (2014–15), Ellison hosts a panel of the art-world figures Bettina Korek, Jori Finkel, and Catherine Opie to discuss the meaning of art. "We have an all-female panel joining us today," she begins. "Is that an issue? Because we only have women on this show and we don't feel the need to question or discuss that." Ellison then goes on to complement the beauty of her guests, before asking questions such as whether contemporary art is dumb, whether truth is beauty, whether art is off-putting, and whether celebrities and athletes are themselves artists. At one point, Finkel calls Ellison a "romantic." The panel determines Paris Hilton not to be an artist because there is no "consciousness" in her actions, nor is she "critical" of them. Ellison addresses "the value of the female perspective" and alludes to the fact that men sell more art than women, but in doing so, cheekily reminds the viewers throughout the segment that she is hosting an "all-female panel." With *Touching the Art*, Ellison worked to destabilize traditional modes of viewership using a talk-show format to address everything from eco art to pornography, discussions that are themselves performative.

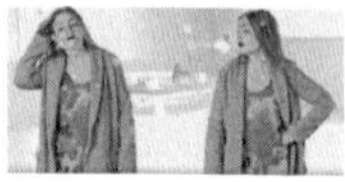

pp. 22–23

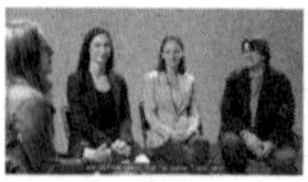

p. 24

Of note in Ellison's unapologetically feminist talk-show-host persona was that she used it to address a particular community within the internet rather than any viewer that happened upon her show. This raises the question of what kinds of audiences "new self" artists are helping to foster. On one side of this spectrum are the alt-right, who have used meme and viral video culture to spread hate messages. Chief among them is Baked Alaska, the online alt-right nationalist persona of former Buzzfeed spokesman Tim Gionet, who stars in a series of doltish online music videos about building walls and loving Trump. Far less vacuous and far more celebratory are the internet's thriving queer communities and the artists who perform for them. In his *Reifying Desire 1–6* (2011–16), the artist Jacolby Satterwhite brings analogue tropes to the digital realm. Using 3-D composites of utilitarian items—clothing, forks, knives, and television screens—as well as life-drawing sketches by his mother (an amateur artist and musician), Satterwhite populates a universe full of drafted characters, adding to it vogue dancers (a once-underground queer movement that has gained a degree of mainstream popularity) pulled from video stills and green-screen performances. At times, these sensuous bodies float within Satterwhite's space, colliding orgasmically into one another. At others, they don costumes such as ornate African attire or the knock-off sports apparel sold by city vendors, becoming characters who begin to desire one another until everyone comes together in a sexual embrace.

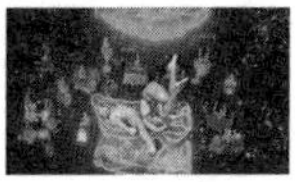
pp. 24–25

By queering the internet, it becomes a space by which anyone can be who they fully envision themselves to be. Consider all the users on Second Life who lead lavish and promiscuous lives online to escape more limited lifestyles offline. A queered internet has the potential to evolve liberal individualism and bring contemporary forms of identity to more traditional and mainstream culture. The American artist and filmmaker Wu Tsang was one of the first major figures to draw media attention beyond the art world for being transgender, first identifying as female to male, and subsequently again as a female. In *Wildness* (2012), Tsang documented the Silver Platter, a Los Angeles bar that has been a safe haven for the LGBTQ community since 1963. The film revolved around a weekly performance night, run by young artists including Ashland Mines, that promoted gender fluidity and inclusion. In casting her camera onto this space, where everyone is self-expressive, Tsang considers the ownership of "queerness" and the different ways that queer identification become manifest. *Wildness* also dealt with the self-promotion of identity in an era of social media, with much of the club's patrons documenting their activities through social platforms. The fact that this gave Silver Platter a huge marketing boost was a side effect that removed its status as an "underground" escape for particular members of the queer community.

In 2014, Tsang produced *A day in the life of bliss*, which dealt with humanity's continual quest for self-aggrandizement. Set in a sci-fi future-scape, the protagonist is blis, performed by transgender performance artist Boychild. blis moves through an entangled world of fans who tweet different slogans and catchphrases. blis retreats to their solitary space, performing for the camera actions that look akin to a form of cathartic martial arts. The installation is presented across two video channels through mirrors, which blur the lines between the virtual and physical worlds of the screen and our reality.

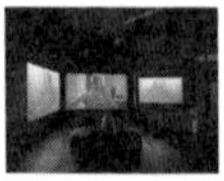

p. 25

Tsang emerged at the same time as many other transgender figures began to make their presence known to a wider public. The multimedia artist Zackary Drucker was first recognized for her role in dealer/curator Jeffrey Deitch's *Artstar*, an unscripted TV program where artists could compete to be presented at Deitch Projects. Drucker later collaborated with her then partner Rhys Ernst, presenting *Relationship* (2008–13) at the 2014 Whitney Biennial. The work was comprised of a sprawling set of images that documented their relationship as they both transitioned—Drucker to female, Ernst to male. The success of the Biennial led to television offers—the two becoming joint consulting producers on the award-winning Amazon TV series *Transparent*, which follows the life of a transitioning family patriarch. Drucker later became a guest star on Caitlyn (formerly Bruce) Jenner's transition documentary TV show *I Am Cait*.

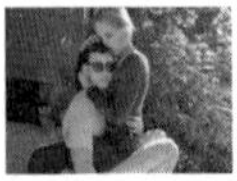

p. 26

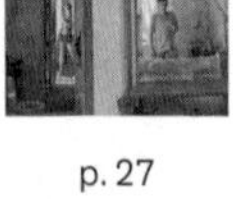

p. 27

Artist Zach Blas is equally interested in the methods by which gender identity is performed and articulated. In 2011, he cofounded a project called *Queer Technologies* (2007–12), which critiqued how gender stereotypes relate to everyday technologies. To question patriarchal purviews such as why plugs and outlets are denoted as "male" or "female," or why computer code displays discernible heteronormative characteristics, Blas started an organization that produced an array of products and branding that included genderless plugs, ports, and software. At venues and conferences around the world, Blas would assemble a "Disingenuous Bar," a play on Apple's Genius Bar, where participants would be invited to purchase queer solutions to their technical problems. Blas's notoriety increased with his *Facial Weaponization Suite* (2011–14), in which he subverted face-recognition technology by creating a series of "fag masks" that would be unrecognizable to any computer, but that could be worn by any human being.

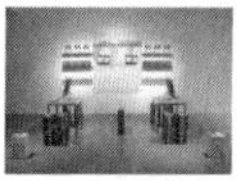

p. 28

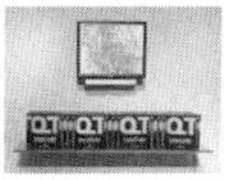

p. 29

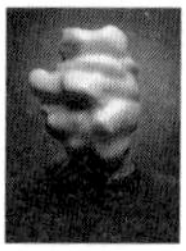

p. 31

The progress of sexual-identity culture has also been led in large part by club culture, which often acts as a bridge between underground and mainstream cultures. The art-music collective House of Ladosha has, since 2007, created performances at club nights that deconstruct masculine connotations of hip-hop culture, influenced by seminal queer films such as *Paris Is Burning* (1990), which introduced vogue dancing to a non-club audience and later impacted popular culture when Madonna appropriated its tropes for her hit single "Vogue." As a collective, House of Ladosha often wear provocative apparel bearing slogans such as "Cunt Life," which speak to the reclamation of the hip-hop genre from heteronormative male culture. Its breakout member, Juliana Huxtable, a DJ, poet, and artist, has since become a poster child for the transgender movement. In the 2015 New Museum Triennial, the exhibition's curators presented self-portraits and poetry by Huxtable alongside a 3-D-printed rendering of her body by the artist Frank Benson. This ornate and luminescent sculpture illustrated a woman in the flux of gender

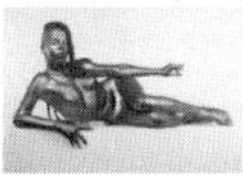

p. 31

with a beautiful, voluptuous female body, bearing an equally beautiful penis.

These cultural shifts have occurred in tandem with the global rise and awareness of queer and transgender issues. Rupaul, an early champion of drag, remains a popular TV personality, but has since been joined by others, such as Laverne Cox, who stars in the Netflix TV program *Orange Is the New Black*. Chelsea Manning, the American whistleblower, received extra notoriety regarding her tumultuous gender-transition issues. After threatening suicide while in a male military prison, artists and activists the world over campaigned for her freedom. She was pardoned by former President Barack Obama near the end of his term, and was released in May 2017.

As many of these lives and projects illustrate, we now live in a world where notions of selfhood have become increasingly malleable. How we see ourselves, and how we see others, is now mediated by social-media platforms and a desire to push beyond antecedent cultures. While we live in a milieu that is far from utopic, as evidenced by the horrific violence waged in 2016 by a Muslim fundamentalist upon the patrons of the gay nightclub Pulse—at the time one of the most brutal mass shootings in the United States—we can still see seeds of hope that these tragic events remain outliers, while many more queer and minority people can live without being seen as "other." The digital realm has the capacity to enable new forms of expression that were previously nonexistent and, as we use these forms to evolve our culture, the capacity to thrive.

Touch Me

> Yeah! Come on, come on, come on, come on
> Now touch me, babe
> Can't you see that I am not afraid?
> What was that promise that you made?
> Why won't you tell me what she said?
> What was that promise that you made?
>
> The Doors, "Touch Me" (1968)

Touch is one of the sensory functions that enables us to access our spatial environment. As digital media have become increasingly haptic or touchable, the way we physically engage with the world is altering. While tactility is traditionally explored by what we can experience with our hands, the idea of what we can engage with through "touch" is rapidly evolving. Because the digital realm is most often experienced behind two-dimensional screens, the human hand has had to develop a different set of commands to engage with it, such as swipes, taps, and clicks. Rather than dimensions, art that engages digital technology has emphasized layers, where links can take you from one screen to another, and where layers can be added and removed like sheets to a stack of vellum pages. The desire to touch is thus transferred from the hand to the finger, where the age-old instinct to hold something in its entirety is refocused on an evolving instinct to poke at a particularity. I want to focus on how tactility has been transformed by new technologies and what potential lies ahead for its continued evolution. First, I want to consider how creative materials such as paint and artistic objects such as sculpture are being transposed through processes of computer programming and 3-D printing. I will then move on to consider how virtual augmented-reality software and applications are changing the way artists are conceiving work.

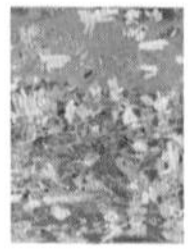
p. 32

Let us begin by considering how a historical art material like paint, which has traditionally taken on various analogue forms (acrylic, oil, and water), now encompasses digital forms that have the potential for physical realization. The artist Petra Cortright works as a sort of virtual painter, using Photoshop as her canvas and an array of digital brushes—tools that apply the element of digital imagery—downloaded from the artist-minded social-media site DeviantArt, where they are traded like gaming cards. Even a quick look at DeviantArt is enough to glimpse the near infinite "brushes" one can find there. One user offers a tool that can swab various types of grasses and plants across the screen; another user has on display a brush that can render various types of smoke. By layering a multitude of such configurations onto each other, Cortright creates kaleidoscopic executions that look like future Impressionist paintings, which led to Artsy calling her "the Monet of the 21st century." After finalizing her compositions, Cortright transfers them onto an aluminum panel—the results are luminescent, textured objects that sit uncomfortably in the world: they are neither digital nor tactile paintings, yet the hand of the artist is undeniably present.

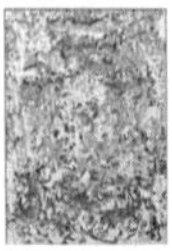
p. 32

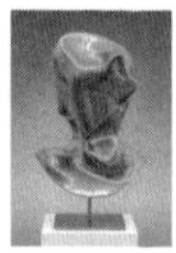
pp. 32-33

Jon Rafman similarly adopts processes that seek to physicalize the virtual. In his series *New Age Demanded* (2012–present), the artist created a group of virtual avatars—thumbnails in the shape of human heads—on which he imposed deconstructed versions of canonical modernist works, then used a 3-D printer to carefully materialize these profiles into delicate sculptures. Because many of these objects—made out of impermanent materials such as resin, fiber, and foam—are so palpably fragile, they contradict their more durable virtual versions. This challenges the hierarchy of originality between a work's analogue and digital forms, whether a blueprint for art is more or less valuable than its frail (and replicable) realization, and where the desire for tactile experience now lies, whether in a physical object or its virtual counterpart. As I noted in my previous chapter, Rafman has explored how simulation can provide sensual stimulation. In Rafman's bi-reality installation

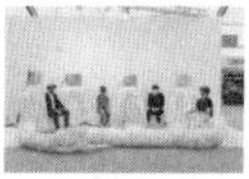

p. 33

piece *Trans-dimensional Serpent* (2016), visitors are invited into a meticulously decorated room occupied by a giant ophidian creature whose curves serve as chairs to which VR goggles are connected. Upon donning this headgear, visitors are transposed to the point of view of the serpent as it maneuvers through a macabre world of dancing mythical creatures. One feels as if they are dangling off the serpent's body and could easily engage with this alternate universe. Watching people interact with this world, one can see their desire to do so as they reach out with their hands and maneuver their bodies, forming a performance in their own right. The territory created by this simulation address virtual reality's growing influence on the human senses, and causes one to wonder just how cybernetic the human species is becoming.

The idea of a human that is half-organic, half-mechanized is no longer the province of science fiction, but like many things first imagined as fantastic, these developments may at first seem like marvels of the future, only to be quickly acknowledged as touchstones of our actual technological advances. Many of these creations owe their existences to ongoing conversations between scientists who can invent them and artists who can humanize them. For example, the artist Aleksandra Domanović creates work that addresses how technological advancements engage with historically marginalized bodies. In her project about the Belgrade Hand Prosthesis, Domanović examines the world's first robotic prosthetic—developed in 1964 in Belgrade in former Yugoslavia. Using the design of the original invention, as well as the hands of female scientists associated with the original project, Domanović devised a series of 3-D printouts to develop a semiotic language that liberates heteronormative conventions. In *Torches of Freedom* (2013), a prosthetic hand peeks out from a wall holding a cigarette. The title derives from a phrase once used as a slogan by advertisers targeting the women's liberation movement, encouraging women to purchase and use a product that was at the time associated with masculine aspiration. *Relay Runner (Sanija Hyseni 1979)*

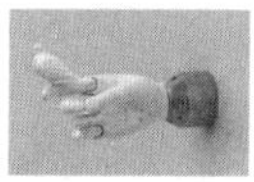

p. 34

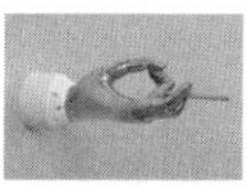

p. 35

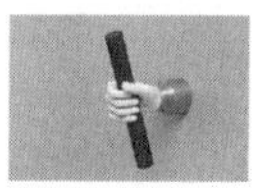

p. 34

(2013) shows a hand holding what looks like the end of a wooden flagpole, a reference to the Relay of Youth, an annual event held in honor of President Tito's birthday in which boys and girls could participate. But Domanović's purview of the marginalized extends beyond that of examining the sidelined female. In *Alan's Apple* (2013), the eponymous fruit is held in a tight grip, a reference to the tragic figure and founder of modern computing, Alan Turing, who committed suicide after consuming a cynaide-laced apple following persecution by the British government for being gay. In the artist's sculpture, however, the apple remains uneaten, a utopic allusion to the growing acceptance of homosexuality in mainstream culture.

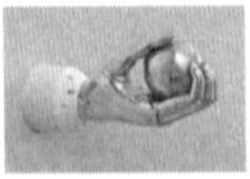

p. 35

As a corrective historical project to reveal the marginalized figures of technology, Domanović's hands can be read as a "transhuman" work. In his book *To Be a Machine: Adventures among Cyborgs, Utopians, Hackers, and the Futurists Solving the Modest Problem of Death* (2017), the writer Mark O'Connell defines the term as "a liberation movement advocating nothing less than a total emancipation from biology itself." While this may sound like the aspiration of a purely post-gender society, O'Connell cautions that "there is another way of seeing this, an equal and opposite interpretation, which is that this apparent liberation would in reality be nothing less than a final and total enslavement to technology." It's a dichotomy we have little time to consider as technologists such as Elon Musk and Sergey Brin are developing driverless cars, augmented apparel, synthetic foods, and ever-sophisticated possibilities for artificial environments. But as we move forward as a society and species, how do we ensure that our advancements properly address questions of acquiescence and inequality?

The artist Oliver Laric, who collaborated with Domanović on the previously mentioned VVORK project, is another key artist whose work considers how technology, in the wrong hands, can be manipulated and abused. In his work *Versions (Missile Variations)* (2010), Laric responded to media stories in 2008 reporting that Iran had launched missile tests. These stories were supported by an image

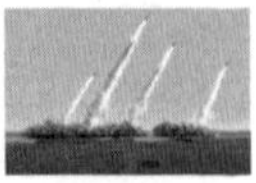

p. 37

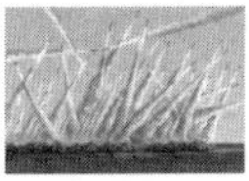

p. 36

of rockets bursting into the sky that was falsified by the Iranian government. When it was discovered that the image had been doctored—an extra missile had been copied and pasted into the frame—internet users the world over took to the web and rendered their own "versions" of this image, photoshopping hysterical and absurd renderings of what the military testing might look like. Laric then aggregated a selection of these images and had them airbrushed onto canvas, thus materializing a digital image into physical space. Interestingly, *Versions* highlights an actual example of "fake news," before the alt-right had usurped the term to mean anything postulated by mainstream media, and may provide one of the last universally agreed-upon examples of chicanery before truth became politicized.

p. 36

Pivoting off *Versions*, Laric created a ten-minute video that illustrated the mutability and manipulation of different images, such as Disney's self-plagiarizing animations and the virtual restorations of Italian sculptures, which sought to address the power of reproduction and representation. What Laric is engaging with is itself a variation on the fundamental question posited by Walter Benjamin as to whether the reproduction of a work of art destroys the "aura" of the original. In the case of Laric, a reproduction is autonomous from the "truth" of an original—it develops its own political autonomy in the world and thus possesses not only its own aura but an agency capable of manipulating our hermeneutic senses.

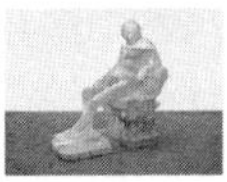

p. 38

But one cannot speak about digital manipulation without speaking of the ways people now communicate. A perfect example of this is the advent of the emoticon and later the emoji. In *:)* (2014) the artist Antoine Catala cleverly rendered a text-based smiley face as a 3-D-printed robotic sculpture that moved about the gallery floor, liberating it from the confines of our smartphones and instant messengers to be given life and character. But Catala is also interested in more complicated configurations and propositions that we take for granted using alphabetic graphemes. For example in *(::( )::) (band-aid)* (2014), Catala created a leviathan of an

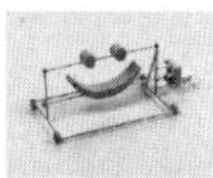

p. 39

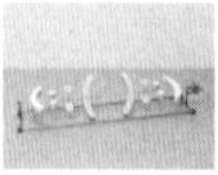

emoji that resembles something algorithmic as much as it does lexical. Catala expanded upon this semiotic binary with a project that debuted at the 2015 New pp. 38–39 Museum Triennial called *Distant Feel*, in which Catala proposed a new twenty-first-century symbol for "empathy," a joiner to the oft-used "peace" symbol: "E3." The logo was presented in a floating case that resembles a fish tank. Indeed, the sculpture was encased within a living medium—tank-grown coral. On his website, Catala notes that *Distant Feel* "acknowledges that it's paradoxically OK to be distant and encourages us to express our empathy in an effective way. [...] This project is about encouraging people to affirm their bond and to express it via all means of communication." *Distant Feel* can thus be considered an advertising campaign (indeed, Catala worked with the advertising agency Droga5 on this project) to let the virtual and the physical coexist in peace and compassion.

In order for this to happen, we would have to recognize how materiality, for better or worse, bridges these two states of being together. One cannot engage with the virtual without an apparatus to do so. And as recent exposés have shown us, our hunger for these devices, such as the iPhone, is met by workers in compromised spaces who are vastly overworked in often unsanitary and unsafe conditions, and underpaid to the point of being regarded as slaves. This is evidenced in the work of artist Josh Tonsfeldt, who considers devices that "plug us in" in ways

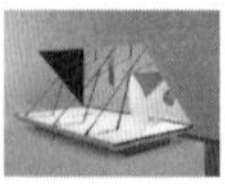

most of us do not (or rather, would not). In *Untitled* (2015), an LCD television screen is unbuckled from its backing and opened coffin-like for the viewer to see. p. 39 The screen is propped up, and from within the housing a shimmering light appears. The interiority of the object is exposed, showing various objects placed inside: a dust mask that formed the shape of a face, fragments of a found-footage film that flickered on and off, and two slivers of screen that stood vertically within. I found them strangely inviting, as if one could stick their hand inside and feel its unnaturally smooth surface, but I recognized also that the screen could easily cut through my skin, perhaps even amputate me if it were to slam shut. I recalled a *Guardian* article in which a worker at a flatscreen factory recounted having both of her hands "flattened like tortillas" in a gruesome incident. I felt unsettled that this was an object that I used in my everyday life, and only now could see how threatening a device could be when disconnected from its manufactured purpose.

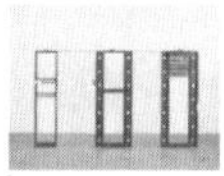
p. 40

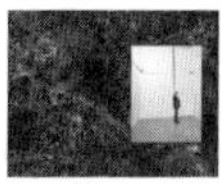
p. 43

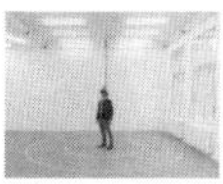
p. 42

More harmonious engagements between the virtual and the physical can be found in works such as Ben Schumacher's *Rebirth of the Bathhouse, server room detail 1:1* (2014), where the artist, working with architect Andrea Macias-Yanez, created a series of "speculative executions" that used a variety of simulation technologies and databases to create abstracted, yet detailed 3-D renderings of the interior of a shuttered New York City bathhouse. Schumacher's purpose was not to propose an interior plan, but to interrogate our growing reliance on computer data to automate propositions about what would be the most ideal real-world construction. Rather than critique the computer-generated environment, Daniel Steegmann Mangrané's virtual-reality piece *Phantom (Kingdom of all the animals and all the beasts is my name)* (2014–15) examines the relationship between the physicality of an individual and a space remote from it. To do this, Mangrané used Oculus Rift glasses to allow people to be transported to the Mata Atlântica rainforest in southern Brazil. The experience is psychedelic, like taking a drug: one can freely and clumsily roam around this virtual rendition of a real geographic location, grabbing and reaching for materials that cannot be touched, yet stimulated, even astonished, by the verisimilitude. If an artist can bring us a rainforest, what other environments, relationships, and feelings could be mediated through such technologies?

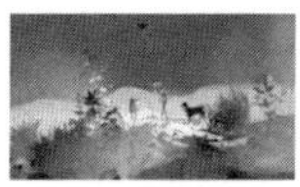
p. 42

Among the most provocative simulation artists is Ian Cheng. A key figure in the debate around "simulation," he proposes that simulations are a habitat for stories that possess "open-ended dynamics" programmed to take on their own narratives, and which can evolve in whatever form that program enables. In Cheng's trilogy *Emissaries*, the stories run amok, allowing for

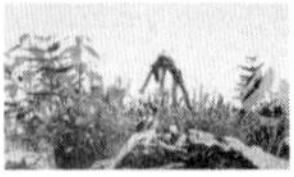

p. 43

wide interpretation. For the first part, *Emissary Forks at Perfection* (2015–16), Cheng created what he calls a "Darwinian playground," a virtual realm projected onto a mammoth screen where a colorful panoply of animals and figures roams around a semitropical landscape. When I watched it, bushes were tumbling about and flying in the air, while landscapes collapsed into themselves, only to reform later. In *Emissary Forks for You* (2016), the viewer can be found using a tablet, and is guided around the gallery by the avatar of a dog that appears throughout the trilogy. After I had been given one, the dog led me through a universe that seemed chained to him, a landscape that he was attempting to run away from. He would jump and try and untangle himself from it, and then be weighted down by its existence. As he directed me this way and that, other gallery patrons began to stare at me: I had become once again an unwitting performer, just as I had been in Rafman's and Mangrané's installations. This eschewing of "classical narrative determinism," again to quote Cheng, raises a fundamental question about how we will navigate the world in our future. Will our minds crave stories founded on evolving algorithms? Will we hunger for different forms of touch based on virtual experiences? Will sex and desire become extra-bodily? Whatever may be the case, if our near past has proven, the future of experience is bound to change.

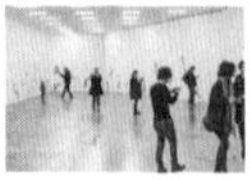

p. 45

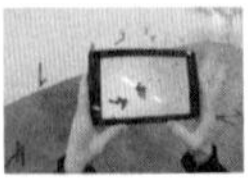

p. 44

Don't Control Me

> Somebody's watching me
> And now I'm nervous
> And I shouldn't be
> Somebody's got their eye on me
>
> Thompson Twins, "We Are Detective" (1983)

Britain is on high security alert, afraid of the potential threat of terrorism. I am once again at an airport, Heathrow, this time in security control where, despite my acquired peevish Britishness, I am harangued and harassed by the guards. Finally, they let me go and hand me back my cell phone. I attempt to call a loved one, but the lithium-ion battery on my phone is drained. Wandering in agitation, I spot a neon sign above a kiosk that advertises "tech, travel, relax," purchasing from the vendor a portable phone charger, my fifth in a month. I am still shaken and want nothing more than to use my phone. I find an outlet at a nearby waiting area and plug in my charger, waiting impatiently for the Apple logo to reappear on the screen so that I can make my call. On the floor, my ear against a device unnaturally warmed by electricity, I listen to the endless rings. No answer. I try another number, desperate to make contact with a familiar voice. My neck starts to pulse in pain as it sandwiches the phone between my head and shoulder. Again, no answer. Finally, I began tapping at various apps on my phone such as my email, Apple News, and Twitter, where I scroll through endless hashtags, re-tweets, and favorites, letting myself get lost in the streaming oceans of other people's subconsciousness. When I get up again, it is to relieve my bowels, taxed by the flight and detainment. I make my way to the bathroom and notice a security camera positioned right near the entrance. It brings to mind that observation once made by an artist friend: "You're still being watched by some governmental power, even when you are taking a shit. It's like when you were in your bedroom as a young boy first learning to masturbate, that feeling that 'God' was watching you, and how that made you feel as though you were doing something wrong. Well, that's how we are meant to feel now all the time, because the big guy, in the form of the NSA or the GCHQ, is always watching us."

A few days later, I find myself on the roof of a car park at Bold Tendencies, a public-arts space in Peckham, London. I am floating above the city; its skyline, the metropolis, sits at my feet. Though I am in the open air, no one can see me here. James Bridle is sitting next to me staring at the empty sky with a pair of binoculars. A small plane swooshes by. Bridle jumps up with excitement; I remain seated, confused at his reaction. "It's a Metropolitan Police plane," he informs me. "They are watching us." I look back up at the plane, suddenly feeling quite vulnerable as an Arab who has the attention of the police. "Why?" I ask Bridle, my voice slightly betraying my anxiety. "Terror alert," he says, and without any further explanation begins to walk across the roof, heading in the direction of the plane. It's no coincidence that Bridle (and by proxy, myself) have caught the attention of the police. He installed on the rooftop three pseudo airbases complete with a hanger made from three large metal containers. One stored a giant Helikite aerostat balloon, another exhibited its findings, and a third acted as a performance space / workshop where people could go to learn more about and engage with the balloon. The heart of this assemblage was the giant Helikite, a combination of a helium balloon and a kite, which was originally developed by the military for advanced surveillance. Bridle's balloon, passengered by a plush doll and outfitted with a Darknet router and camera, hovered over the car park, creating a rebellious blemish on London's skyline of corporate skyscrapers.

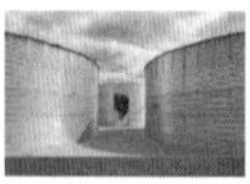

p. 46

Over the summer of 2014, Bridle's balloon captured South London's urban landscape, shooting hours of footage that streamed at the hanger as a form of abstract visual poetry, with landscapes and masses of people resembling fragments of a jigsaw puzzle. Bridle would periodically send TinyLetter updates about the project, which he

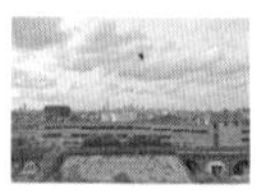

pp. 46–47

called *The Right To Flight* (2014), that detailed how various London communities had become engaged with the work, from collaborations with fellow artists, to youth groups curious about meteorology, to even a hot-air-balloon enthusiasts' club. In effect, Bridle had turned the tools of surveillance back on itself to become a tool for communal outreach, which plays into his long-standing belief that the so-called invisible monitoring of our lives could, and indeed should, be made visible. In *Drone Shadow* (2012), Bridle outlined in chalk skeletal shapes of drone planes—unmanned surveillance vehicles—sketching them at a 1:1 scale on the ground of the environments that they would hover over, and urban areas in particular. This question of making the invisible visible has been a preoccupation for a number of artists who have sought to encourage everyday citizens to consider the means not only by which they "see" the world but also how they themselves are, more and more, being "seen"—by corporations, agencies, institutions, and society. Bridle, in particular, has interrogated this theory in both his visual and written work under the aegis of activism. "In the decade or so I've been making work, the legacy of 9/11 and the global war on terror has infiltrated every area of life," he said in a 2017 interview with the *Evening Standard*. "As someone who often explores the ways in which technology shapes culture, I've seen particularly how the internet has turned from being an open community into a place of total surveillance and growing paranoia and division. This is mirrored in the physical world—not least in London, which has become crowded with security cameras and other apparatuses just as the tone of our political discourse has become more fractured and divisive. I don't think it's possible to make work that's about the world today without addressing these subjects to some extent."

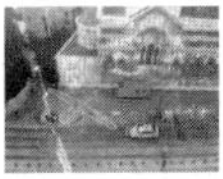
p. 47

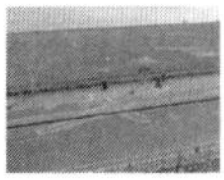
p. 46

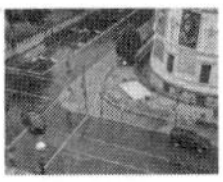
pp. 46–47

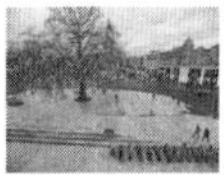
p. 47

Discourse around issues of public surveillance exploded in 2013 after the *Guardian* reporter Glenn Greenwald published a series of articles documenting the reach of American and British surveillance programs gathered from former National Security Agency contractor Edward Snowden. Greenwald was joined by filmmaker Laura Poitras who later released the footage

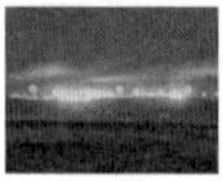

p. 48

in what would become an Oscar-award-winning documentary, *Citizenfour* (2014). Poitras's director of photography for the film was the artist Trevor Paglen, known for his visual iconography of surveillance and the hidden sites of power and communication. His photographs have included classified military and intelligence locations and undersea communication cables, while other visual works by Paglen include a cube made from irradiated glass excavated from the Fukushima Exclusion Zone and a visual record of contemporary civilization

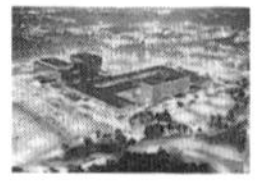

p. 49

launched into orbit. By taking classified sites and information out of invisibility and making them viewable to the general public,

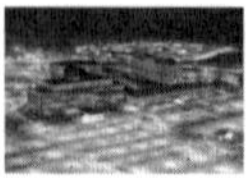

p. 49

Paglen is building civic consciousness of these sources of governmental power over its citizens. Another key factor of Paglen's work is distribution—he allows his visual work to be downloaded and used by any media or public source without demanding licensing fees. In creating works of art with the intent of distribution that, in fact, rely on wide circulation to be effective, one could also argue that Paglen is chal-

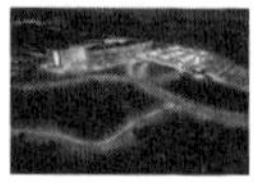

p. 48

lenging the notion of authenticity and "aura," and, like Bridle, he is fond of building a terminology to describe his work. One such term, "Experimental Geography," was coined by Paglen to discern what practices radicalize our notions of geography. Paglen has also adopted the late documentarian Harun Farocki's methodological term "operational images" to consider what the world looks like to machines. For his work *Sight Machine* (2017), Paglen collaborated with the tech collective Obscura Digital and the award-winning chamber group the Kronos Quartet, in which a screen lofted above all five members visualized them as a machine would. While this "machine vision" was somewhat crude and rudimentary, bearing a semblance to animated crayon sketches, there is undoubtedly a future for the visual intelligence of machines, one that could impact the formal and aesthetic makeup of images.

But are machines ready to become artists? In a study produced in 2017 by the Artificial Intelligence Lab at Rutgers University, a team of researchers explored a machine's ability to generate "human-level" art. To do this, the team developed two AI programs, the Generative Adversarial Network (GAN) and the Creative Adversarial Network (CAN). GAN was tasked with finding how accurately machines could replicate human-developed artistic practices, such as Baroque, Color Field, Rococo, and Abstract Expressionism. With CAN, however, the researchers sought to determine how well machines could deviate from any human-made practices yet still create works that could be recognizable to any human being as having artistic intent. When people were asked to identify the work of a "real" artist from a "machine," the study found that 53 percent of them could not "distinguish art generated by the proposed system from art generated by contemporary artists and shown at top art fairs." What is also worth noting is that this study group also preferred the computer images to the human ones, ranking them higher in categories of "intentionality," "visual structure," "communicability," and "inspiration."

While AI technologies can consider the future of artificial aesthetics that trigger human stimulation, interface technologies may be splintering the universality of our species by filtering how we see the world. After Rhizome's annual Seven on Seven conference, where technologists and artists are teamed together to develop unimagined technological potentials, artist Taryn Simon and the late activist and technologist Aaron Swartz created a

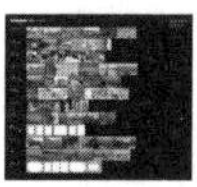
p. 50

platform that indexes top image results for given search terms across local engines throughout the world. Enter a word such as "Arab," for example, into the search engine and one will notice a whole array of different results than for the USA, UK, and New Zealand. In these countries, the results are identical—a series of innocuous-looking Arab men sporting kaffiyehs—a traditional male headdress. In Russia, however, these regular Arab men are replaced by fashion models who not only wear kaffiyehs on their heads but seductive looks on their faces. Contrast this with the Israeli result for Arab, which depicts a goofy-faced Yasser Arafat alongside Arab men with mugshot-style portraits; or the Indian result for Arab, which swaps all figurative results with architectural ones. Simon told the *New Yorker* that *Image Atlas* (2012) "investigates the engines that deliver us supposedly neutral statistical data. We are presented with the 'top' results when we search for words or images online in a way that is definitive. But really, 'top' images represent mass taste at a given moment that is inevitably shaped by political and cultural events, trends, etc. We have begun to naturalize the way a search engine works: we trust it to deliver us the best information. The Image Atlas reveals how subjective and contingent the process of search really is."

The project also exists on a tragic note, as Swartz, its co-creator, would end his life only five months after *Image Atlas* was launched in August 2012. Swartz was a keen and noted hacktivist, working to address and maintain online civil liberties and freedoms. Swartz had helped develop RSS web feeds, Creative Commons, and Reddit, and was engaged in many online activist campaigns to keep the internet independent of government intervention. Prior to and after developing *Image Atlas*, Swartz was in the process of fighting federal prosecution charges of wire and computer fraud, including "illegally" downloading a series of JSTOR articles and texts while a fellow at MIT. Facing up to fifty years in prison along with a million-dollar fine, Swartz hung himself in his Brooklyn apartment that January. He has since become a martyr for a generation of online activists and people who believe that the knowledge the internet contains should be freely accessible to all.

The torchbearer of this utopian ideal is Google, the internet's foremost provider for all the world's information. Google is the great vehicle of the digital world, letting users wander wherever their need or imagination takes them, but with its permissiveness comes broad penetration and permeation into everyday lives, including a necessity for surveillance in order for some of its tools, such as Google Street View, to function with great accuracy. Using a fleet of cars equipped with photographic equipment, Google has since 2007 mapped out nearly every human-occupied corner of the planet using panoramic images of neighborhoods and roads stitched together so that users can embark on virtual tours of these places. Looking at a typical Street View panorama however, one notices that these photographic images are unfiltered, meaning along with the mundane reality of store

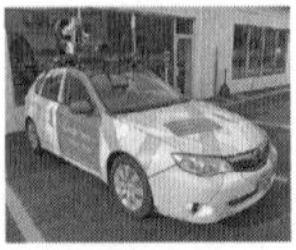

p. 51

fronts and porches that exist on these streets, Google Street View has also invariably captured all kinds of human activity within its interstices. In *The Nine Eyes of Google Street View* (2008–ongoing), Jon Rafman has collected some of the unintentional

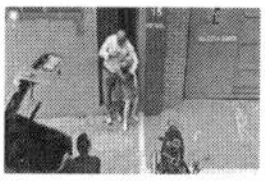

p. 50

interplays and exchanges Google's street cars happened to capture on its cameras: a woman held at gunpoint, two women pulling each other's hair in a deserted street, a dead animal in the middle of a barren road, identical twins standing next to a pool of water, young girls playing hopscotch, and so forth. What *The Nine Eyes of Google Street View*

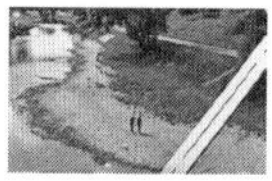

p. 52

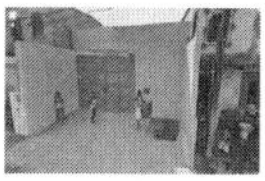

pp. 52–53

reveals is how data captured by machines cannot account for human subjectivity, that they do not consider what it is they see, they just document it. As the project has grown, Rafman has made use of volunteers to send him images that keep the project ongoing.

But Google's human component, its employees, do know the differences between right and wrong, which is what makes Andrew Norman-Wilson's project *Workers Leaving the Googleplex*

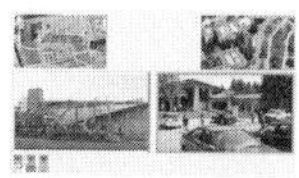

pp. 54–55

(2011) so disturbing. In 2007, Norman-Wilson had been hired as a contractor to work as a temporary nine-to-fiver at Google's headquarters in Mountain View, California, where he was offered some, but not all, of the benefits of a full-time Google employee. During his employment, he became aware that the company's employees were assigned different colored badges pertaining to their rank. One group in particular stood out, a highly confidential group of yellow-badge employees who worked a graveyard shift that began at 4 a.m. and finished up the next afternoon around 2 p.m. Norman-Wilson decided to interview some of these workers, which led him to discover that the group's primary function was to scan books for Google's Books program, a task considered so low that the staff privileges Google full-timers took for granted, such as free meals and shuttle cars, were denied to all yellow-badged employees. One interviewee told Norman-Wilson that though he disliked his job, it "paid the bills." When Google found out about Norman-Wilson's interviews, he was accused of illegally undertaking an "exposé" and was duly fired by both Google and the temp agency that had gotten him hired in the first place. But Google did not seek to claim the footage Norman-Wilson had shot, which he later uploaded as a video that soon went viral on YouTube. *Workers Leaving the Googleplex* not only disrupted Google's image of a utopian company and "don't be evil" idealism, it also demonstrated its participation in a capitalist labor loop commonly invisible from the public. Don't be evil indeed.

The birth of the digital age has revitalized these kinds of activist art and artists to such a degree that oftentimes we depend on them to make sense of political and social issues that can, at times, seem opaque or unknown. In Constant Dullaart's *The Censored Internet* (2013–14), a series of flags hung at half-mast within a room depict the nineteen countries accused of being "enemies of the Internet" by Reporters Without Borders, among them the United States, Saudi Arabia, China, and Russia. The flags are covered in LED spotlights that change in color, making each flag at various times indiscernible, a metaphor for subverting online restrictions imposed by various governmental institutions. But because the internet engenders such considerations, artists are now taking its utopic idealism into the real world in interesting ways. In her exhibition "Everything Must Go" at The Third Line in Dubai in 2017, Sophia Al-Maria presented two video works, *Black Friday* and *The Litany* (both 2016), that followed the aforementioned philosophies behind the Gruen transfer, Austrian architect Victor Gruen's dictum for turning malls into spaces that can only be meaningfully engaged through consumerism. In *Black Friday*, a large vertical screen envelops us with an image of two escalators that lead to the main floor of a windowless mall lit as if by hellfire, a vision that echoes the basement elevators of the Twin Towers. Al-Maria presses the allegory further by transforming the iconography of Western shopping malls into Islamic-tinged architectural motifs. A sermon, voiced by actor Sam Neill, evokes an Old Testament prophet of doom. The central marble bay within the heart of the mall is made to resemble a mausoleum. A menacing soundtrack overtakes us, a far cry

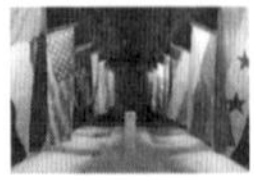
p. 55

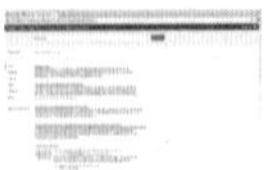
pp. 54–55

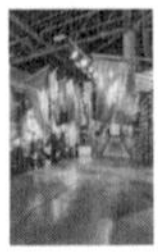
p. 54

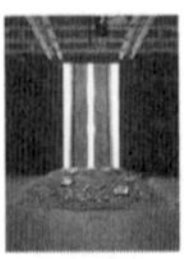
p. 56

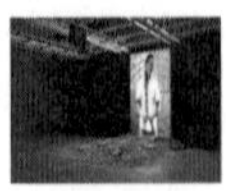
pp. 56–57

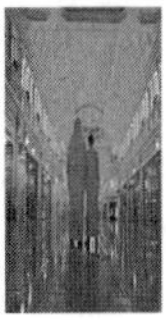

p. 57

from the cheesy muzak often streamed at gallerias, quaking the viewer with its apocalyptic bassline. In *The Litany*, a plethora of outmoded mobile-phone screens rest at the base of the elongated video projection. These products explode with sounds. Among the nearly one hundred recycled phones, individual videos play advertisements and war patter on their screens in high-pitched squeals, as if this outdated technology were screaming in fury at its former users. Lining the walls of the adjacent gallery space were prints bearing phrases such as "CASHFLOW EXFOLIANT," "POST-TRUTH PLUMPER," and "DIRTY BALM," lifted from political playbooks and cosmetic adjectives and hung against the backdrops of demolished buildings and satellite maps like a hyper-saturated wainscoting. These are the magic words that give power to the "beauty industrial complex" as Al-Maria calls it, who in turn grants them a new power charged by these poetic phrasings.

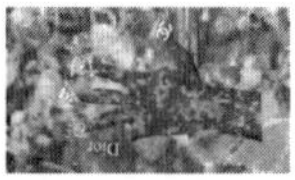

pp. 56–57

The corporatization of spaces of image making has been intensely mined by New York–based art collective DIS, whose multiplatform practice encompasses a magazine, merchandise, curatorial projects, and multimedia artworks. For their exhibition "Ocean of Images" (2015) at the Museum of Modern Art in New York, the collective produced several works, including a video that consisted of four interlinked LED screens with slow-motion footage of the drag queen Conchita Wurst, an Austrian transgender pop recording artist. Wurst came to fame after winning the 2014 Eurovision song contest with the song "Rise Like a Phoenix," a number that undoubtedly spoke to transgender representation on mass-media platforms. The video of Conchita shows slow-motion images of the drag queen moving, a wind machine blowing her hair, while a giant "X" and "MoMA" marked her face and body, resembling a copyright watermark. The piece became an advertising campaign for the exhibition, but also a critique of how institutions seek to commoditize, brand, and "own" the image of figures from popular culture. The piece itself was called *Positive Ambiguity (beard, lecturn, teleprompter, wind machine, confidence)* (2015)—whether that was a slogan or a title for the work remained unclear to me.

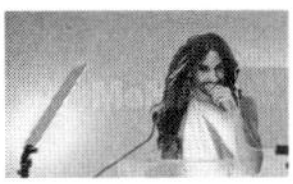

p. 57

The culture of commoditization and capitalization of the image is articulated in the work of writer and artist Hito Steyerl, who has sought to explore the contradictions of how artists and everyday people utilize image technologies. A major argument can be found in Steyerl's text "In Defense of the Poor Image," first published in *e-flux journal*, which functioned as a kind of manifesto for constantly downloaded, re-uploaded, degraded images often found on the internet—image decay in quality with the velocity of user engagement. To Steyerl, a poor image is not a worthless image, but rather it is emblematic of a life lived online. Likewise, Steyerl argues that a loss of image quality functions as a kind of resistance to appropriation from the media powers that be. The poor image is free to exist, be seen, and as W. J. T. Mitchell, a distinguished professor of art history at the University of Chicago would argue, would like to be free to see itself. Conversely, the poor image gives us what Zach Blas has called a kind of "opacity" from constant viewership.

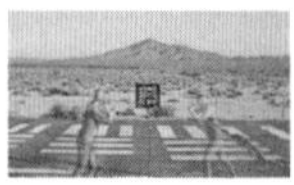

p. 58

In her landmark installation *How Not to Be Seen: A Fucking Didactic Educational .MOV File* (2013), Steyerl takes as her starting point the giant pixels constructed on the parched earth of the Mojave Desert by the American government, who used them as calibration test sites for its surveillance equipment. Steyerl transforms this site into a place where numerous characters wearing pixel-looking boxes on their heads bound in and out of visibility. The film is shot in the style of an educational film and presented in a room that mirrors the ecosystem depicted in the film. Alongside these pixel creatures, green "render ghosts" appear, which resemble figures used by corporations as stand-ins for real people. Are they people who live inside our imagination, struggling to be seen? Or are they potential future beings of which we can only glimpse here?

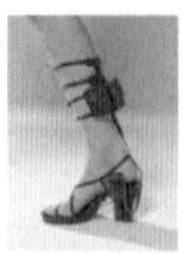

p. 60

The power of surveillance is not always one that lies in the hands of government agencies and private corporations. It also is a tool that we can use on each other and ourselves. In *Surveillance Shoe* (2000), artist Jill Magid, then a student at the ACT program at MIT, created a shoe embedded with a camera which she wore as she walked around the city. But rather than record the world at ground level, Magid outfitted her camera to give us a lopsided angle up her skirt. She noted, "It is as if the city is a scroll, and with the kick of my free leg, I can unroll it." I read this work as an intimate foreshadowing of the kinds of "closeness" that these technologies would play in the future. Indeed, as a teenager in the year 2000, and with the advent of the first cell-phone cameras with video functionality, one of the primary concerns of government officials in Saudi Arabia, where my Egyptian family lived for a brief time, was that young boys would use these camera phones to take similar-angled and invasive pictures of young women. In Magid's piece, that perversion is reversed, so that Magid can control an angle of surveillance that no CCTV camera would be able to capture.

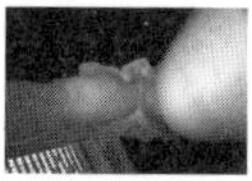

pp. 60–61

The Iraqi-American artist Wafaa Bilal has also used his body as a site of perpetual surveillance to controversial ends. In *The 3rdi* (2010–11), Bilal, who is a professor at New York University's Tisch School of the Arts, underwent a surgical procedure to have a camera implemented into the back of his head. A website was created to accompany the project, which broadcast the photographs that were shot from the camera once a minute. The project was due to extend over the course of the year. Bilal's stated purpose was to blur the boundaries between the "public and private imagination," and to consider the role and state of the cyborg in the twenty-first century. "Most of the time, we don't live in the places we live in," he told the *Chronicle of Higher Education*. "We don't exist in the city we exist in. Perhaps physically we exist, but mentally we are somewhere else." Often the material he collected was mundane: walls, streets, and campus surroundings. However, working as a professor at a private university, Bilal's *3rdi* raised privacy concerns with his students and colleagues, who had not agreed to be filmed by Bilal's omnipresent camera. NYU eventually forced him to cover the camera when he teaching. Eventually, Bilal had the implant removed after his body rejected it, causing him intense pain. The age of the cyborg, it seems, still has some kinks to work out before it can be set upon us.

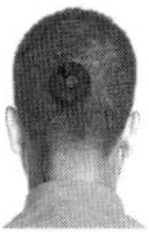

p. 61

Play with Me

Ring around the rosie
Hopscotch, Monopoly
Red light, green light
G. I. Joes and Barbies

Hide and seek, kick the can
Cowboys and Indians
Wiffle ball, paper dolls
Hacky sack and hangman

Tag you're it, cops and robbers
Jungle gym, chutes and ladders
Tic tac toe, Mister Rogers
Marco Polo, London bridges

Simon says, steal the bacon
Time out, trick or treat
Electric company
Olly olly oxen free

Do you, want to, play with me

Extreme, "Play with Me" (1989)

In October 2015, for a project commissioned by the Jeu de Paume museum in Paris, the artist Constant Dullaart paid $5,000 for 2.5 million Instagram followers being sold on eBay. The followers he purchased were distributed among thirty Instagram accounts that the artist felt were all actively commodifying social-media audiences. Comprising artists, institutions, curators, collectors, galleries, critics, and a single collective, these accounts were each given 100,000 followers, rendering everyone similarly important, at least on Instagram. In our age of hyper-capitalism, one can argue that Dullaart's stunt was an act of social-media socialism, a critique of follower-based statuses, and a commentary on the shallow ways these audiences are created. Dullaart's stated intent was to give "a warped perspective on the 'attention economy,' of course, in my eyes desperately necessary in our present age of hyper-capitalism," and his observations couldn't have arrived at a more appropriate time. Within an ever-expanding world of online avatarism, a parallel culture of customization and enhancement—from followers to virtual makeovers—can be idealized with the right amount of money.

The strangest online activities can now be bought through the delegated, scalable, mechanical, physical workforces employed by Amazon's Mechanical Turk service and Fivvver.com. These laborers work overtime playing online games to develop experienced computer-game characters to be sold to wealthier players who don't want to spend the days or weeks needed for typical character advancement. Gaming culture in particular, where many post-millennial digital technologies first developed, has long nurtured vendor-like interactions within the virtual realm.

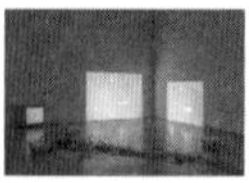
p. 62

For artists, the possibility for critical engagement with gaming culture has manifested in playful ways. Cory Arcangel, widely regarded as one of the biggest pioneers of internet-engaged art, first came to prominence with *Super Mario Clouds* (2002–ongoing), in which he took an old Super Mario Brothers game cartridge and erased everything but the clouds. He also released instructions for how users could do this themselves at home. Looking at this pre-YouTube work, one can trace not only an archaeology of gaming technologies, but also the kinds of visual "progress" we have made, such as the enhanced resolution enabled by different forms of video-sharing sites and social media. Arcangel has remained engaged with the culture of gaming, creating over the years a webisode series of solitaire games, self-playing video bowling games that only bowl gutter balls, and an old Japanese Famicom racing game with every element removed except the road—a relic for aesthetic appreciation. This culture of play is more broadly evidenced in

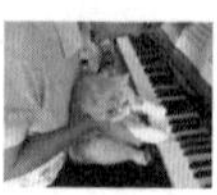
pp. 62–63

Arcangel's *Drei Klavierstücke op. 11* (2009). In this YouTube video, Arcangel has painstakingly taken YouTube videos of cats bouncing on and off pianos to create a cat-generated rendition of Arnold Schoenberg's Op. 11. Call it a *cat-orchestra*!

Eva and Franco Mattes have equally made a consistent effort to engage with gaming technologies. In *Freedom* (2010), Eva played a violent first-person-shooter game set in a desolate war zone. During the performance, in which other players unwittingly took part, she pleads for other users not to shoot her. "This is an art performance," Eva tells the other players, who nonetheless shoot her every time she speaks. Freedom speaks to the trigger-happy nature of violence in video games, and the player's inherent unawareness that they may be simulating a particularly violent act. An equally disturbing observation is made in the couple's piece *My Generation* (2010), where an old-school computer is placed in a pile of debris within a gallery space. As you inch closer, the sound of screaming and shouting emanates from the computer speakers, while on its screen is a series of videos of youths turning violent and striking their consoles over video-game mishaps. *My Generation* contemplates a world whereby violence is engendered through gaming technologies; but it can also be seen to offer a counterargument, that violent video games also put forward a cathartic space for aggression that would otherwise manifest in the real world.

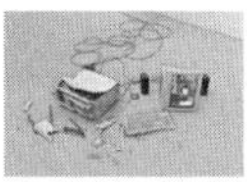

p. 63

But while some games offer violent individual experiences, others are more communally engaging. Among the more popular of these social-gaming experiences is karaoke, which has also evolved to allow users to create their own "set lists." In *More Songs of Innocence and of Experience* (2013), the duo Thomson and Craighead collated spam and scam emails, transforming them into karaoke songs that blurred romanticism and realism, with lyrical narrations intended to evoke the spirit of Charles Dickens's novel *Our Mutual Friend*. One song begins: "Dear Sir, I know that this might be a surprise to you since we have not met before." Another: "I am the wife of the late Libyan leader Colonel Muaamar Ghadafi [*sic*]." Other games offer social sensorial experiences. In *Factory of the*

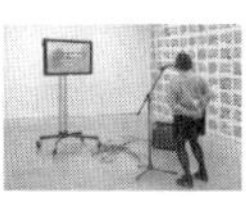

pp. 62–63

Sun (2015), for example, Hito Steyerl explored the hazards and pleasures of image circulation by immersing the viewer into an installation that resembled the video-game-like film *Tron* (1982). The spectator entered into a darkened box where the floors and ceilings were rendered as bright-blue shimmering grids. A series of deck chairs was placed in front of a metal-mounted screen on which a high-octane film that jumps between news reportage and dance footage reveals the potential indulgence of sitting before a virtual world as we would a television screen, hinting at the possibility of a future for virtual couch potatoes.

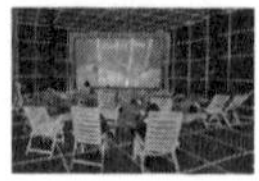

p. 64

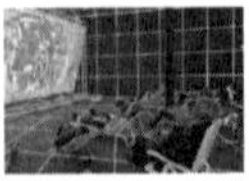

pp. 64–65

Questions about our collective future were raised in DIS's inspired, immersive installation *The Island (Ken)* (2015), which premiered that same year at the New Museum Triennial curated by Lauren Cornell and Ryan Trecartin. The premise of the project at first is seemingly simple. You are in a kitchen designed by luxury bath and kitchen supplier Dornbracht. The surfaces are lush, sleek, and inviting—a picture of gratifying seduction. But look again and this kitchen is also a bathroom, a hybrid model comprised of two of the most showroom-y lifestyle setups. The work's mash-up quality is akin to what can be done through digital appropriation and manipulation: the two worlds here collide uninterruptedly into one. The space was also used as a platform for critical, yet playful engagement—participants could schedule a bath or have a meal cooked for them—while also functioning as a platform for public programs that investigated how technology evolves our culture. Like much of DIS's work, *The Island (Ken)* is an uncomfortable amalgam that blurs the lines between aesthetics, art, and promotional material.

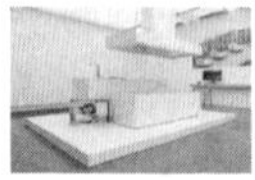

p. 65

The concept of play is an important point to dwell on here, in that much of these projects have been devised as a kind of reengagement with an original experience. Rather than exist as mere appropriations, these replications reimagine how we might engage with technology, even prepare and train us for new technologies that might otherwise bewilder us. Headlines these days are filled with how, for instance, VR technology is helping human interactions such as studying complex surgical procedures, or engaging with refugees housed in UN encampments, or even, as was highlighted in a *Creators Project* feature, helping us to understand a fundamental human fear: what it means to die. The embrace of virtual reality owes much to an emergent generation that grew up playing video games and thereby learned to engage with virtual environments, customizable avatars, and often fellow players. It may be through these tropes that gaming culture could be credited for having helped us to prepare for our increasingly customizable world experiences. Open your profile in something as utilitarian as a Lyft account and you'll be given the option of adding a profile pic and selecting traits such as a favorite music genre. You can also rate each driver as you would a Yelp review and award him up to five stars depending on how "enjoyable" your ride was or how much small talk you had to endure. In *Hitch (http://tryhit.ch)* (2017), artist Chris Collins created a website that parodies the experience of taking taxicab-style services such as Uber or Lyft. When you enter the site, a picture of a hand holding a mobile device invites you to take a "Hitch" with them. By clicking on the image, you are then presented with an attractive-looking car and welcomed by a pair of eyes that look at you from the windshield. "Welcome aboard, and thanks for choosing Hitch, the only on-demand autonomous vehicle service that's fast, fun, and completely free! I'm BART and I'll be your driver this afternoon. Please make yourself comfortable, and let me know when you're ready to begin your ride." As you start, a series of questions and prompts are put forward—"Are you comfortable?"; "Do you need the air conditioning turned up?"; "Is there any music that you would like to listen to?"—revealing how these late-capitalist platforms create tailor-made services based on "likes" and "star rankings." So while you might feel that you are experiencing a simulation, or playing a game, the artist is in fact demonstrating the homogenization that often underlies these experiences.

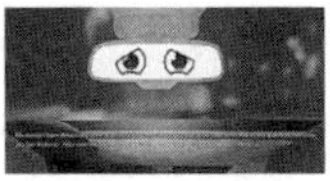

pp. 64–65

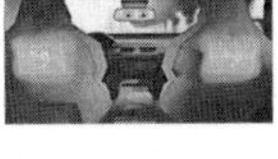

p. 65

But does the internet's inherent heterogeneity come with its own detriments? Consider artist Rafaël Rozendaal, who has long used the internet to play with and explore absolute creative

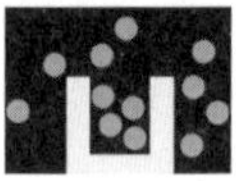

p. 66

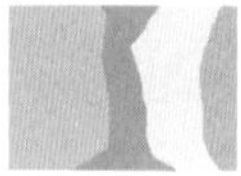

pp. 66–67

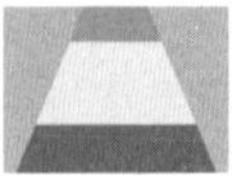

p. 67

freedom. In *Lots Of Many .com* (2017), a series of red balls are seen bursting out of a blue container. As one clicks on these red balls, they start to proliferate, filling the screen but never quite overtaking it. In *Floating The. com* (2016), numerous colors, walls, glaciers, buildings—I'm not sure—flow into each other in an endless cyclical loop. In *Future Is Uncertain . com* (2013), a multicolored conveyer belt stands before us. Move the pointer toward the top of the screen and it starts to accelerate, faster and faster, as if one is moving into an abyss of our own making. Move the pointer toward the bottom and our progress slows to a crawl. "My interest in the internet is the freedom to do whatever I want," Rozendaal told the *Creative Independent*. "To me it's unique. Throughout cultural history there's always been someone asking the maker, 'Are you sure?' Whether it's a publisher, or a curator, or a gallerist, or an editor. There's always someone like, 'Yeah that's great.' With the internet, for good or bad, you do whatever you do without thinking, and you publish immediately. Early on, I was attracted to that and very hopeful. I'm not so hopeful about it anymore. I don't know if it's a good idea. But to me, as an artist, there's something about it... If I want to make a farting website, and the next website has clouds, and the next website is abstract, and the one after that has a dog, no one is like, 'What do those have to do with each other? Why are you putting them together?'"

Automation here becomes a sort of limitation in that it cannot be anything other than what it offers. User interaction is minimized to a single command. It's possible to go further, to create virtual environments that play and engage with you but that you cannot interact with in return. For the Hammer Museum's "Made in LA 2016" biennial, web-art pioneer Guthrie Lonergan created an M&M's candy mascot that lived on the museum's website where it would "speak" to its visitors using awkward turns of phrase such as: "The observer would be engaged, and so I determined to look back to confront, to establish a dialogue. The issues were too important ...," or "My work is a visual, not verbal experience, then." To make this project, Lonergan fed self-authored statements from

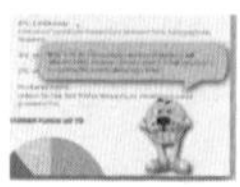

p. 68

artists' websites into a voice-automation software, which were then spoken by a changing cast of M&M's avatars throughout the exhibition. The resulting feedback for the project was rather hilarious.

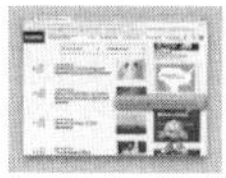
p. 69

Users could not discern the role or function of the M&M's and many accused it of being mere product placement. One user noted, "What the fucking hell is up with the M&Ms on the hammer website? I hope they paid you a lot of money." Another expressed worry and agitation: "Hello, What is up with the little M&M guy in the corner of

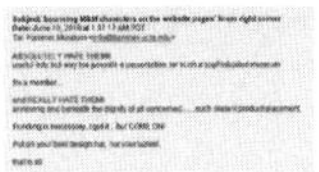
p. 69

your website? Can't tell if you have been hacked or I have. Either way the widget is terribly annoying." Lonergan appeared to be trolling visitors who disdained the "branding" of contemporary art when they were in fact experiencing art at its most contemporary, art that is responsive to internet culture and its diverse machinations. In fact, Lonergan's title for the piece, *Built with Indexhibit* (2016), refers to an early and ongoing platform that allows artists to create and share websites of their portfolios. But who knows how many of the Hammer's visitors were able to piece this together.

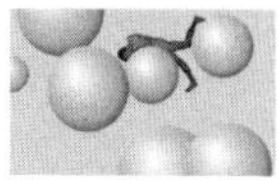
p. 68

Don't Shoot Me; I'm Ready for an Uprising

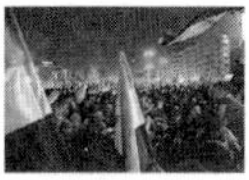

p. 70

Wading through images of the Egyptian revolution of 2011 on a search engine has become an ongoing pastime of mine. This interest came about after the death of my grandfather in January of 2011, during the revolution. Since then, the only way I could relate to my country of birth was through Egypt's images of recent conflict. I would study them. In all of these photographs mediating an event for global public viewing, a motif recurred: images of a mass of bodies, a corpus efflorescing as one singular body. This visual vocabulary also applied to the protestors outside Capitol Hill fighting a different conflict against the gross inequalities of financial capital—the Occupy movement.

As one begins to examine the conditions of image making after the rise of the internet, one cannot help but be seduced by the potential of using the collective figure of the body as an allegory for a greater struggle: a melee that traverses first-, second-, and third-world social, economic, and political conditions. Does protest become as trendy as sex? Can we eat it, can we devour it, or rather, does it devour us?

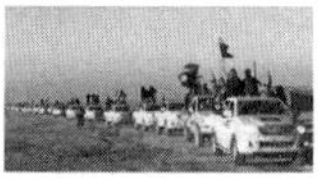

pp. 70–71

If we skip to the context of the present, more than six years on from the Egyptian revolution of 2011, can we synonymize the formal conditions of image making surrounding ISIS to that of the liberator revolutionary body? Indeed, in so many recent images, groups of protestors or militias are portrayed as a singular whole: pulsating, progressing into an infinite visual valley—or is it an archipelago?

It is easy to see a corpus of placards as extensions of the body, reaching for the sky. Is there a message that we must decipher therein?

In terms of image making in the age of the internet, this chapter seeks to extend beyond the limits of art and into the realm of the political, focusing on Egypt and its revolution.

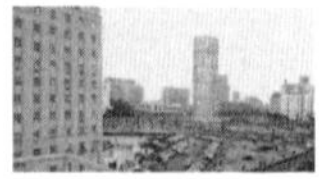
pp. 70–71

I first began thinking of Tahrir Square (Freedom Square) and other sites of revolution when I saw a digitally rendered photo by the artist Iman Issa of a glistening monument in the middle of the cityscape. The piece is called *Proposal for a Crystal Building* (2003). In 2014, it was produced as a sculpture. I had been thinking through the concept of revolution and the language around it partly because my grandfather was an activist who was fervent about the Egyptian public's potential to overthrow President Hosni Mubarak's regime. I followed my grandfather's thinking over a number of years and took particular concern with how the images of so-called revolution were presented after his death in 2011.

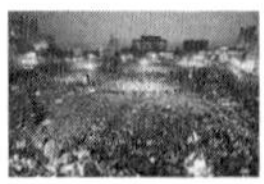
p. 71

One of the primary images that circulated around news media was an aerial view of Tahrir Square lit up at night during the Egyptian revolution. The picture circulated rapidly and quickly became a metaphor for numerous political movements taking place across the Arab world, from Tunisia to Syria. I became concerned, however, when this aerial view started to appear throughout images of the Arab uprisings, rendering many of the activists faceless from the media. Was the internet liberating us with new forms of documentation and image circulation, or was it reinscribing the distanciation techniques commonly adopted by news media that have sought to hold the other at a distance?

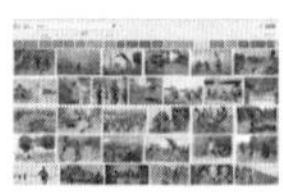
p. 72

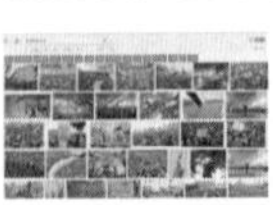
p. 73

Another question emerged: How were these images of conflict indexed on search engines such as Google? At the time of writing, if you image-searched "Iraq War" as a keyword, for example, one receives a series of options: "combat," "casualties," "fighting," "soldiers in action," "2003," and so forth. When you click on each quadrant you get more detailed and violent images of conflict. If one searches "Egyptian Revolution," one receives another series of accumulated sets of images. In this case, "social media," "2013," "protests,"

"1919," and "1952." I click on 1919 and see images of the Egyptian revolution of 1919—archival images that I could never have fathomed existed. What appears are detailed images of marching bodies, flagpoles, and buildings, which, through their postures, collectively look as if they are about to overthrow some entity.

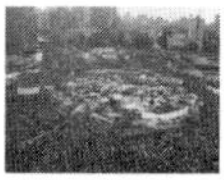
p. 72

Click on the option "2013," and the first image it yields is the iconic aerial view of Tahrir Square. But wasn't this 2011, I ask myself? I start to realize that there is a temporal disjuncture happening here. An image from 2013 looks like an image from 2012 looks like an image from 2011. These are just crowds gathered in Tahrir Square. Does the internet flatten time so that it becomes indiscernible, so that conflict in the third-world context becomes part of one homogenous whole? There is an occasional close-up in this search: an image from the Associated Press of a woman screaming in front of the camera. But the rest of the images that I see are ones of floating bodies in space. I click on the images to find their sources but many do not have a date, time, or author attributed to them. One then must ask: Is the internet really a scrupulously indexical zone? And if not, might it in fact be re-entrenching colonial paradigms?

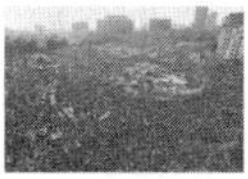
p. 73

In an exhibition at the ICA, London, in 2014, I curated a show titled "Whose Gaze Is It Anyway?" It included ephemera that were derived from appropriated material from cinema as a means to reflect on the "sensationalized" nature of the images from the Arab world that were circulating globally. The show's title pertains here: Whose gaze is it that we think about when we look at online images of postcolonial territories? Are we looking at a colonized image? Is this image colonized by the West or by the militancy of its local context? Can it be liberated through its circulation, where writers, audiences, and historians can decode it?

I am asking a lot of hard-to-answer questions, including this one: Does simply querying open the door to new ways of thinking about these images? I am not certain, but I want to know whether the militant image, the image of revolution, is ours to parse and share, as was so commonly done during the so-called Twitter Revolution. When it comes to the Arab image, is the image of the Arab a manifestation of some kind of fantasy, and if so, whose fantasy is it? Is it the sensualized fantasy of Egyptian cinema with starlets such as Soad Hosny and Shadia acting as pliable subjects to their male counterparts? Or is it the image of Arab B movies such as *Way to Hell* starring sex kittens such as Randa Fariba? Or is it the image of the white British actor Peter O'Toole on a camel in *Lawrence of Arabia*, hands raised against a desert sky? Or is it an image propagated by artists such as Jumana Manna and Sille Storihle who, in their film *The Goodness Regime* (2013), portrayed the revolutionary conflict that led to the formation of the state of Israel and the numerous ensuing intifadas with all of the characters played and personified by children?

It's important to consider what revolution we're talking about when we discuss revolution in the Arab world. Are we speaking of the Egyptian revolution of 1919, the formation of Israel in 1948, the revolution that led to the overthrow of the monarchy in Egypt in 1952, the Arab-Israeli war of 1967, which led to the collapse of the pan-Arab ideal, or are we strictly talking about 2011 because that is the revolution that has been most documented online? Certainly. I will focus on how the revolutionary image circulates and what form it takes in 2011, and what content it produces.

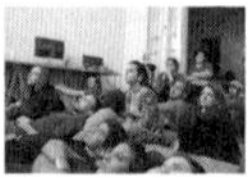
p. 74

Mosireen is an independent media collective that formed after the Egyptian revolution of 2011 as a counterpoint to the lack of free press in Egypt and the Arab world. It was initially composed of a group of filmmakers and activists who wanted, as they stated on their website and YouTube channels, to "empower citizens through media." They used cinema and the documentary form to subvert political systems, and they professed to balance the truth in light of precarious coverage from news media that proclaimed to be "independent." Mosireen quickly grew in international renown, becoming the most-watched not-for-profit organization on YouTube and garnering global press attention for their documentary coverage of the unfolding political situation in Egypt after the 2011 revolution.

There was a focus on aesthetics throughout their documentary videos; these were meaningful pieces of "work," as much art as political dispatches. They were also strategic in the

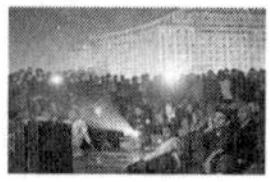
p. 75

way that they focused and gathered around key social and political events that took place in the country, such as the the massacre of Coptic Christians in October 2011, the brutal attacks on female protestors, and the violent breakup of peaceful sit-ins. They interspersed this activity with community building through educational workshops, as well as a project called Tahrir Cinema, which used film to draw together diverse groups of people from different social and economic classes.

In *Blood at Night, Grief by Day (Maspero 9/10/11)* (2011), the collective produced one of the most evocative documentaries of the post-Arab uprising in Egypt. The film, which documents the massacre against Coptic Christians in Cairo in front of the

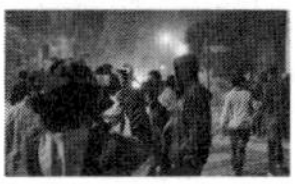
p. 74

Maspero television building, begins with chaotic crowds. Then a narrator appears, anxiously updating us on the facts. Darkness. Crowds. Appropriated footage is interspersed: a military truck smashing into civilians. Coffins laden with white roses appear. A screaming women, begging, "Why are they doing this to us?" A mother weeps over a coffin. Racing cameras evoke the chaos of the situation. Howling mothers scream again. Civilians run away from the military. Hysterical crying. A man holding a blood drenched shirt says, "I am sure this is my brother, I am certain this is my brother," commenting on the absence of what he believes to be his dead sibling.

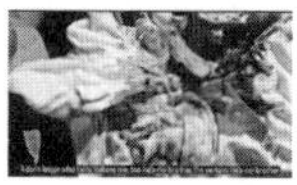
p. 74

He says this calmly. But then there is more howling that enters the narrative from elsewhere. Dead bodies lie on the floor, uncovered.

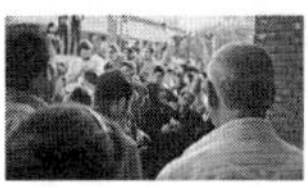
p. 75

Crowds, again. A mother is in lament, holding her dead child's arm against her chest. Dead bodies lay flat on the ground with images of Christ placed atop them. We see members of the collective occupying this space—a church, a community hall? Appropriated footage of cars crashing into civilians. Squashed bodies and faces. A space of retreat: a coffin. Silence. The end.

When I first saw this video, I wept. I felt angry, confused, but I also sensed that the internet had granted this collective an agency to share this information, where I could see it from a distance. My grandfather had lived in Asyut, Egypt, his whole life, where one of the largest Coptic populations in the country live. He was a figure who, through his role as a community doctor, promoted interreligious dialogue. The video left me itching with thoughts and questions about its form, its content, and its aesthetics.

Its use of appropriation, its sound design, its fragmented cinema verité narrative style all lent a sense of credibility to the work. But it also stirred something else that felt as if it were authored from inside the experience of violence. The film seemed to function as a kind of catharsis. I could feel the anxiety of whoever produced the film. The constant return to weeping mothers was almost a stand-in for the filmmakers who made this film, themselves weeping, grieving, working through their emotions.

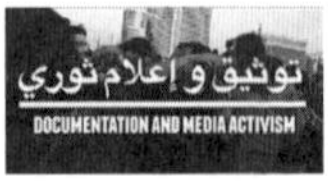

p. 75

One of the defining features of Mosireen's work is the notion of testimony. These videos serve as evidence, documents that are revealing hidden truths. They are clearly "framed" as a form of resistance to dominant news media. Within this paradigm of "reframing" the truth, a suggestion of utopia emerges. It also fulfills an audience hunger for liveness and immediacy. Indeed, we continually want to be inside the event, as opposed to waiting for new media to catch up. The internet allows us this. But still, who is this collective? Is it always a single voice or are we experiencing multiple voices? These are questions, not criticisms.

Some might argue that the violence presented on-screen is a form of sensationalism, but one could equally argue that this is one of the fundamental principles of documentary filmmaking as articulated by John Grierson—that the "raw material" is the greatest barometer of the truth. What, then, are the image tactics that we should use in this day and age? Could it be that the close-up becomes a form of resistance? A close-up of a face laced with bullet wounds from Demotix, a photo agency that proclaimed to be the "news by you," is one example of a space where these images could be found.

It is also important to consider whether these images function as a form of digital activism. When they circulate online through social-media networks, do they have the same agency as bodies in space? Or is the virtual sphere simply a space to "activate" and initiate bodies into space? The latter is a question that Judith Butler tackles in her book *Notes toward a Performative Theory of Assembly* (2015). One can argue that the best form of activism emerges through mainstream entertainment platforms. For example, after the revolution, a group of filmmakers made a series of short films collectively called *18 Days* (2011), which was screened at the Cannes Film Festival. Ibrahim El Batout directed a film called *Winter of Discontent* (2012), which revealed some of the impetuses behind the Egyptian revolution, while Jehane Noujaim's *The Square* (2013) offered a documentary view of the revolution, capturing the lives of many activists, including members of Mosireen. It was nominated for an Academy Award, the first time Egypt had made it into the competition at the Oscars. The film was later acquired by Netflix, thus becoming freely available to its subscribers as an introduction to the revolution and its aftermath.

Others have proclaimed that a kind of artistic co-option has taken place as artists aestheticize the conflict. Nermine Hammam photographed Egyptian military men on tanks and then used image-manipulation techniques to place them in serene, photogenic environments. Certainly, a great number of exhibitions emerged after the revolution and a spotlight was shone on artists from the region. But did the revolution also become a kind of gold rush?

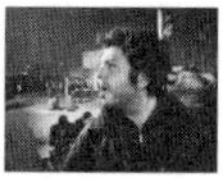

p. 76

One example can be found in Ahmed Basiony, a young Egyptian artist who was killed during the first eighteen days of the Egyptian revolution. Basiony quickly became a martyr figure after his death. He had the perfect profile: in his early thirties, father of two, and with a youthful visage and smiling face. His image became plastered across the streets on posters and placards, and he grew to international prominence after his death, having previously been a complete unknown outside of Egypt. In 2011, the interim minister of culture in Egypt, Emad Abu Ghazi, decided that Ahmed Basiony would represent the country at the Venice Biennale. A multichannel video installation was presented, devised in collaboration with artist Shady El Noshokaty, friend and mentor of the artist. The work consisted of documentation of a performance, *Thirty Days of Running in the Place*, that the artist staged outside of the Cairo Opera House in

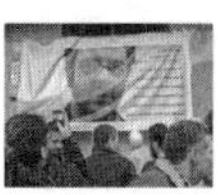

p. 76

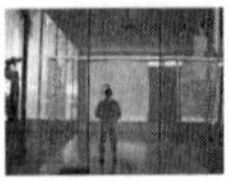
p. 78

2010, where he ran in the same place for an extended period of time with body sensors attached to him, which produced a visualization of his circadian rhythms. This footage was countered with recordings of the revolution taken on the artist's mobile phone, which was found on his laptop after his death. Some believed this to have been the starting point for a potential new work.

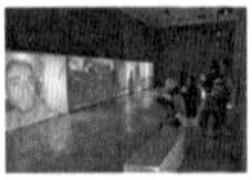
pp. 78–79

The installation at the Venice Biennale was also called *30 Days of Running in the Space* (2011). Basiony's footage of the revolution was also shown a year later at documenta 13, the largest exhibition of contemporary art, held every five years. Many within Egypt's artistic community criticized the presentation at Venice as a form of co-option by the interim regime, a craven attempt to signal that they were breaking ties with the past. Others believed that the authorship of the Venice installation was questionable and that the catalogue produced in collaboration with the American University in Cairo Press (AUC Press) was a poor decision, considering the AUC's downtown campus rooftop was believed by many to have been used by the Mubarak regime as a base to shoot down protestors.

The curatorial statement for the exhibition also raised fundamental questions in that it did not seek to position the work of Basiony as art, but rather focused on the artist's biography and his death. It read:

> On January the 28th, Ahmed Basiony died of gunshot wounds inflicted by snipers from the Egyptian Police Forces on Tahrir Square during the start of the 25 January 2011 revolution. He leaves behind a wife and two children (of 6 and 1 years of age).
>
> Basiony has quickly became a symbol to protestors of the sacrifices they had to endure in the course of their struggle. An emblem of exhilarating creativity to all new generations in Egypt and the Middle East at large, his work is being honoured as a metaphor for change in a new, post-revolutionary Egypt. Ahmed Basiony's most significant projects: 'Thirty Days of Running in the Place' (2010), will feature alongside documentary footage filmed by the artist himself in Tahrir Square, in the

days before his death on 28th January 2011. A testament to the way the world watched Egypt's revolution through hundreds of media channels.

The statement, which was authored in collaboration with El Noshokaty, the exhibition's cocurator at Venice, highlighted some questions about the role that art and artists can play in narrating the revolution. Should they hold this burden? Should Basiony's legacy be tied to that of his death?

As time went on, different forms of creative production began to fuel the revolutionary discourse. Graffiti became a popular form of expression, and artists such as Ganzeer came to global prominence for their politically critical slogans. In Syria, comic-book artist Ali Farzat created cartoons criticizing President Assad, which circulated widely until he had his hands wounded by pro-Assad forces, rendering him unable to sketch. Other artists took on different forms: the collective Masasit Mati created a YouTube series called *Top Goon*, exploring the everyday tragedy of life in Syria through a puppet show of all of the major political players, drawing a large international audience on YouTube. Another Syrian collective emerged simultaneously: Abounaddara was a cohort of self-taught and volunteer filmmakers who produced what they called "emergency cinema." Their work was shown at the 56th Venice Biennale in 2015 before they decided to pull out of the exhibition, and following Basiony, were featured in the next edition of documenta.

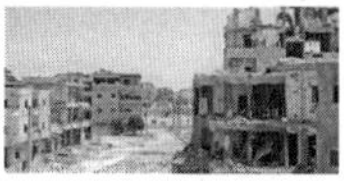

p. 79

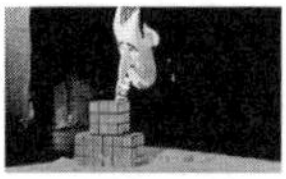

pp. 78-79

We must ask what is happening with these image networks and this mediation of narrative. Might the circulation and redistribution of these images create counter-truths? Or, being consumed piecemeal at art exhibitions and biennales, do they create their own myths, independent of reality? Either way, online "viral" culture still promises catalytic power, one that has the potential to engage a broader audience.

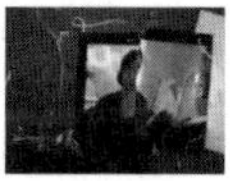

p. 79

The issue with much of this cultural production is that it is often surrounded by language from media, which is suggestive of “new dawns” and “new beginnings,” yet the current political situation, especially in metropolitan areas, is evermore violent.

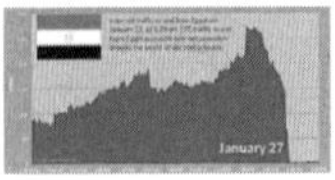

pp. 80–81

It’s important to consider where the revolutionary image will live. Will it continue to live online? And if so, is this a viable option? On January 28, 2011, President Mubarak was able to switch the internet in Egypt off, leaving the country without connectivity. If we are subjected to state control, there is an imperative to find alternative, non-online spaces to allow these images to be archived and endure.

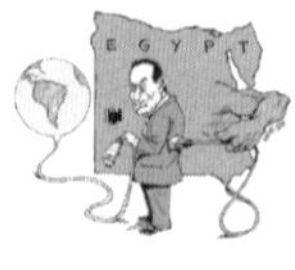

p. 81

We should also consider who has access to these platforms and these arenas. In poorer countries in East and West Africa, the internet has played less of an influential role in terms of circulation and distribution even though these regions are equally marred by conflict. One assumes that this is because access to these tools is less available. This brings me to another revolutionary, or perhaps counterrevolutionary, image that emerged after the shootings at the LGBTQ Pulse nightclub in Orlando in 2016. In response to this horrific attack, a campaign was launched on social media called #twomenkissing, which presented men kissing and celebrating their love for one another in solidarity with the victims of the Orlando attack. There are two intrinsic problems in this online activism. First, “two men kissing” excludes the diversity of individuals within the nightclub: the women and transgender individuals who were also victims. Second, the campaign would have only been restricted to those who lived in openly liberal metropolitan centers as opposed to conservative constituencies, where such expressions of affection would be considered taboo.

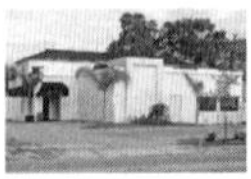
p. 80

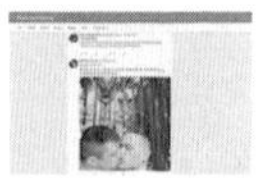
pp. 80–81

Thus, one can pose the question again: Do the forms of activism that exist online promote extant colonial power structures that exclude specific minority groups? I have sought to consider this concept of life at stake since the Egyptian revolution in 2011, when the politics of the everyday turned into violence against the human body on a global scale, from Istanbul to Damascus to Cairo. In Orlando, one could argue that this was a situation where the "body"—specifically the LGBTQ body's biosocial and political function as a minority, liberated dissident sexual subject—was completely annihilated in plain sight.

But, in their endless proliferation, the kissing faces of #twomenkissing also made clear another function, the production of the body-conscious gay male as an aspirational pursuit unto itself, and so a confirmation not of community but of a self-satisfying sense of selfness. This is not to admonish the role and function of a more confrontational, male-led image in queer society, but rather, to raise a different set of questions: Whose image culture are we partaking in, and indeed, who are the authors of these images? How do we engender a framework that enables a context, not only for grief, but that would also allow one to speak back to the simplistic, paradigmatic structure of good and evil, of love and hatred?

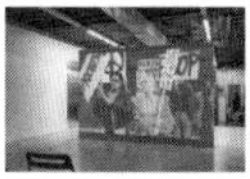
p. 81

What should we do as agents of the image, as producers and proprietors of them? Should we say "Goodbye!" to the culture of individualism that has been enabled by social-media broadcasting tools, in favor of a polyphonic, creolized notion of community? These are the questions that we must ask ourselves as we move forward into the ever-evolving twenty-first century.

Toward a New Digital Metabolism

I have used this book to grapple with the context of an image's aesthetic within a digital landscape. As I have shown, an image has evolved beyond not only physicality, but also beyond an "aura" of originality. The continual evolution of the internet, the ubiquity of mobile devices, and an array of software applications have led to a kind of image circulation that is unparalleled to what has come before. But we no longer just examine an image, we metabolize it: taking it in, processing it, and then repurposing it for new public consumption. With a smartphone, one can take a photo of a preexisting work of art, tweak and crop the photo through a set of filters and tools, then share it on a social-media site where it can be liked by someone halfway across the world, all within the span of a minute. With each customizable layer given to an image, a new formal image is produced, one that is removed from the original context and aesthetic created by its primary author. The form in which it gets shared is but one variation among hundreds, with many leading back to an "original" work (e.g., the Mona Lisa) or to a new kind of work that eludes the notion of originality altogether. With an ever-expanding database of manipulated imagery, we must reconsider the agency and "aura" of art in the digital age, where the internet itself has become a gallery, and where traditional notions of art—its spatiality, its tactileness, its dimensionality, its authenticity—are no longer the dominating attributes in how we look at visual work.

As articulated previously in this book, the late art critic John Berger expounded upon Walter Benjamin's theories of art in the age of mechanical reproduction in his seminal text *Ways of Seeing*. Though published over forty-five years ago, many of Berger's observations still hold true, and even in a post-digital age, art remains distillable to a set of qualities. Art is still valued for possessing beauty, whether it be founded in aesthetics or philosophy; artists are valued for creating work that emerges from an interior honesty and that responds to some truth of reality; genius remains the highest form of praise and appraisal of an artist's work, one that cements their place within society, and at times, even human history; art's form is still evaluated on its execution and composition, which can be debated on grounds of taste and merit; and because this notion of art is endemic to culture, its status or state is essential to civilization.

In other ways we have indeed moved beyond the considerations of Benjamin and Berger. Art can now be synthesized down to its characteristics, as demonstrated by projects such as Artsy's Art Genome Project, which maps out an image's "genes," that is, discernible traits, such as eras, disciplines, materials, that are further broken down into nearly one thousand characteristics, then rebuilt and bridged together through algorithms. While longtime patrons of the arts might argue that such advances actually work to destabilize the value economy, to remain sentimental about old ways of thinking is to stagnate how we consider art in a digital era.

This is not to say that there is a demographic in the art world that would prefer a return to a pre-digital past, but rather as technology advances, so must we constantly reexamine our notions of art, which now exist in a state of digital flux. We must also adapt a sort of "accelerationism," a term propelled into modernity by cultural theorists such as Robin Mackay and Armen Avanessian, who proposed in their coedited anthology *#Accelerate: The Accelerationist Reader* (2014) that rather than retreat against new technology, we must find ways of "repurposing" it, even if that means asking difficult questions such as "Can a computer teach me ways that can help me further my ideological positions? Can it teach me ways to extract myself from my entrenched mental habits?"

In *Ghosts of My Life: Writings on Depression, Hauntology and Lost Futures* (2014), the late theorist Mark Fisher touched on another idea—that of a "hauntology" of culture. "When the present has given up on the future," he writes, "we must listen for the relics of the future in the un-activated potentials of the past." Fisher noted how artistic disciplines such as music remain steeped in the lore of the past, where production techniques are calibrated to make Adele and Amy Winehouse sound as if they had been recording nearly half a century ago. Were we to hold all music production to a former ideal, we would be in effect "canceling the future." Fisher warns against this temporal lag, which he believes will only keep us in outmoded notions of materialism.

These fretful conditions have long been the trope of sci-fi writers who have turned the fear of the future into a fruitful literary trope. And today's science-fiction writers are no longer the prophets of alien invasion or robots run amok, but near-future speculators and allegorists. Take, for example, Charlie Brooker's TV show *Black Mirror*, which opened its third season in 2016 with an episode called "Nosedive," where social-media "likes" have become universal capital. You cannot rent a car or attend an event without having gained and maintained a consistent approval rating. Even more intriguing is how, through performed actions, status can be accrued, generated, yet also diminished and lost. One could form a positive counter-reading to this episode's intent, which is to consider how social media might disrupt traditional capitalist hierarchies. Or should we be evermore wary of Constant Dullaart's motives to gain social-media currency by using actual capital? The future as a concept is something that we have always approached with both excitement and trepidation, but more often than not, when we speak of the future, we are often referring to the present. By habit, our discussions primarily encapsulate extant technologies, the current versions of our smart devices—our phones, our speakers, our watches, which serves only to ground us in the here and now and precludes critical discussions of where we could and should be.

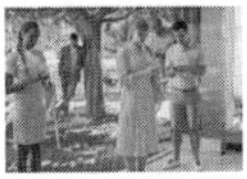

p. 82

In 2017, the artist Simon Denny staged an exhibition at the Hammer Museum, Los Angeles, which sought to imagine a whole different potential for living and transacting. In *Blockchain Future States* (2017), Denny presented a work based on the potentials of the blockchain, the underlying mechanism that enables the functioning of cryptocurrencies such as Bitcoin, an encrypted digital currency that operates independently of traditional banking

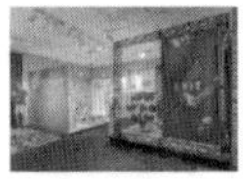

pp. 82–83

systems. Here, he presented a promotional film where three representative forms of finance companies, assembled as a mock trade fair, illustrate the different ways that the blockchain could be dependably applied to everyday lives. "Trust is guaranteed," says the narrator, who waxes on about blockchain's innovative security technology. "The blockchain is indestructible and incorruptible. It is public and transparent. It is the truth." In Denny's proposition, the future is here, but we have yet to be sold on it.

In order to embrace technology, we must be able to "see" it. In *A Convention of Tiny Movements* (2015), the artist Lawrence Abu Hamdan worked with researchers at MIT to instrumentalize a tool being developed known as the visual microphone, a device that records the sound waves of our speech patterns, and thus creates a new form of surveillance when decoded. Utilizing this technology before it was acquired by intelligence agencies, Abu Hamdan staged an intervention at the Armory Show in New York, where he filled the fair with glistening potato chip packets at every end, their empty wrappers strewn across the VIP lounges and public areas, making sounds when stepped on that masked our speech identities. Hamdan's project addresses the possibility of controlling how technology can be used against us, or even redirected at others, but it also allowed for conversations regarding the democratization of such technologies and how they might be used for alternative purposes. In the 1990s, pioneering artists such as Olia Lialina, JODI, and Mark Amerika exposed the machinations of technologies such as hypertext that were then beginning to become commonplace, repurposing them to reveal and provoke new narrative structures through code.

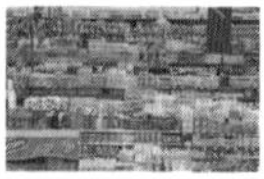

p. 85

Virtual and augmented reality is a clear route to thinking through our post-contemporary condition, "the body without organs," as articulated by Deleuze and Guattari and Antonin Artaud, who were among the first to foresee our future corporeal state. Ian Cheng's self-playing simulations and Jon Rafman's virtual-reality portals function as key examples of this kind of experience. Though virtual realities and the artificial intelligences that inhabit them may one day overtake us, they may also develop in surprisingly harmonious ways for humanity, where virtual

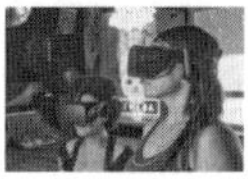
pp. 84–85

environments, or virtual procedures, or virtual events may come into normality, even banality. DiMoDA, the brainchild of the Chicago-based duo Alfredo Salazar-Caro and William Robertson, houses virtual art exhibitions navigable through VR headsets. But this is a mere scratch on the surface of things. Google, with its numerous VR platforms, including the sketchpad Tilt Brush and the headwear VIVE, along with competitors Oculus and Khora, are but a few of the companies that are extending the real into the virtual, making these technologies accessible to artists and audiences alike. These platforms will create new spaces for experiences and will be undoubtedly stretched beyond their formal limits. Indeed, artist Jeremy Bailey, an early adopter of the Xbox Kinect, a motion-sensor gaming device, used the apparatus to create augmented-reality performances, games, and other artistic scenarios, far from the intent of the Kinect's original function.

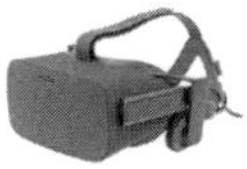
p. 85

Internet culture isn't just upon us, it's widespread. At the time of this writing, the San Francisco Museum of Modern Art has launched a program called Send Me, where audiences can text in requests such as "Show me an artwork that is red." In turn, Send Me would send back a whole variety of works embodying that color from its collection. Airport lounges are now filled with citizens speaking into thin air, with white Apple wireless headphones (AirPods) dangling from their ears, making them look like techno zombies. Friends continue testing new dating apps in pursuit of "perfect" love and everyday citizens are increasingly perplexed by the state of global politics in what has been dubbed a "post-truth" era. We have faith that online-petition sites such as change.org can elicit change. We believe we have the power to conquer the alt-right extremist believers who congregate online to mobilize offline in places such as Charlottesville. We are determined to insure that malicious figures such as Donald Trump can be repelled from ever again achieving office. We have the technology to unite, and if we cannot use it to create the environments these technologies or their creators actually believe they are bringing to reality, then we are fated to careen toward a post-apocalyptic era. But even still, the artists will be there, making work such as *The Hereafter Institute* (2015), where artist Gabriel Barcia-Colombo created a fictional company that can care for your digital self after your physical body is long gone.

Yet it is evident that so many of these tools, created by corporations, have been used to promote a neoliberal model of aesthetic experience. The artist Zach Blas calls the resistance to this ideological standpoint "contra-internet." Templating his thoughts on Paul B. Preciado's *Manifiesto contrasexual* (2002) and utilizing the work of technologists such as Alexander Galloway and Eugene Thacker, who have promoted how alternative digital spaces such as the deep web could be used for beneficial means, Blas argued:

- Critique the internet as a neoliberal structural model
- Acknowledge its classicism
- Refuse its standardization
- Find ways to radicalize it
- Consult alternatives
- Imagine that there is a space beyond the internet

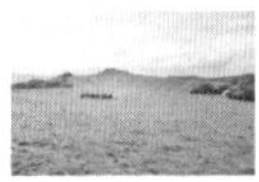
p. 86

Other artists such as Angelo Plessas have imagined the advent of non-digital safe spaces where one can detox from online society. In his yearly event *Eternal Internet Brotherhood and Sisterhood*, Plessas has created global campsites that offer discussions about the polemical conflicts the internet engenders. Inviting artists who engage with the internet as a primary tool for production and distribution, the event becomes a think tank for speaking, writing, and debating freely on what it might mean to exist in an alternative universe, whereby the internet returns to being a tool rather than a crutch, to enable the practice of art making.

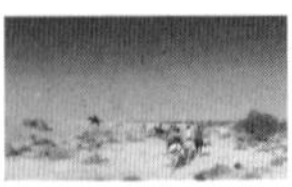
p. 87

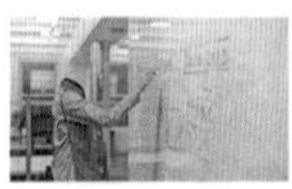
pp. 86–87

The collective DIS have also engaged with the force of the internet, having launched *Dis.Art*, what they're calling a "PBS for an emerging culture," a Netflix-like channel for "genre-nonconforming edutainment." A twisted hybrid of education and entertainment, the collective is subverting the way so-called millennials consume

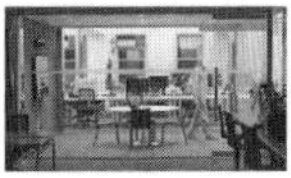

p. 86

information. Their TV channel, they argue, is a counterstrategy that allows artists to respond to social changes. While such resources for information and news remain under threat, they may also be an outmoded source for younger generations.

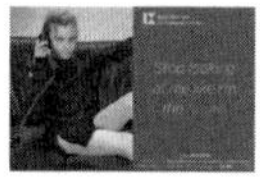

p. 87

While these examples exemplify how we deal with the digital age, it remains daunting how we keep up with its quickening evolutions. With all the endless operating-system updates, app-version upgrades, and generational devices that now emerge twice a year, at what point will we become too exhausted to go on? In a 2016 conversation with the architect Todd Reisz, we discussed “metabolic architecture,” a concept founded by Japanese architect Kenzō Tange, who believed that the architecture of cities should function like living organisms that keep growing and adapting in response not only to their environments, but to the needs of their inhabitants. There is something metabolic about the digital age, with its microchips and wireless connections, which enable virtual portals that keep us all patched in like a giant, intelligent creature with hyperlinked minds, where all of human knowledge is at our fingertips. But just as easily, this architecture can keep me under surveillance or manipulate my habits. I return to Zach Blas’s contra-internet manifesto: refuse to be standardized. There is a need to understand the tools that we use and to avoid risking homogeneity. “Hello, World” is most often the first phrase typed into a computer to introduce the influential C++ computer language to novice programmers. As new languages have emerged, however, it is perhaps time to say “goodbye” to the Internet’s perceived utopia, in order to create our own environments where we individually optimize its functionality and, in turn, our very existence.

Afterword

I wrote this book in the balmy heat of a Chicago summer in 2017, yet by the time this piece of writing reaches bookshelves in 2018, so much that I have exemplified will have been altered, or evolved, or even made obsolete. Indeed, even as I was considering pieces to highlight in my conclusion, I kept happening upon new technological innovations now in development that could bring hypothetical artistic practices, platforms, and aesthetic experiences into reality. I walk this path to the future filled with excitement, not because I wish to see the analogue world pass fully into a digital utopia, but because I see art as the foremost way of humanizing and engaging with this impending future. We're already aboard for the ride but we can't know where we are going, unless we keep our eyes open.

ALGORITHMIC PLAYLIST 1
Confessions, or My Most Played Videos on YouTube

When Adele paid tribute to George Michael at the 2017 Grammy Awards, I was devastated and subsequently moved by her ethereal, slowed-down take of the late singer's spirited hit "Fastlove." A song about quick hookups and hard sex became a song of constant longing to be noticed and desired by someone, anyone. On morning and evening runs down my street in Chicago, toward the cemetery at the end of North Glenwood Avenue in Edgewater, I would loop a YouTube upload of Adele's cover, the only high-quality audio version I could find, to play over and over. In the space of six months, I had listened to the song over 500 times, which added up to roughly 2,500 minutes, nearly 42 hours, almost 2 days. As crazy as that seems, all that time was, of course, spent running. Surely a good thing!

I point this out because not only do I know that Adele's cover of "Fastlove" is my most played online video, YouTube knows this too. Everyone has online habits that can be broken down and analyzed, even by external sources. In fact, Spotify has made an ad campaign based on extreme plays. On a billboard in Times Square, one reads: "Dear person who played 'Sorry' 42 times on Valentine's Day, what did you do?" Data crunching is no longer the province of statisticians, it has become cultural, allowing users an objective look at their tastes and engagements. For example, looking at some of my most streamed YouTube videos for music, it is obvious that my musical preferences gravitate toward saccharine, retro, and reverential compositions; not exactly the kinds of tunes that personal trainers encourage to put on to rev you up for aerobic activity. But whenever I plugged in my ear buds, these were the songs in which I wanted to lose myself, imagining how I would perform them at some Las Vegas lounge.

After "Fastlove," my second-most played YouTube music video was a smartphone-recorded rendition of Prince's "Purple Rain" performed impromptu by the cast of *The Color Purple* days after the artist's death. It was one of Jennifer Hudson's last performances with that cast and she killed it! I played that recording, despite its poor lo-fi quality, 377 times, roughly 1,885 minutes, or 31 hours, enraptured without fail every single time.

But I didn't always play these songs from beginning to end. Sometimes I jumped ahead to hear a specific high note or climax. This process of dragging a cursor or pin along a segment of the waveform is called "scrubbing," and out of my most played videos, most of the ones included on that list were ones I visited just to scrub to a specific note from a beloved song, often from studio tracks, but also to nuances that appear in live performances, late-night show appearances, reality-TV auditions, or anything else that had been unofficially recorded.

Here are eleven selections from my "Most Played" playlist:

1. Adele, "Fastlove." Written by George Michael. Recorded live at the 2017 Grammy Awards.
2. The cast of the Broadway musical *The Color Purple* (feat. Jennifer Hudson and Cynthia Erivo), "Purple Rain." Written by Prince. Recorded live at Bernard B. Jacobs Theater, New York City, April 21, 2016.
2. Sam Smith, "Writing's on the Wall." Written by Sam Smith and Jimmy Napes. Recorded live on the *Graham Norton Show*, 2015.
3. Sheryl Crow, "Safe and Sound." Written by Sheryl Crow. Recorded live at the Nippon Budokan, Tokyo, 2002.
4. Christina Aguilera, "At Last." Written by Mack Gordon and Harry Warren. Based on a cover by Etta James. Recorded live at VH1's TV special "Men Strike Back," 2000.
5. Idina Menzel, "Defying Gravity." Written by Stephen Schwartz. Recorded on the "Live: Barefoot at the Symphony" tour, 2012.

6. Trent Harmon, "Chandelier." Written by Sia. Recorded live for *American Idol*'s 14th season, 2015.
7. Kelly Clarkson, "Piece by Piece." Written by Greg Kurstin. Recorded live for *American Idol*'s "Farewell Season," 2016.
8. Patti Smith, "A Hard Rain's A-Gonna Fall." Written by Bob Dylan. Recorded live at the 2016 Nobel Prize ceremony, Stockholm.
9. Mariah Carey, "Vision of Love." Written by Mariah Carey and Ben Margulies. Recorded live on *Saturday Night Live*, October 27, 1990.
10. Whitney Houston, "Star-Spangled Banner." Written by Francis Scott Key and John Stafford Smith. Recorded live at Super Bowl XXV in Tampa, Florida, 1991.

There you go. I have no shame in reliving Mariah's big-hair days, no shame in listening to Whitney belt out the American national anthem, no shame in losing hours of my life to hearing Jennifer Hudson sing Prince, no shame in replaying Sheryl Crow's howling-till-it-cracks performances, no shame in loving Sam Smith's gentle vocal lisp, no shame in reliving Kelly Clarkson's most famous *American Idol* moments. This is my meme culture. This is my playlist. You're welcome to test it out, maybe something new will have taken its place by the time you are reading this book, something just as ostentatiously sentimental. I don't care. May all my street credibility blow up into thin ringlets of smoke!

ALGORITHMIC PLAYLIST 2
What Should I Watch?

It's a Friday morning and I am at home, having taken the day off to rest a sprained back muscle. I am sitting on my swivel lounge chair, something I probably shouldn't do, as I have been advised to lay flat on my back and to get up only to occasionally perform stretch exercises. But I want to be able to sit up and watch TV. Ten years ago, this would have involved flipping through channels, but now broadcast television has given way to streaming networks. With my Amazon Fire TV streaming device I have been able to aggregate my accounts with Amazon Prime, Netflix, HBO, and whatever else I would like to view on demand.

Here is a list of what I view during a morning of streaming surfing:

I Love Dick
I've been reading this book by Chris Kraus twenty years too late. She's a genius of the most epic proportions. She articulates very female but also very queer expressions of sexuality and desire. Jill Soloway's adaptation is commendable in many respects, but Kevin Bacon as Dick Hebdige, the infamous media scholar—why, oh why? He has the sexiness of an infomercial actor and the brains of a slab of bacon. Bad casting call.

Into the Forest
Too creepy; didn't watch.

Westworld
I don't mind science fiction so long as it's set in the future. I have no love for ultra-masculine cowboys or the Wild West.

Feud
What a divine portrayal of one of my favorite Hollywood rivalries, Joan Crawford and Bette Davis. I think that Jessica Lange whoops Susan Sarandon's ass in this depiction.

I forgot she was even acting. Ryan Murphy is genius. Who would have thought he would ever ascend beyond his former FX series, *Nip/Tuck*?

Big Little Lies
I would never live in Monterey, California, after this, or maybe I would. I was so seduced by the seascapes, but couldn't stop shirking from the violent, passive aggressiveness of seaside society. Getting to know Nicole Kidman over seven hours gave me a newfound love for her. As an abused spouse, she was pitch perfect. Reese Witherspoon was unlike I had ever seen her. Biting. Laura Dern made me compassionate about even the toughest of ice queens. Recommend!

Catastrophe
Bumbling husband Rob Delaney is the perfect counterpart to Sharon Horgan's lacerating Irish witticisms. Isn't he everyone's perfect husband? Don't we all want to spend quality time on the toilet quietly releasing our bowels, uninterrupted, with newspaper in hand?

RuPaul's Drag Race
Who said reality TV was dead? *RuPaul's Drag Race* is a mash-up of *America's Next Top Model* meets *Project Runway* meets *The Real World* with a heavy dose of identity politics thrown in.

Veep
Julia Louis-Dreyfus. Enough said.

The Good Fight
Part of the reason I moved to Chicago was because of how glamorized it was in *The Good Wife*. Alicia Florrick's facial expressions, which could move from desire to fear to anger in seconds, stirred feelings in me that are impossible to put into words. *The Good Fight*, its recent spin-off, is just about fine. We are lucky to have lawyer Diane Lockhart still being played by Christine Baranski.

Broad City
Rerun. Re-watch.

America's Next Top Model: Cycle 22
I got bored of this show after *Cycle 7*, that is until the producers started pitting

boys against girls to create sexual dynamism and dramatic dynamo that added an intriguing layer of narrative. I was truly inspired and in love with just about all of it, especially this season's winner, Nyle, a gorgeous deaf activist.

Unbreakable Kimmy Schmidt
Titus Andromedon's "Lemonade-ing" post-cruise-ship tour was one of the greatest moments in TV history. "I'm pretty but tough, like a diamond," he says. "Or beef jerky in a ball gown."

Sense 8
The Wachowski sisters! My heart breaks that this show is gone, canceled. I wanted to be part of the "Sensates," to be a member of their cluster.

Glow
I don't know what Netflix was thinking with this female boxing drama. I can't believe this was recommended to me and that I watched four episodes. I want my 3.5 hours back. Delete.

ALGORITHMIC PLAYLIST 3
Top Ten Social-Media "Friend" Suggestions

Facebook

1. Andy Sawyer, librarian at the Science-Fiction Foundation, University of Liverpool (1 mutual friend)
2. Paul Hewitt (4 mutual friends)
3. Bruce Munro Wright (6 mutual friends) (friended) (real-life friend)
4. Nick Leech, columnist and feature writer at the *National* (15 mutual friends)
5. Ann Webb (no mutual friends) (I did meet this person however, only four days before writing this. Creepy!)
6. Krista Thompson (3 mutual friends) (friended) (real-life friend)
7. Teju Cole, writer (1 mutual friend) (not sure if it's a fake profile or not)
8. Christopher Griffin, Courtauld Institute (6 mutual friends)
9. Esther May Campbell (13 mutual friends)
10. Eric Liknaitzky (no mutual friends) (creepy, he's a high school student)

Instagram

1. defneayas_, followed by antoniamcarver +7 more
2. theneurologist, followed by milovanfarronato
3. kpp305, followed by monieulitz
4. sculptinator, followed by victoriamaysiddall
5. ghawde, follows you
6. capriceh55, followed by mbkayne
7. studioteresacol-lins, followed by mrbenstephenson
8. eatsecondbreak-fasts, new to Instagram
9. garyfmetzner, follows you
10. alfredtarazi, followed by antoniamcarver +7 more

Twitter

1. @urbananalytics
2. @guardian
3. @ToyotaSD
4. @udibc
5. @michaelgeller
6. @chefdannygrant
7. @IntracorpCanada
8. @NewYorker
9. @eightbar_chi
10. @dzeij_dii

LinkedIn

1. Rachel Coker (intern where I work)
2. Juliane Victor
3. Arnout Mampaey
4. Amanprit Sandhu (went to college with her)
5. Paul Kelly
6. Allan Sekula (dead)
7. Chang Sun
8. Jussi Parikka
9. Miriam Sakwa
10. Victoria Beesley (went to college with her)

ALGORITHMIC PLAYLIST 4
Myself

Most searched keywords for those stalking Omar Kholeif on Google: Art After the Internet, age, MCA Chicago, born, email, books, Jeddah childhood, circa 1994, Instagram, bio

People who search for Omar Kholeif also search for: James Richards, Sarah Perks,

Jason Wood, Sophia Al-Maria

Number of results for Omar Kholeif on Google: 27,100 results

Number of results for Omar Kholeif on Yahoo: 3,920 results

Number of results for Omar Kholeif on Duck Duck Go: 79

Number of results for Omar Kholeif on Bing: 442

ALGORITHMIC PLAYLIST 5
Suggestions from Amazon That Appeared as I Wrote This Book

More items to consider

- *The Happiness Equation: Want Nothing + Do Anything = Have Everything* by Neil Pasricha
- *The Seventh Sense: Power, Fortune, and Survival in the Age of Networks* by Joshua Cooper Ramo
- *Pause: Harnessing the Life-Changing Power of Giving Yourself a Break* by Rachael O'Meara
- *Bad Choices: How Algorithms Can Help You Think Smarter and Happier* by Ali Almossawi
- *The School of Greatness: A Real-World Guide to Living Bigger, Loving Deeper, and Leaving a Legacy* by Lewis Howes
- *Stick with It: A Scientifically Proven Process for Changing Your Life—for Good* by Sean Young
- *Simply Brilliant: How Great Organizations Do Ordinary Things In Extraordinary Ways* by William C. Taylor

Inspired by my shopping trends

– *The Liberal Imagination* by Lionel Trilling
– *Mimesis: The Representation of Reality in Western Literature* by Erich Auerbach
– *The Protestant Ethic and the "Spirit" of Capitalism* by Max Weber
– *Young Radicals: In the War for American Ideals* by Jeremy McCarter
– *The Reckless Mind: Intellectuals in Politics* by Mark Lilla
– *Escape from Freedom* by Erich Fromm

Recommendations for you
– *Time* by Amelia Groom
– *The Transhumanist Wager* by Zoltan Istvan
– *The Body Builders: Inside the Science of the Engineered Human* by Adam Piore
– *Heart of the Machine: Our Future in a World of Artificial Emotional Intelligence* by Richard Yonck

For a night in
– *Queen Sugar*
– *Love & Hip Hop: Hollywood*
– *The Truman Show*
– *Daughters of the Dust*

New for you
– *Famously Single*
– *Claws*
– *Face Off: Divide & Conquer*
– *Big Brother*

(Am I a reality-TV whore?)

SELECTED BIBLIOGRAPHY

Alpyadin, Ethem. *Machine Learning: The New AI*. Cambridge, MA: MIT Press, 2016.

Barry, Robert. *The Music of the Future*. London: Repeater Books, 2017.

Basar, Shumon, Douglas Coupland, and Hans Ulrich Obrist, eds. *The Age of Earthquakes: A Guide to the Extreme Present*. London: Penguin, 2015.

Berger, John. *Ways of Seeing*. London: Penguin, 1972.

Bridle, James. "The New Aesthetic and Its Politics." *booktwo.org.com* (blog), June 12, 2013. http://booktwo.org/notebook/new-aesthetic-politics.

Butler, Judith. *Notes Toward a Performative Theory of Assembly*. Cambridge, MA: Harvard University Press, 2015.

Carr, Nicholas. *The Shallows: What the Internet Is Doing to Our Brains*. New York: W. W. Norton & Company, 2011.

Coupland, Douglas. *Bit Rot*. London: William Heinemann, 2016.

Debord, Guy. *The Society of the Spectacle*. Translated by Donald Nicholson-Smith. New York: Zone Books, 1994.

Deleuze, Gilles and Felix Guattari. *A Thousand Plateaus: Capitalism and Schizophrenia*. Translated by Brian Massumi. Minneapolis: University of Minnesota Press, 1987.

Fisher, Mark. *Ghosts of My Life: Writings on Depression, Hauntology and Lost Futures*. London: Zero Books, 2014.

Foster, Hal. *The Art-Architecture Complex*. London: Verso, 2013.

Goldsmith, Kenneth. *Wasting Time on the Internet*. New York: Harper Perennial, 2016.

Goodfellow, Ian, Yoshua Bengio, and Aaron Courville, eds. *Deep Learning*. Cambridge, MA: MIT Press, 2016.

Greengard, Samuel. *The Internet of Things*. Cambridge, MA: MIT Press, 2015.

Gronlund, Melissa. *Contemporary Art and Digital Culture*. London: Routledge, 2016.

Jenkins, Henry. *Convergence Culture: Where Old and New Media Collide*. New York: NYU Press, 2008.

Kholeif, Omar, ed. *You Are Here: Art after the Internet*. Manchester: Cornerhouse, 2014.

Kholeif, Omar. "Metabolic History." In *The Rumors of the World: Rethinking Trust in the Age of the Internet*, edited by Omar Kholeif. Berlin: Sternberg Press, 2015.

Klein, Naomi. "Cross-Embedded Media: An Introduction." *Vision, Memory, Media*, edited by Omar Kholeif and Andreas Brøgger. Liverpool: Liverpool University Press, 2011.

Mackay, Robin and Armen Avanessian, eds. *#Accelerate: The Accelerationist Reader*. Falmouth: Urbanomic, 2014.

McLuhan, Marshall. *Understanding Media: The Extensions of Man*. Cambridge, MA: MIT Press, 1964.

Mitchell, W. J. T. *What Do Pictures Want? The Lives and Loves of Images*. Chicago: University of Chicago Press, 2005.

Morris, Catherine. *9 Evenings Reconsidered: Art, Theater, and Engineering*. Cambridge, MA: MIT Press, 2006.

Nagle, Angela. *Kill All Normies: Online Culture Wars from 4Chan and Tumblr to Trump and the Alt-Right*. London: Zero Books, 2017.

O'Connell, Mark. *To Be a Machine: Adventures among Cyborgs, Utopians, Hackers, and the Futurists Solving the Modest Problem of Death*. New York: Doubleday, 2017.

Paglen, Trevor and Rebecca Solnit. *Invisible: Covert Operations and Classified Landscapes*. New York: Aperture, 2010.

Paik, Nam June. "Media Planning for the Postindustrial Society: The 21st Century Is Now Only 26 Years Away," 1974. *Medien Kunst Netz*. http://medienkunstnetz.de/source-text/33.

Poitras, Laura and Jay Sanders. *Astro Noise: A Survival Guide for Living under Total Surveillance*. New York: Whitney Museum of American Art, 2016.

Steyerl, Hito. *The Wretched of the Screen*. Berlin: Sternberg Press, 2013.

Swartz, Aaron. "Freedom to Connect: Aaron Swartz (1986–2013) on Victory to Save Open Internet, Fight Online Censors." *Democracy Now*, January 14, 2012. http://democracynow.org/2013/1/14/freedom_to_connect_aaron_swartz_1986.

Zuckerman, Ethan. *Digital Cosmopolitans: Why We Think the Internet Connects Us, Why It Doesn't, and How to Rewire It*. New York: W. W. Norton & Company, 2013.

ORGANIZATIONS

Abandon Normal Devices
andfestival.org.uk

Ars Electronica
aec.at

Arsenal - Institute for Film and Video Art
arsenal-berlin.de/en/home.html

Centre for Contemporary Art, Glasgow
cca-glasgow. com

Edith-Russ-Haus für Medienkunst
edith-russ-haus.de/home.html

Electronic Arts Intermix
eai.org

Eyebeam
eyebeam.org

FACT (Foundation for Art and Creative Technology)
fact.co.uk

HOME
homemcr.org

Impakt Festival
impakt.nl

Julia Stoschek Collection
julia-stoschek-collection.net

Light Industry
lightindustry.org

LUX
lux.org.uk

MAAT - Museum of Art, Architecture and Technology
maat.pt/en

MIT Program in Art, Culture and Technology
act.mit.edu

Nam June Paik Art Center
njpac-en.ggcf.kr

NEW INC
newinc.org

Rhizome
rhizome.org

SPACE STUDIOS
spacestudios.org

The Kitchen
thekitchen.org

V Tape
vtape.org

V2_, Lab for the Unstable Media
v2.nl

Video Data Bank
vdb.org

Werkleitz Festival
werkleitz.de

Western Front
front.bc.ca

Worm
worm.org

Zabludwoicz Collection
zabludowiczcollection.com

ZKM | Zentrum für Kunst und Medien
zkm.de

PLATFORMS

Artsy
artsy.net

Contemporary Art Daily
contemporaryartdaily.com

Streaming Museum
streamingmuseum.org

s[edition]
seditionart.com

Paddle8
paddle8.com

art:i:curate
articurate.net

UbuWeb
ubuweb.com

CREDITS

Every effort has been made to contact the rightful owners with regards to copyrights and permissions. We apologize for any inadvertent errors or omissions.

COVER
Martin Parr, *Louvre, Paris, France*, 2012. © Martin Parr / Magnum Photos / Agentur Focus.

LOOKING AT ART AFTER THE INTERNET
p. 10 Whitney Museum of American Art, view from 12th Avenue, 2015. The new building, designed by Renzo Piano Building Workshop, opened May 1, 2015 at 99 Gansevoort Street, New York, NY. Photo: Timothy Schenck. Courtesy of Whitney Museum.

p. 11 Tate Modern's new extension, the Blavatnik Building, by Herzog and de Meuron, London, June 19, 2016. © Eric Flamant | Dreamstime.com.

p. 10 The north face of Daniel Libeskind's Michael Lee-Chin Crystal extension to the Royal Ontario Museum, Toronto, January 28, 2008. © Gary Blakeley | Dreamstime.com.

p. 11 Philippe Parreno, *Anywhen*, 2016. Installation view of Hyundai Commission 2016, Tate Modern, London. Courtesy of Pilar Corrias, London; Gladstone Gallery; and Esther Schipper, Berlin. Photo: Andrea Rossetti. © Philippe Parreno.

p. 12 Eva and Franco Mattes, *BEFNOED*, 2016. Video, screen, custom wall bracket, various cables. Dimensions variable. Exhibition view, Carroll/Fletcher, London. Courtesy of the artists.

pp. 12–13 3-D cat jump GIF, 2015. Courtesy of giphy.com. https://giphy.com/gifs/cat-3d-jump-mOGyA3JDNxQIO.

p. 12 Trump GIF, 2017. Courtesy of giphy.com. https://giphy.com/gifs/cat-trump-jLWcWtRG8QAkU.

pp. 12–13 Trevor Paglen, *Autonomy Cube*, 2015. Plexiglas cube, computer components, 50 × 50 × 50 cm. Courtesy of the artist; Metro Pictures, New York; Altman Siegel Gallery, San Francisco.

p. 13 Trevor Paglen, *Autonomy Cube*, 2015. Plexiglas cube, computer components, 40 x 40 × 40 cm. Courtesy of the artist; Metro Pictures, New York; Altman Siegel Gallery, San Francisco.

pp. 14–15 James Bridle, *Citizen Ex*, 2015. Website and browser extension, http://citizen-ex.com. Courtesy of the artist.

p. 14 Exterior environment of DiMoDA, 2015. From "DiMoDA 2.0: Morphé Presence." Courtesy of DiMoDA.

pp. 14–15 "DiMoDA 2.0: Morphé Presence," Superchief Gallery, Brooklyn, September 9–October 14, 2016. Works from left to right: Theo Triantafyllidis, *Self Portrait (Interior)*, 2016; Rosa Menkman, *DCT: Syphoning. The 64th Interval*, 2016. Courtesy of DiMoDA.

p. 15 Theo Triantafyllidis, *Self Portrait (Interior)*, 2016. In "DiMoDA 2.0: Morphé Presence." Courtesy of DiMoDA.

p. 16 Rosa Menkman, *DCT: Syphoning. The 64th Interval*, 2016. VR for Occulus Rift. In "DiMoDA 2.0: Morphé Presence." Courtesy of DiMoDA.

p. 17 Theo Triantafyllidis, *Self Portrait (Interior)*, 2016. In "DiMoDA 2.0: Morphé Presence." Courtesy of DiMoDA.

THE NEW SELF
pp. 18–19 Mendi + Keith Obadike, *Blackness for Sale*, 2001. Courtesy of the artists.

p. 18 Jayson Musson as Hennessy Youngman, 2010. Courtesy of the artist and Salon 94, New York.

pp. 18–20 Ryan Trecartin, *P.opular S.ky (section ish)*, 2009. HD video, 43:51 min. Courtesy of Regen Projects, Los Angeles; and Sprüth Magers. © Ryan Trecartin.

pp. 20–21 Ryan Trecartin, *Sibling Topics (section a)*, 2009. HD video, 51:26 min. Courtesy of Regen Projects, Los Angeles; and Sprüth Magers. © Ryan Trecartin.

pp. 20–21 Ryan Trecartin, *KCorealNC.K (section a)*, 2009. HD video, 33:05 min. Courtesy of Regen Projects, Los Angeles; and Sprüth Magers. © Ryan Trecartin.

p. 22 Jeremy Bailey, *The Web I Want*, 2015. Courtesy of the artist.

p. 23 Jeremy Bailey, *The Future of Television*, 2012. Courtesy of the artist.

p. 22 Amalia Ulman, *Excellences & Perfections (Instagram Update, 1st June 2014)*, 2015. Courtesy of the artist and Arcadia Missa.

pp. 22–23 Casey Jane Ellison, *The Right & Left Brains of Casey Jane's—Episode 1*, October 15, 2015. Video, 4:10 min. Courtesy of the artist and BB Dakota.

p. 24 Casey Jane Ellison, *Touching the Art—Episode 1: Catherine Opie, Bettina Korek, Jori Finkel*, July 17, 2014. Video, 6:43 minutes. Courtesy of the artist and Ovation.

p. 25 Casey Jane Ellison, *IT'S SO IMPORTANT TO SEEM WONDERFUL*, December 17, 2012. Video, 5:48 min. Courtesy of the artist and MOCAtv, the Museum of Contemporary Art, Los Angeles.

pp. 24–25 Jacolby Satterwhite, *Reifying Desire 6*, 2014. 3-D animation and video. Courtesy of the artist.

p. 25 Wu Tsang, *A day in the life of bliss*, 2014. Two-channel HD video installation, surround sound, projection screens, mirror, two-way mirror, seating, 20 min. Installation view: "A day in the life of bliss," Galerie Isabella Bortolozzi, Berlin, May 2, 2014–July 31, 2015. Courtesy of the artist and Galerie Isabella Bortolozzi, Berlin.

pp. 26–27 Wu Tsang, *A day in the life of bliss*, 2014. Two-channel HD video installation, surround sound, projection screens, mirror, two-way mirror, seating, 20 min. Installation view: ICA, London, April 22–June 21, 2015. Photo: Mark Blower. Courtesy of the artist and Galerie Isabella Bortolozzi, Berlin.

p. 27 Zackary Drucker and Rhys Ernst, *Relationship, #58*, 2008–14. Chromogenic print, 23 × 30 in. Courtesy of the artists and Luis De Jesus Los Angeles.

p. 26 Zackary Drucker and Rhys Ernst, *Relationship, #23 (The Longest Day of the Year)*, 2008–14. Chromogenic print, 13.3 × 20 in. Courtesy of the artists and Luis De Jesus Los Angeles.

p. 27 Zackary Drucker and Rhys Ernst, *Relationship, #33*, 2008–14. Chromogenic print, 7 x 10 in. Courtesy of the artists and Luis De Jesus Los Angeles.

p. 28 Zach Blas, *Queer Technologies: Disingenuous Bar*, 2008. Installation detail, New Wight Gallery, University of California, Los Angeles, 2008. Courtesy of the artist.

p. 29 Zach Blas, *Queer Technologies: Technologies: transCoder: Queer Programming Anti-Language*, 2011. Installation detail, "SPECULATIVE," Los Angeles Contemporary Exhibitions (LACE), 2011. Courtesy of the artist.

p. 28 Zach Blas, *Queer Technologies: Gay Bombs: User's Manual*, 2008. Installation detail, New Wight Gallery, University of California, Los Angeles. Courtesy of the artist.

pp. 28–29 Zach Blas, *Queer Technologies: Gay Bombs*, 2011. Installation detail, "SPECULATIVE," Los Angeles Contemporary Exhibitions (LACE). Courtesy of the artist.

p. 29 Zach Blas, *Queer Technologies: ENgenderingGenderChangers*, 2008. Installation detail, "Exit Strategies," New Wight Gallery, University of California, Los Angeles. Courtesy of the artist.

pp. 30–31 Zach Blas, *Facial Weaponization Suite*, 2015. Installation detail, "The Theory of Colour," curated by Cuauhtémoc Medina, Helena Chávez, and Alejandra Labastida. Museo Universitario Arte Contemporáneo (MUAC), Mexico City, September 27, 2014–February 7, 2015. Courtesy of the artist.

p. 31 Zach Blas, *Facial Weaponization Suite: Fag Face Mask*, Los Angeles, October 20, 2012. Photo: Christopher O'Leary. Courtesy of the artist.

p. 30 Zach Blas, *Facial Weaponization Suite: Fag Face Scanning Station*, 2013. Reclaim: pride with ONE Archives and RECAPS Magazine, Christopher Street West Pride Festival, West Hollywood, June 8, 2013. Photo: David Evans Frantz. Courtesy of the artist.

p. 31 Frank Benson, *Juliana*, 2014–15. Bronze and polyurethane acrylic paint, 138 × 122 × 61 cm. Courtesy of the artist and Sadie Coles HQ.

TOUCH ME

p. 32 Petra Cortright, *Call Trees VC++*, 2014. Digital painting on aluminium, 121.92 × 91.44 cm. Photo: Mark Woods. Courtesy of the artist and Foxy Production, New York.

p. 32 Petra Cortright, *photo_graphicStudentCreditCard:foun@clicnetSRVR*, 2016. Digital painting on Belgian linen, 169.86 x 120.97 cm. Photo: Mark Woods. Courtesy of the artist and Foxy Production, New York.

pp. 32–33 Jon Rafman, *New Age Demanded (Futurisimo Red to Green)*, 2013. 3-D polyamide print, auto body paint, 45 × 30 × 34 cm. Courtesy of the artist and Seventeen.

p. 33 Jon Rafman, *New Age Demanded (Richter)*, 2011. Mixed media, archival pigment print, 244 × 183 cm. Courtesy of the artist and Seventeen.

p. 32 Jon Rafman, *New Age Demanded (Kline)*, 2011. Mixed media, archival pigment print, 244 × 183 cm. Courtesy of the artist and Seventeen.

p. 32 Jon Rafman, *New Age Demanded (Globular Marble)*, 2014. Archival pigment print mounted on dibond, 152.4 × 101.6 cm. Courtesy of the artist and Seventeen.

p. 33 Jon Rafman, *New Age Demanded (Sface Oak)*, 2017. CNC-milled wood, varnish, 56 × 46 × 29 cm. Courtesy of the artist and Seventeen.

p. 33 Jon Rafman, *Trans-dimensional Serpent*, 2016. Oculus Rift VR headsets, custom-built personal computers, VR program, fiberglass, faux-leather, LEDs, 4:30 min. Unique installation, 600 × 400 × 150 cm. Installation view, Seventeen at Frieze Focus London, 2016. Photo: Damian Griffiths. Courtesy of the artist and Seventeen.

p. 34 Aleksandra Domanović, *Little Sister II*, 2013. Laser-sintered PA plastic, polyurethane, Soft-Touch & brass finish, 9 × 11 × 22 cm. Courtesy of the artist and Tanya Leighton, Berlin.

p. 35 Aleksandra Domanović, *Torches of Freedom*, 2013. Laser-sintered PA plastic, polyurethane, Soft-Touch & brass finish, 9 x 11 × 26 cm. Courtesy of the artist and Varon Collection, Monaco.

p. 34 Aleksandra Domanović, *Relay Runner (Sanija Hyseni 1979)*, 2013. Laser-sintered PA plastic, polyurethane, Soft-Touch & brass finish, 9 × 23 × 27 cm. Courtesy of the artist and Tanya Leighton, Berlin.

p. 35 Aleksandra Domanović, *Alan's Apple*, 2013. Laser-sintered PA plastic, polyurethane, Soft-Touch & brass finish, 9 × 11 × 19.5 cm. Courtesy of the artist and Tanya Leighton, Berlin.

pp. 36–37 Oliver Laric, *Versions (Missile Variations)*, 2010. Airbrush on dibond, 70 x 100 cm. Courtesy of the artist and Tanya Leighton, Berlin.

p. 38 Oliver Laric, *Sleeping Boy*, 2016. Stereolithography and selective laser sintering, polyamide, polished epoxy, TuskXC2700T, 55 x 111.5 × 101.5 cm. Courtesy of the artist and Tanya Leighton, Berlin.

pp. 38–39 Antoine Catala, *:)*, 2014. 3-D printed ABS plastic, steel, motor, plasti-dip, electronics, 27.94 × 50.80 × 30.48 cm. Photo: Andy Keate. Courtesy of the artist; 47 Canal, New York; and Pilar Corrias, London.

pp. 38–39 Antoine Catala, *(::( )::) (band-aid)*, 2014. Foam coated in plastic, motor, steel, plastic, electronics, power supply, 27.94 × 121.92 × 30.48 cm. Photo: Andy Keate. Courtesy of the artist; 47 Canal, New York; and Pilar Corrias, London.

p. 39 Josh Tonsfeldt, *Untitled*, 2015. LCD television, digital video, carbon fiber, fiberglass, CFL tubes, dust mask, pigment print on hydrographic film, pigment inks, resin, 76.2 × 139.7 × 152.4 cm. Courtesy of the artist and Simon Preston Gallery, New York.

pp. 40–41 Ben Schumacher, *Rebirth of the Bathhouse, server room detail 1:1*, 2014. Cable management racks, glass, polymer powder print, vinyl, steel, 213.4 × 30.5 × 375.9 cm. Photo: © Genevieve Hanson. Courtesy of the artist and Bortolami, New York.

p. 42 Daniel Steegmann Mangrané, *Phantom (Kingdom of all the animals and all the beasts is my name)*, 2014–15. Oculus Rift VR headset, Unity 3-D forest scan, motion-capture technology, custom ceiling grid. Developed by ScanLAB Projects, London. As installed, 380 × 579 × 408 cm, installation height variable. Exhibition view: "Spiral

Forest (kingdom of all the animals and all the beast is my name)," Esther Schipper, Berlin, 2015. Photo: © Andrea Rossetti. Courtesy of the artist and Esther Schipper, Berlin.

p. 43 Daniel Steegmann Mangrané, *Phantom (Kingdom of all the animals and all the beasts is my name)*, 2014–15. Oculus Rift virtual reality headset, Unity 3-D forest scan, motion capture technology, custom ceiling grid. Developed by ScanLAB Projects, London. As installed, 380 × 579 × 408 cm, installation height variable. Photo: © Daniel Steegmann Mangrané. Courtesy of the artist and Esther Schipper, Berlin.

pp. 42–43 Ian Cheng, *Emissary Forks at Perfection*, 2015–16. Live simulation and story, infinite duration, sound, dimensions variable. Courtesy of the artist; Pilar Corrias, London; Gladstone Gallery; and Standard (Oslo).

pp. 44–45 Ian Cheng, *Emissary Forks for You*, 2016. Live simulation; infinite duration, sound, Google Tango tablets. Courtesy of the artist and Migros Museum für Gegenwartskunst.

DON'T CONTROL ME

pp. 46–47 James Bridle, *The Right To Flight*, 2014. Installation, London, UK. http://right-to-flight.com. Courtesy of the artist.

p. 47 James Bridle, *Drone Shadow 002*, 2012. Installation, Istanbul, Turkey. http://booktwo.org/notebook/drone-shadows/. Courtesy of the artist.

p. 46 James Bridle, *Drone Shadow 003*, 2013. Installation, Brighton, UK. http://booktwo.org/notebook/drone-shadows-dispositions/. Courtesy of the artist.

p. 46–47 James Bridle, *Drone Shadow 004*, 2013. Installation, Washington, DC, USA. Courtesy of the artist.

p. 47 James Bridle, *Drone Shadow 006*, 2013. Installation, London, UK. Photo: Steve Stills/stevestills.com. Courtesy of the artist.

p. 48 Trevor Paglen, *NSA/GCHQ Surveillance Base, Bude, Cornwall, UK*, 2015. C-print, 91.44 × 121.92 cm. Courtesy of the artist; Metro Pictures, New York; Altman Siegel Gallery, San Francisco.

p. 49 Trevor Paglen, *National Security Agency, Ft. Meade, Maryland*, 2014. C-print, 45.72 × 68.58 cm. Courtesy of the artist; Metro Pictures, New York; Altman Siegel Gallery, San Francisco.

p. 48 Trevor Paglen, *National Geospatial-Intelligence Agency, Springfield, Virginia*, 2014. C-print, 45.72 × 68.58 cm. Courtesy of the artist; Metro Pictures, New York; Altman Siegel Gallery, San Francisco.

pp. 48–49 Trevor Paglen, *National Reconnaissance Office, Chantilly, Virginia*, 2014. C-print, 45.72 × 68.58 cm. Courtesy of the artist; Metro Pictures, New York; Altman Siegel Gallery, San Francisco.

p. 49 Trevor Paglen, *National Security Agency, Ft. Meade, Maryland*, 2013. C-print, 90.49 × 134.62 cm. Courtesy of the artist; Metro Pictures, New York; Altman Siegel Gallery, San Francisco.

p. 50 Taryn Simon and Aaron Swartz, *Image Atlas, Border, 9/30/16, 12:19 PM (Eastern Standard Time)*, 2012. Courtesy of the artists and Gagosian.

p. 51 Google Street View car, Subaru Service Center, Jersey City, NJ, November 2, 2016. Photo: Luigi Novi. © Luigi Novi / Wikimedia Commons / CC 4.0.

p. 50 Jon Rafman, *24 Rua Maria Ortiz, Santo André, São Paulo, Brazil*, 2012. From the series "The Nine Eyes of Google Street View," 2008–ongoing. Archival pigment print mounted on dibond, 101.6 × 162.6 cm. Courtesy of the artist.

p. 51 Jon Rafman, *353 Rua Bento Freitas, São Paulo, Brazil*, 2010. From the series "The Nine Eyes of Google Street View," 2008–ongoing. Archival pigment print mounted on dibond, 101.6 × 162.6 cm. Courtesy of the artist.

p. 52 Jon Rafman, *Havlíčkovo nábřeží, Ostrava, Czech Republic*, 2013. From the series "The Nine Eyes of Google Street View," 2008–ongoing. Archival pigment print mounted on dibond, 91 × 121 cm. Courtesy of the artist.

pp. 52–53 Jon Rafman, *176 Rua Ligia Maria, Salvador, Bahia, Brazil*, 2013. From the series "The Nine Eyes of Google Street View," 2008–ongoing. Archival pigment print mounted on dibond, 101.6 × 162.6 cm. Courtesy of the artist.

p. 53 Jon Rafman, *Unknown Road, Carltonville, Johannesburg, South Africa*, 2012. From the series "The Nine Eyes of Google Street View," 2008–ongoing. Archival pigment print mounted on dibond, 101.6 x 162.6 cm. Courtesy of the artist.

p. 52 Jon Rafman, *77 S Gabouri St, Ste. Genevieve, Missouri, United States*, 2017. From the series "The Nine Eyes of Google Street View," 2008–ongoing. Archival pigment print mounted on dibond, 101.6 × 172.7 cm. Courtesy of the artist.

pp. 52–53 Jon Rafman, *Mexico 45, Silao Guanajuato, Mexico*, 2011. From the series "The Nine Eyes of Google Street View," 2008–ongoing. Archival pigment print mounted on dibond, 101.6 × 162.6 cm. Courtesy of the artist.

p. 53 Jon Rafman, *75 Na Podskaiku, Humenne, Presov Region, Slovakia #1*, 2012. From the series "The Nine Eyes of Google Street View," 2008–ongoing. Archival pigment print mounted on dibond, 101.6 × 162.6 cm. Courtesy of the artist.

pp. 54–55 Andrew Norman Wilson, *Workers Leaving the Googleplex*, 2009–11. HD video, 11 min. Courtesy of the artist.

pp. 54–55 Constant Dullaart, *The Censored Internet*, 2013–14. Website, custom router, flags, LED lights. Courtesy of the artist and Carroll/Fletcher, London.

p. 55 Constant Dullart, *Rave Lecture*, 2013–15. Performative lecture series. Courtesy of the artist and Upstream Gallery Amsterdam.

pp. 56–57 Sophia Al-Maria, *Black Friday*, 2016. Digital video, color, sound, 16:36 min. Installation view, Whitney Museum of American Art, New York, 2016. Courtesy of the artist and The Third Line.

pp. 56–57 Sophia Al-Maria, *The Litany*, 2016. Sand, glitter, glass, smartphones, computer screens, tablet computers, USB cables with multichannel looped digital video, color and b/w, sound; durations variable. Courtesy of the artist and The Third Line.

p. 57 DIS, *Positive Ambiguity (beard, lecturn, teleprompter, wind machine, confidence)*, 2015. Courtesy of DIS and Project Native Informant, London.

pp. 58–61 Hito Steyerl, *How Not to Be Seen: A Fucking Didactic Educational .MOV File*, 2013. HD video, single screen in architectural environment, 15:52 min. Image: CC 4.0 Hito Steyerl. Courtesy of the artist and Andew Kreps Gallery, New York.

p. 60 Jill Magid, *Surveillance Shoe*, 2000. IR surveillance camera, battery pack, wireless transmitter. Courtesy of Jill Magid; Labor, Mexico City; Untilthen, Paris.

pp. 60–61 Jill Magid, *Surveillance Shoe*, 2000. B/w surveillance footage produced from surveillance shoe, 6 min. Courtesy of Jill Magid; Labor, Mexico City; Untilthen, Paris.

p. 61 Wafaa Bilal, *3rdi*, 2010–11. Year-long performance. © Wafaa Bilal. Courtesy of Wafaa Bilal and Mathaf: Arab Museum of Modern Art.

PLAY WITH ME

p. 62 Cory Arcangel, *Super Mario Clouds*, 2002–ongoing. Installation view. Handmade hacked Super Mario Brothers cartridge and Nintendo NES video game system. Photo: Daniel Terna. Image courtesy of Cory Arcangel. © Cory Arcangel.

pp. 62–63 Cory Arcangel, *Drei Klavierstücke op. 11*, 2009. Single-channel video, YouTube, 15:58 min. Image courtesy of Cory Arcangel. © Cory Arcangel.

p. 63 Eva and Franco Mattes, *My Generation*, 2010. Video, 13:18 min., broken computer, CRT monitor, loudspeakers, keyboard, mouse, various cables. Dimensions variable. Exhibition view, Fotomuseum Winterthur. Photo: Christian Schwager. Courtesy of the artists.

pp. 62–63 Thomson and Craighead, *More Songs of Innocence and of Experience*, 2013. Karaoke videos, mic, amp, and unicol stand. Installation view. Courtesy of the artists.

pp. 63–65 Hito Steyerl, *Factory of the Sun*, 2015. Installation view: German Pavillion, 56th Venice Biennale, 2015. Photo: Manuel Reinartz. Courtesy of the artist and Andrew Kreps Gallery, New York.

p. 65 DIS, *The Island (KEN)*, 2015. Installation view, "CO-WORKERS," Musée d'Art Moderne de la Ville de Paris, 2015. Courtesy of DIS and Project Native Informant.

pp. 64–65 Chris Collins, *Hitch (http://tryhit.ch)*, 2017. Artist website. Courtesy of the artist.

p. 66 Rafaël Rozendaal, *Lots Of Many .com*, 2017. Dimensions variable, duration infinite. Courtesy of the artist.

pp. 66–67 Rafaël Rozendaal, *Floating The .com*, 2016. Dimensions variable, duration infinite. Courtesy of the artist.

p. 67 Rafaël Rozendaal, *Future Is Uncertain .com*, 2013. Dimensions variable, duration infinite. Courtesy of the artist.

p. 66 Rafaël Rozendaal, *Float Bounce .com*, 2016. Dimensions variable, duration infinite. Courtesy of the artist and Takuma Collection.

pp. 66–67 Rafaël Rozendaal, *Remotely Distant .com*, 2014. Dimensions variable, duration infinite. Courtesy of the artist.

p. 67 Rafaël Rozendaal, *Neo Geo City .com*, 2014. Dimensions Variable, duration infinite. Courtesy of the artist and collection of Jeremy Bailey.

p. 68 Guthrie Lonergan, *guthrielonergan.com*, 2008. Website. Courtesy of the artist.

pp. 68–69 Guthrie Lonergan, *Built with Indexhibit*, 2016. Museum website widget. Courtesy of the artist.

p. 69 Email of complaint to the Hammer Museum about Guthrie Lonergan's *Built with Indexhibit*, June 10, 2016. Courtesy of the artist.

DON'T SHOOT ME; I'M READY FOR AN UPRISING

p. 70 Egyptian revolution, Cairo, January 25, 2011. © Edwardgerges | Dreamstime.com.

pp. 70–71 Image from a militant website posted January 7, 2014, showing a convoy of vehicles and fighters from ISIS in Iraq's Anbar Province. © picture alliance/AP Photo.

pp. 70–71 Iman Issa, *Proposal for a Crystal Building*, 2003. Detail, treated image of the structure in the center of Tahrir Square, 29.7 × 42 cm. Courtesy of the artist and Rodeo, London.

p. 71 Egyptians gather in Tahrir Square, June 2, 2012. Photo: Fredrik Persson. © picture alliance/dpa.

p. 72 Google search result for "Iraq war," November 15, 2017, 11:40 a.m. Courtesy of Google.

p. 73 Google search result for "Egyptian revolution," November 15, 2017, 11:40 a.m. Courtesy of Google.

p. 72 Tahrir Square, February 8, 2011. Photo: Lilian Wagdy / The Egyptian Liberal / Wikicommons / CC-2.0.

p. 73 Supporters of presidential candidate Mohamed Morsi demonstrate against disputed election results, Tahrir Square, June 24, 2012. Photo: Mohamed Messara. © picture alliance/dpa.

pp. 74–75 Mosireen, Tuesday Night Screenings, Cairo, November 15, 2011. Photo: Mosireen / Flickr / CC BY-NC-SA 2.0.

p. 75 Mosireen, Tahrir Cinema, Tahrir Square, December 2, 2011. Photo: Mosireen / Flickr / CC BY-NC-SA 2.0.

pp. 74–75 Mosireen, *Blood at Night, Grief by Day (Maspero 9/10/11)*, October 11, 2011. Video. Courtesy of Mosireen.

p. 75 Mosireen, *About Mosireen*, 2012. Video. Courtesy of Mosireen. https://vimeo.com/37895234.

pp. 76–77 Ahmed Basiony in Tahrir Square, Cairo, January 28, 2011 (Friday of Rage). Photo courtesy of Magdi Mostafa.

p. 77 Ahmed Basiony and Magdi Mostafa in Tahrir Square, Cairo, January 28, 2011 (Friday of Rage). Photo courtesy of Magdi Mostafa.

pp. 76–77 Poster of Ahmed Basiony, Tahrir Square, Cairo, February 4, 2011. Photo courtesy of Magdi Mostafa.

pp. 76–77 Egyptian newspaper showing those killed in the revolution, February 2011. Photo courtesy of Magdi Mostafa.

p. 78 Ahmed Basiony, *Thirty Days Running in the Place*, 2010. Live performance, January 2010. Courtesy of the artist's family.

pp. 78–79 Ahmed Basiony, *30 Days of Running in the Space*, 2011. Installation view, The Egyptian Pavillion, 54th Venice Biennale. Photo: Magdi Mostafa. Courtesy of the artist's family.

p. 79 Neighborhood in Raqqa, Syria, destroyed during the Syrian Civil War, August 1, 2017. © Mahmoud Bali (VOA) / Applodion / Wikimedia Commons / CC-0.

pp. 78–79 Masasit Mati, *Top Goon*, "Who Wants to Kill a Million?," episode 2, November 27, 2011. YouTube series, 6:25 min. Courtesy of Masarit Mati.

p. 79 Maha Maamoun, *Night Visitor: The Night of Counting the Years*, 2011. Single-channel video, 8 min. Courtesy of the artist and Gypsum Gallery.

pp. 80–81 Graph showing the Egyptian internet being shut off at 5:20 p.m. EST, January 27, 2011. Courtesy of Arbor Networks.

p. 81 Carlos Latuff, *Mubarak shuts down Internet! Egypt will shut down Mubarak!*, January 28, 2011. Cartoon. Courtesy of Carlos Latuff / Wikicommons / CC-0.

p. 80 Pulse Nightclub, Orlando, Florida, 2006. Courtesy of Rick Singh / Xaosflux / Wikicommons / CC-0.

pp. 80–81 #twomenkissing Twitter campaign, summer 2017. Courtesy of Twitter.

p. 81 Juliana Huxtable, *A Split During Laughter at the Rally*, 2017. Courtesy of the artist; Reena Spaulings, New York; Project Native Informant, London.

TOWARD A NEW DIGITAL METABOLISM

p. 82 *Black Mirror*, "Nosedive," season 3, episode 1, October 21, 2016. Image courtesy of © House of Tomorrow Limited 2016; David Dettman (photographer); Endemol Shine International Limited.

pp. 82–84 Simon Denny, *Blockchain Future States*, 2017. Installation view, Hammer Museum, Los Angeles, 2017. Courtesy of the artist and Galerie Buchholz, Berlin/Cologne/New York.

p. 85 Lawrence Abu Hamdan, *A Convention of Tiny Movements, 2015—Spinneys Supermarket, Achrafieh Beirut August 2017*, 2015. C-type print mounted to aluminium, 110 × 195 cm. © Lawrence Abu Hamdan. Courtesy of Maureen Paley, London.

p. 84 "DiMoDA 2.0: Morphé Presence," RISD Museum, Providence, RI, January 6–April 30, 2017. Screens from left to right, Miyo Van Stenis, Rosa Menkman, Theo Triantafyllidis. Courtesy of DiMoDA.

pp. 84–85 Visitors wearing VR headsets at "DiMoDA 2.0: Morphé Presence," Superchief Gallery Gallery, Brooklyn, September 9–October 14, 2016. Courtesy of DiMoDA.

p. 85 The Oculus Rift CV1 (Consumer Version 1), a VR headset made by Oculus VR and released in 2016. Photo: Evan-Amos, 14 July 2017 / Wikicommons / CC-0.

p. 86 Angelo Plessas, *6th Eternal Internet Brotherhood/Sisterhood*, Lebensbogen, Zierenberg, May 2017. Courtesy of the artist.

p. 87 Angelo Plessas, *Eternal Internet Brotherhood/Sisterhood*, Palestine, 2014. Workshop by urbanist Mia Lundstrom. Photo: Vincent Charlebois. Courtesy of the artist.

pp. 86–87 DIS, *General Intellects with McKenzie Wark*, 2017. Courtesy of DIS and Project Native Informant, London.

p. 87 *Not in the Berlin Biennale ad campaign*, 2016. Image: Not in the Berlin Biennale. Courtesy of Roe Etheridge, Babak Radboy, and Chris Kraus.

SONG LYRIC CREDITS

p. 133 The Doors, "Touch Me," 1968. Words and music: Robby Krieger. © 1968 (renewed), Doors Music Co. All rights reserved. Used by permission of Alfred Music.

p. 141 Thompson Twins, "We Are Detective," 1983. Words and music: Tom Bailey, Alannah Joy Currie, Joseph Martin Leeway. © Universal Music Publishing MGB Ltd. / Musik Ed. Discoton Musik GmbH.

p. 153 Extreme, "Play with Me," 1989. Words and music: Nuno Bettencourt, Gary Francis Cherone. © Color Me Blind Music / Almo Music Corp. / Rondor Musikverlag GmbH.

Author Biography

Omar Kholeif, PhD, FRSA, is a writer, curator, and broadcaster whose work focuses on the intersection of art, politics, urbanism, and emerging technologies. He currently holds the position of Manilow Senior Curator and Director of Global Initiatives at the Museum of Contemporary Art Chicago. Prior to this, he was curator at London's Whitechapel Gallery; senior curator at Cornerhouse and HOME, Manchester; and curator at FACT (Foundation for Art and Creative Technology), Liverpool. Kholeif has curated or cocurated over one hundred exhibitions, commissions, and special projects over the last decade, including the Cyprus Pavilion at the 56th Venice Biennale, 2015; the Abraaj Group Art Prize, 2015; the Liverpool Biennial 2012; and the forthcoming V-A-C Pavilion at the 58th Venice Biennale and the Sharjah Biennial 14 in 2019. Author and editor of over two dozen books and catalogues, he also writes widely on art and culture for media outlets such as the *Guardian*, *Artforum*, *Art Papers*, *Mousse*, *frieze*, *Wired*, and *Art Monthly*.